Faces of Béxar

Faces of Béxar

Early San Antonio & Texas

JESÚS F. DE LA TEJA

TEXAS A&M UNIVERSITY PRESS • *College Station*

Copyright © 2016
by Jesús F. de la Teja
All rights reserved
Second printing, 2019

This paper meets the requirements
of ANSI/NISO Z39.48-1992 (Permanence of Paper).
Binding materials have been chosen for durability.
Manufactured in the United States of America

LIBRARY OF CONGRESS CATALOGING-IN-PUBLICATION DATA

Names: Teja, Jesús F. de la, 1956– author.
Title: Faces of Béxar: early San Antonio and Texas / Jesús F. de la Teja.
Description: First edition. | College Station: Texas A&M University Press, [2016] | Includes bibliographical references and index.
Identifiers: LCCN 2015036245 | ISBN 9781623494018 (printed case: alk. paper) | ISBN 9781623497897 (paper) | ISBN 9781623494025 (ebook)
Subjects: LCSH: San Antonio (Tex.)—History. | Spanish Americans—Texas—San Antonio—History. | Mexican Americans—Texas—San Antonio—History. | Texas—History—To 1846.
Classification: LCC F394.S21157 T44 2016 | DDC 976.4/351—dc23
LC record available at http://lccn.loc.gov/2015036245

Cover art: Theodore Gentilz, *Convité para el baile*.
Courtesy of Daughters of the Republic of Texas Library, San Antonio, Texas.

Contents

List of Illustrations / vi
Preface / vii
Introduction / 1

1. Spanish Colonial Texas / 11
2. "A Fine Country with Broad Plains—The Most Beautiful in New Spain": Views of Land and Nature in Colonial San Antonio / 35
3. Forgotten Founders: The Military Settlers of Eighteenth-Century San Antonio de Béxar / 53
4. "To the Last Drop of Our Blood": Defending King and Empire in San Antonio / 67
5. The Saltillo Fair and Its San Antonio Connections / 79
6. Why Urbano and María Trinidad Can't Get Married: Social Relations in Late Colonial San Antonio / 93
7. "Buena gana tenía de ir a jugar": The Recreational World of Early San Antonio, Texas, 1718–1845 / 119
8. Discovering the Tejano Community in "Early" Texas / 139
9. Rebellion on the Frontier / 161
10. The Colonization and Independence of Texas: A Tejano Perspective / 181

Bibliographic Essay / 199
Index / 215

Illustrations

All paintings by Theodore Gentilz

Convité para el baile
Mexican Market, Pay Day, Coal Miners, San Felipe, Coahuila, Mexico
Ojo de Agua San Pedro
On the Trail
Comanches on the War Path
Aguador: Water Seller
San Juan Capistrano
Corrida de la sandía
La cocina
La Purísima Concepción de Acuña
Stick Stock

Preface

Articles and book chapters are to history what short stories are to fiction: an opportunity to develop a more limited theme or topic than the type treated in a book-length work. Sometimes authors are asked to write on a single theme but from different geographical, biographical, or chronological perspectives. At other times a historian gets an idea that does not quite merit a book but that has the potential to illuminate a topic in a particular context that is part of a historiographical trend. And, sometimes, a historian wants to "stake out" a particular subject by publishing preliminary findings to be developed in book form at a future date. In time, if enough of those articles and chapters accumulate, a pattern may emerge that the author believes to warrant collective republication.

For more than twenty-five years I have been researching and writing on the history of early San Antonio, Spanish and Mexican Texas, and the Texas Revolution. In that timespan I have been invited or gotten the idea to write articles and book chapters in all of the contexts mentioned above. The earliest of those invitations came shortly after I had passed my PhD exams at the University of Texas at Austin (UT) and begun work on my dissertation. In the mid-1980s the Texas State Historical Association was preparing a volume of the *Southwestern Historical Quarterly* dedicated to the sesquicentennial of Texas independence, and the editors had asked John Wheat, Spanish translator at what was then the Barker Texas History Center at the University of Texas, to contribute an article on Mexican Texas. He invited me to be his co-author, and the topic we developed was a social and economic overview of San Antonio from the eve of Mexican independence to the eve of the Texas Revolution.[1] If there had been any doubts in my mind about my choice of professions, working on that article dispelled them once and for all.

An article on San Antonio in the 1820s was a natural extension of my dissertation topic, a socio-economic history of San Antonio in the eighteenth century. That subject was itself an extension of the work I had been doing for James A. Michener, who was responsible for my transformation into a historian of early Texas. In fall 1981 I was in my first semester at UT as a doctoral student in Latin American history when the opportunity of a lifetime presented itself. The Pulitzer prize–winning author of *Tales from the South Pacific, Hawaii,* and *Centennial* was coming to campus, with the history department as host. A couple of professors, including Latin Americanist Eric Van Young, whose class "The Great Estate in Latin America" I was taking, were asked to suggest possible research assistants. On Van Young's recommendation I was interviewed for one of the two slots and, amazingly enough, got it. My only qualifications for the assistantship were my bilingual skills and an interest in late-colonial Mexico. I had arrived in Texas (my surname notwithstanding) not too long before, had not read any Texas history, and had not even made it to the San Antonio missions yet. Needless to say, it was an audacious act to take on the assignment. It was also a life-changing opportunity.

Over the course of the two-and-a-half years that I worked as a research assistant for Jim Michener, I reoriented my scholarly interests to Spanish Texas from the involvement of Mexico and Gran Colombia in an abortive Cuban independence movement during the Spanish American wars of independence. Aside from the practical aspects of the move—I was working hard to learn early Texas history for my assignment with Michener—I had become aware that the historiography of Spanish Texas, specifically San Antonio, lacked a solid social and economic component. Most of what had been written about Spanish Texas emphasized the missions as institutions, the efforts of explorers, the political administration of the province, narrative accounts of conflicts with Indians and royalist troops during the Mexican War of Independence, and the arrival of Anglo Americans. There were plenty of picture books and broad general narratives but little in the way of understanding how society functioned. In fact, much of what there was tended to be rather disparaging and dismissive—lazy Mexicans, lazy Indians, lazy half-breeds, all waiting around until intrepid and industrious Americans claimed Texas from the virtual wilderness in which it had been mired for three centuries.[2]

The proof that there was a fuller, richer, more complex, and more inclusive history was right there in the records I had been working with, first to help in the Michener project and then for my dissertation. In the late nineteenth century, the University of Texas had become the repository of much of San Antonio's archival material from the Spanish colonial period while the State Library and Archives had become the home for the records of Nacogdoches and elsewhere. In the first half of the twentieth century, such eminent borderlands scholars as Herbert E. Bolton, Carlos Castañeda, and Charles W. Hackett (among others) had brought to Austin copies of vast amounts of materials from Mexican and Spanish repositories and begun the work of translating and publishing them. Even the Church of

Jesus Christ, Latter Day Saints had contributed to the effort, copies of its microfilm of transcriptions of land grants and wills from the Bexar County Clerk's Office winding up in UT's Tarlton Law Library. The archives of the Texas General Land Office contained important records documenting some of the earliest land distributions in Texas outside San Antonio's city limits as well as documentation on the transfer of mission lands to private hands at the end of the eighteenth and early nineteenth centuries. The Catholic Archives of Texas in Austin and the archives of the Archdiocese of San Antonio held a considerable number of records vital to understanding the population of Spanish Texas.

This is not to say that I was the first to mine these rich archival veins. As far back as the 1960s, Robert Weddle had begun producing important works on the Spanish Texas frontier based not only on the records already in Texas but eventually on others that he collected himself in European repositories. Mardith Schuetz had produced a masterful dissertation on San Antonio's mission Indians, while Alicia Tjarks had written her dissertation and then an article on the demographics of early San Antonio. James McReynolds had written a dissertation on family life in Nacogdoches that started with the town's founding in 1779 and went through the mid-nineteenth century. Although not properly in Spanish Texas, Laredo had received attention from Gilberto Hinojosa, whose dissertation on the town from its founding in 1755 to the mid-nineteenth century was published by Texas A&M University Press in 1983. Jack Jackson's encyclopedic narrative of the development of ranching in Spanish Texas appeared in 1986. These works and those of earlier scholars working from more traditional perspectives informed my own work, which aimed to provide a comprehensive account of San Antonio's first century of existence as a military-civilian community.[3]

I completed my dissertation, "Land and Society in 18th-Century San Antonio de Béxar, a Community on New Spain's Northern Frontier," in 1988 and soon started reworking it for publication. It finally appeared in 1995 as *San Antonio de Béxar: A Community on New Spain's Northern Frontier*, after I had joined the faculty at what is now Texas State University.[4] Much as I covered a broad range of topics in the book, including demographics, economics, and politics, it turned out that *San Antonio de Béxar* was not nearly as comprehensive as I had thought it was. Changes in scholarly fashions, both among historians and the public, my own expanding set of interests, and concern for filling in pieces of the story that I should have realized were missing to begin with have taken me back to San Antonio time and again.

In fact, I was taken back to San Antonio in what proved to be a very important way even before I got to work on revising my dissertation for publication. Again, the opportunity was associated with my work for Michener. In 1989, Debbie Brothers, who had worked on the Michener project, and her business partner Tom Munnerlyn approached me about retranslating Juan Seguín's memoirs for publication. I explained that the memoirs were only available in the 1858 English-language edition but that it might be a good idea to annotate them and provide an introductory essay. I was familiar with the Seguín family, as it was one I had highlighted in my dissertation, so I saw working on the memoirs as a way of linking the Spanish colonial period to the Texas Revolution. The work gradually expanded to include a number of documents associated with Juan's participation in the growing schism between Texas and the rest of Mexico and became *A Revolution Remembered: The Memoirs and Related Correspondence of Juan N. Seguín.*[5]

By the time *A Revolution Remembered* appeared, I was working as an assistant professor of history at Texas State. But the work had begun while I worked in the Archives and Records Division of the Texas General Land Office (GLO). I was hired in 1985 because of my knowledge and skills related to the eighteenth- and early nineteenth-century Spanish-language documentation in that office. Working at the GLO gave me a very different perspective on early Texas history, especially an appreciation of the role of land and genealogy and of the variety of Texas experiences. While employed at the GLO, I met a number of historians working on the Mexican and Republic periods, I came to know local history and genealogy groups whose members traced their ancestors that far back—some even further—and I got to collaborate with other state and local agencies with connections to the state's historical landscape. In other words, I became an archivist and public historian, sensibilities I have brought forward through my career ever since.

After arriving at Texas State, where I taught Mexican American, early Mexican, borderlands, and American Indian history, I continued to be engaged in bringing a more modern understanding of Texas history to the general public. That mission and my eclectic scholarly interests have been the inspiration of my rather broad-ranging research and publication activities. I found that participating in the research projects of others or pursuing a particularly intriguing idea within the context of pre-statehood Texas history allowed me to explore themes just as intellectually rewarding as my dissertation work had been, but without the investment of time that book-length projects require, especially when dealing with topics requiring considerable paleographic work.

Among the ideas I have explored beyond the scope of the essays in this book, none has been more rewarding than my effort to promote an understanding of the Tejano side of the political history of Mexican and revolutionary Texas. Over the course of working on *A Revolution Remembered*, and subsequently, it became obvious to me that numerous Tejanos had played vital roles in the development of Texas in the 1820s and 1830s. They helped organize local, state, and even the national government, they contributed to the debate over the nature of Mexico's political system, they aided and sustained the immigration of Anglo Americans, and they participated politically, economically, and militarily in Texas' revolt against Mexican rule. I became convinced that it was impossible to fully understand the history of Texas during that period without understanding the Tejanos. Moreover, because most of these men were born during the Spanish colonial period, because many of them had roots in Texas going back as far as the founding of the province, and because not a few of them had been active participants in the Mexican War of Independence from Spain, I was also convinced that it was impossible to understand their motivations without understanding that earlier time. And, since that earlier time was the world of eighteenth-century Mexico, I was, and am, determined to make sure that Texans appreciate the Spanish and Mexican side of the state's history. In my edited volume *Tejano Leadership in Mexican and Revolutionary Texas*,[6] I was able to recruit a group of colleagues interested in that period of time to contribute essays on eleven prominent Tejanos, some of them well known and others almost completely lost to the pages of history.

Underlying all of this is my academic background in colonial Mexican history, particularly borderlands history. My work at UT focused on the eighteenth and early nineteenth centuries, which makes my perspective one looking south to north rather one looking east to west. The pioneers I am most interested in came to Texas from Coahuila, Nuevo León, Zacatecas, and points south, rather than from Georgia, Alabama, Tennessee, and other points east and north. Rather than focusing on King Cotton, my reading focused on the silver industry; rather than studying the Great Awakening, I studied the role of the Catholic Church as an instrument of state power—including the Franciscan and Jesuit missionary enterprise from Baja California to the Gulf of Mexico. Although both Anglo America and Spanish Mexico were racialized societies, race expressed itself differently in each, and my sensitivity to the subject has been shaped by my deeper understanding of the Spanish *sistema de castas*.

These interests, both in research and in outreach, have led me to participate in very special programs. When the idea of a state history museum began to take form under the leadership of Lieutenant Governor Bob Bullock back in the mid-1990s, I was consulted about what I thought the museum should concentrate on. Later, when the museum started to take shape, I was fortunate enough to join the content development team. It was a project that taught me a lot about politics and the compromises necessary to present history to a general public. More than fifteen years later, I am still working with the Bob Bullock Texas State History Museum to continue improving how it tells the history of the state to an increasingly diverse and technologically inclined public.

Meanwhile, I also began consulting on Texas history books. During a couple of early adoption cycles, I merely reviewed books and offered comment. Later, I was invited to participate as an author in a US history high school textbook. The opportunity came because of both my support for Texas history education through the Texas State Historical Association and my participation in a college-level Texas history textbook. When Ron Tyler, Paula Marks, and I finished our work for the state history museum, we pondered to what other use we might put our accumulated research, and the answer came back, a college textbook. In it, *Texas Crossroads of North America* (now in a second edition),[7] we employed the themes we developed for the history museum to provide organizing principles for the book. Writing a textbook forces a writer to consider the balance between generalization and detail, narrative and exposition, and text and image. It is also a reminder that at the college level, Texas history textbooks help teach teachers of Texas history.

Along the way, I have acquired an additional interest that finds its way into the present volume in the form of its illustrations. One of the biggest frustrations for historians of early Texas is the dearth of visual material to illustrate the state's history. A handful of items, most prominently a large canvas depicting the Comanche-Norteño destruction of Mission San Saba in 1758 (produced in Mexico City in the following decade), along with an image of a French ship from the La Salle period, a mounted presidio soldier purporting to be from Texas,[8] and various maps, are repeatedly used for lack of other sources. In fact, it is the work of a nineteenth-century French artist Theodore Gentilz that has increasingly graced the work of scholars wanting to use period illustrations on Tejano life.[9]

Although Gentilz worked in the second half of the nineteenth century, his small paintings of life in and around San Antonio, South Texas, and northern Mexico cover themes not treated by other artists. In fact, Gentilz was sympathetic to the Tejano community in a way that other artists were not. His depictions of dances, processions, and life around the missions and in the countryside illustrate a way of life not far removed from what a visitor might have found a century earlier. Clothing styles might have been different in the eighteenth century, but otherwise, the activities, the architecture, and the physical surroundings illustrated in his works are consistent with colonial-period conditions. I have therefore chosen to illustrate each chapter with an appropriate Gentilz painting in hopes that the reader may gain a deeper appreciation of both the subject matter and the art as they play off each other.

I would be remiss if I did not acknowledge some of the intellectual debts I have acquired over the years. Encounters with historians in and outside Texas influenced (and continue to influence) who I am as a historian. I cannot name them all, but three deserve special mention. First, I have to credit Professor Nettie Lee Benson, for whom the world-famous Benson Latin American Collection at UT is named. Miss Nettie not only built that collection into a world-caliber institution, but she also helped shape a number of scholars in Mexican history at work on both sides of the border today. Her special gift for books made her a bottomless pool of bibliographic knowledge. She was as blunt as she was smart about books, and she pushed. I once walked into her office very happy with the third chapter of my dissertation, and before even looking at it, her question to me was, "When are you going to say something new?" She was telling me not to be long winded, to get to the point. I have taken that counsel to heart.

For the six years I worked at the GLO, I had the good fortune to collaborate with Galen Greaser, the agency's official Spanish translator. Galen proved to be not only a marvelous fellow worker but a first-rate colleague. We collaborated on work on the Spanish Collection of the office, we developed finding aids and exhibits together, and we co-wrote an article on the adjudication of South Texas land grants that is often cited by other scholars. His knowledge of Spanish improved my Spanish, and his amazing translation skills taught me a lot about proper technique. I would not be nearly as proficient in translation work without the benefit of Galen's example.

Although I did not come to meet him until after I finished my dissertation and started work on the Seguín project, I count David J. Weber as my guide into the depths of borderlands history. He was at work on *The*

Spanish Frontier in North America when we started our friendship, which lasted until his death in 2009. I already admired David's way with synthesis—he was able to pull together a tremendous amount of material into a cogent whole, as he had proved in *The Mexican Frontier, 1821–1846: The American Southwest under Mexico*, and he always had a way of contextualizing whatever you were doing in ways you had not thought about. By the mid-1990s, he was at work on developing a PhD program in history and a Center for Southwestern Studies at Southern Methodist University, and I was able to take advantage of these pursuits in a small way. At a conference of the Omohundro Institute at UT in 1999, I mentioned to him that what seemed lacking in borderlands studies was communication between those scholars working on Spain's eastern borderlands and those working on New Spain's northern frontier. He agreed, and with the collaboration of Ross Frank, we developed a symposium and book project that resulted in an edited volume, *Choice, Persuasion, and Coercion: Social Control on Spain's North American Frontiers*. I was able to repay David in some small way for all his encouragement and support by writing the essay on him for a book on Texas historians, *Writing the Story of Texas*, edited by Patrick Cox and Kenneth Hendricks.[10]

I came to Texas in 1981 with one agenda, and more than thirty years later here I remain, working on a very different one. I was fortunate to find a career and a family here, and we have done well. Success for Latinos today in many ways comes easier than it did forty years ago, a fact that as a historian I consider every day. And so, aside from the various historians who have influenced the content of my work, I need to acknowledge the debt I owe to the numerous historians who broke through the institutional barriers to careers in higher education for Mexican Americans, among them Arnoldo De León, Andrés Tijerina, Félix Almaráz, and Emilio Zamora, and made the path so much smoother for those of us who followed. This book is dedicated to them.

NOTES

1. Jesús F. de la Teja and John Wheat, "Bexar: Profile of a Tejano Community, 1820–1832," *Southwestern Historical Quarterly* 89, no. 1 (July 1985): 7–34.

2. The most popular example of this perspective is T. R. Fehrenbach, *Lone Star: A History of Texas and Texans* (1968, reprint; Boston: Da Capo Press, 2000).

3. Robert Weddle's oeuvre is too large to list here, but his foundational works, *San Juan Bautista: Gateway to Spanish Texas* (Austin: University of Texas Press, 1968) and *Wilderness Manhunt: The Spanish Search for La Salle* (Austin: University of Texas Press, 1973), made significant contributions to Spanish Texas studies at a time when they had fallen into neglect. Mardith K. Schuetz, "The Indians of the San Antonio Missions, 1718–1821," (PhD diss., University of Texas at Austin,

1980); Alicia V. Tjarks, "Comparative Demographic Analysis of Texas, 1777–1793," *Southwestern Historical Quarterly* 77, no. 3 (Jan. 1974): 291–338; James M. McReynolds, "Family Life in a Borderland Community: Nacogdoches, Texas, 1779–1861," (PhD diss., Texas Tech University, 1978); Gilberto M. Hinojosa, *A Borderlands Town in Transition: Laredo, 1755–1870* (College Station: Texas A&M University Press, 1983); Jack Jackson, *Los Mesteños: Spanish Ranching in Texas, 1721–1821* (College Station: Texas A&M University Press, 1986). Carlos E. Castañeda's seven-volume narrative history of Texas, *Our Catholic Heritage in Texas, 1519–1936* (reprint; New York: Arno Press, 1976), while naturally emphasizing the perspective of the Knights of Columbus, his sponsoring organization, was a tour-de-force of narrative storytelling that remains an essential, though dated, entry point to Texas history, particularly from the sixteenth through early nineteenth centuries. Likewise, Herbert E. Bolton's work on early Texas, collected in *Texas in the Middle Eighteenth Century: Studies in Spanish Colonial History and Administration* (reprint; Austin: University of Texas Press, 1970), is still a useful tool for scholars of Spanish Texas history.

4. Jesús F. de la Teja, *San Antonio de Béxar: A Community on New Spain's Northern Frontier* (Albuquerque: University of New Mexico Press, 1995).

5. Jesús F. de la Teja, ed., *A Revolution Remembered: The Memoirs and Selected Correspondence of Juan N. Seguín* (Austin: State House Press, 1991). I recovered the rights to the book in 2001 and published an edition with the Texas State Historical Association in 2002.

6. Jesús F. de la Teja, ed., *Tejano Leadership in Mexican and Revolutionary Texas* (College Station: Texas A&M University Press, 2010).

7. Jesús F. de la Teja, Ron Tyler, and Nancy Beck Young, *Texas: Crossroads of North America* (2nd ed., Boston: Cengage Learning, 2016).

8. In 2004, I published an article clarifying the provenance and context of the mounted soldier. See "Ramón de Murillo's Plan for the Reform of New Spain's Frontier Defenses," *Southwestern Historical Quarterly* 107, no. 4 (April 2004): 501–33.

9. On the life and work of Theodore Gentilz, see Dorothy Steinbomer Kendall and Carmen Perry, *Gentilz: Artist of the Old Southwest* (Austin: University of Texas Press, 1974).

10. Jesús F. de la Teja and Ross Frank, eds., *Choice, Persuasion, and Coercion: Social Control on Spain's North American Frontiers* (Albuquerque: University of New Mexico Press, 2005); Jesús F. de la Teja, "David J. Weber," in *Writing the Story of Texas*, ed. Patrick Cox and Kenneth Hendrickson (Austin: University of Texas Press, 2013).

Introduction

The present volume presents a broad cross-section of my writings on San Antonio and early Texas over the last twenty years or so and can be seen as expanding on, complementing, and amending my study of eighteenth-century Béxar, *San Antonio de Béxar: A Community on New Spain's Northern Frontier*. The chapters consist of work that appeared in highly specialized books and journals or publications targeting specific audiences. Bringing them together here allows them to reach a broader audience. The topics explored in the individual pieces vary considerably, but they fit together in providing a well-rounded history of San Antonio before its Americanization in the mid-nineteenth century.

San Antonio was a different place before 1850. That may seem ridiculously obvious, but maybe not. We are so accustomed to seeing the modern metropolis with its highways and high rises, its industry and tourism, that we cannot visualize the little hamlet that fit into the area between La Villita and the Witte Museum. Today's urban sprawl is quickly devouring the northwest hills from which Apaches and Comanches once launched their raids. The city long ago swallowed Missions Concepción and San José, to say nothing of the Alamo, then surrounded Capistrano, and is advancing on Espada, the landscape of which, on the other side of Loop 410, still bears some resemblance to the rural community established by Franciscans for regional hunter-gatherers. We travel along the modern Mission Reach Trail next to a channelized San Antonio River and neglect to consider that each of the missions was an autonomous community and that travel even between them could be dangerous and time consuming as well as relatively rare before the 1830s.

And what about the people? With its military bases, its multinational business sector, its international tourist industry, and its diverse higher education community, San Antonio is not the small, isolated, and backward Spanish frontier town that it was before the war with Mexico. How could a metropolis of 1.5 million inhabitants remind anyone of the hamlet of two thousand five hundred that was San Antonio in 1800? Although San Antonio continues to express its connections to Mexico in just about every aspect of life, it is not the city of Mexicans that it was in 1836. Rather, the majority Mexican-American population is a hybrid people whose food, music, artistic aesthetic, and language blend Mexican, American, Asian, European, and, increasingly, African elements. But little remains of the indigenous roots that were so important in the early days, when the town shared its environs with mission communities inhabited by members of area Indian groups, and where autonomous native tribes made regular appearances—welcome and otherwise.

The chapters that follow tell stories that flesh out some of those histories. They spring from my interests in that smaller San Antonio now largely buried, both under the streets and buildings that make up the modern city and by the neglect of our modern society, with its need for a simplistic and trivialized past that does not take up too much room in people's technology-driven lives. They are the product of my concern with understanding San Antonio as a crossroads with roots in a Hispanic civilization that lent its genes to the Alamo City in the same way that English civilization lent its genes to Boston and Philadelphia. They are the product of my drive to show that Spanish Texas history can be just as complex and challenging as the history of any other part of the Atlantic world. And so, the essays in this book cover the entire chronological scope of Texas history from the founding of the province in the 1710s to the advent of Anglo-American hegemony in the 1830s.

In part, the problem in the way early Texas history has been written is the product of the training the historians who told that story received. Or, should I say, the problem is the context of the training? When Mexico lost Texas, Texas became largely lost to Mexican history with the exception of the period covering that loss, which led naturally to discussion of the traumatic war with the United States a decade later. Because Texas (and the rest of the Spanish borderlands) was not part of the English Atlantic seaboard experience, it got little if any coverage in US history textbooks. The American public was taught to see places like Texas, New Mexico, and California as important only from the point at which they became part of American history, while the Mexican public was taught to see Texas only in the context of the struggle with the United States.

In fact, early Texas history belongs to both nations—the United States and Mexico. The border continues today to play an important role in the politics, economics, and cultures of both nations. Understanding where that border came from, how some of the economic imperatives of the region formed, and where a substantial proportion of its population came from are useful for the kind of understanding necessary to address regional issues in an enlightened way. Early Texas history is therefore not irrelevant but vitally important in balancing perspectives, understanding precedents, and making connections across borders and worldviews.

There is more to San Antonio history, however. It is at the heart of what is becoming known as *Tejano history*. As the largest of the Spanish-colonial settlements of Texas, and with a continuous Hispanic story extending back to the early eighteenth century, San Antonio de Béxar is home to the state's oldest established families. Organizations such as Los Bexareños and Canary Islands Descendants Association research, celebrate, and promote ancestors going back to Martín de Alarcón's founding expedition of 1718 and the establishment of the state's first chartered town in 1731. Those settlers, whether Mexican frontiersmen or Old World immigrants, constitute the rootstock of the state's Hispanic population. And, as Andrés Tijerina has commented, "In their search for a link to the founders of Texas, Latinos and Mexican Americans have found a common memory in the Tejano—the native Mexican of Texas—the Texan who was here before the first Anglo American immigrated to Texas."[1] Tejanos, then, form as crucial a foundation for Texas' Latino population as Texians (the name usually applied to the early settlers of Texas from the United States) do for Anglo Texans.

Not that the term *Tejano* is exclusive to the early San Antonio community or is synonymous with the region originally identified as Spanish Texas. Particularly in that part of the state below the Nueces River, which only became part of Texas in 1848, the term has come into use to identify the Hispanic community that settled the region in the late eighteenth and early nineteenth centuries or, simply, Mexican-descent people born in the area.[2] *Tejano* has not caught on universally, however, except in the realm of music, where it denotes that blend of northern Mexican, German, and American influences that are peculiar to Texas east of the Pecos. Consequently, although *Tejano* can be a rather amorphous term, there is no doubt in my mind that in the sense meant by Andrés Tijerina, who first employed it in his early 1970s doctoral dissertation, it applies most aptly to the people of San Antonio who are the subject of the following pages.

The opening chapter of this book, "Spanish Colonial Texas," sets the stage for what follows by offering an introduction to Texas history before 1821. This essay was my contribution to an edited volume by Robert H. Jackson, *New Views of Borderlands History*, following on the heels of David J. Weber's masterful synthesis *The Spanish Frontier in North America*.[3] That book, which appeared in 1992, focused on the United States' side of Spain's story from Florida to California as a single synthetic whole. Jackson, on the other hand, recognized that much of the story of the American side of the borderlands had its roots in the experience of Spanish colonial northern Mexico, an idea earlier explored by Oakah Jones in *Los Paisanos: Spanish Settlers on the Northern Frontier of New Spain*.[4] Moreover, the story of Florida, whose existence might have owed something to French intrigues in the western Gulf of Mexico, was a separate story deserving of distinctive treatment. My essay on Texas was one of five regional chapters, all of which addressed settlement patterns, demographic and economic development, and social structure, as well as provided a family-history case study illustrating Spanish colonial frontier life. Consequently, "Spanish Colonial Texas" allowed me to rethink the way I set up the story of San Antonio as I had done in my book. The result is a depiction that connects Béxar more closely to the indigenous past than I did in *San Antonio de Béxar*.

Although *San Antonio de Béxar* contained chapters on land usage, both urban and rural, and included references to the effects of drought and floods on travel, agriculture, and economic conditions, I had given little thought to the underlying question of natural history. Much of Texas today is the product of human transformations of the landscape to meet modern agricultural, industrial, commercial, and demographic needs. In fact, even in those parts where little change has been made, we whisk by at high speeds in practically hermetically sealed vehicles, stopping when necessary at well-provisioned convenience stores, strategically placed rest stops, and comfortable if monotonous commercial lodging establishments. Along these modern highways one sees herds of cattle and horses, sometimes sheep and goats, on occasion llamas and alpacas. And, one also sees transmission wires, cellphone towers, massive windmill farms, and billboards of all kinds. But what were conditions like for the Spanish explorers who encountered Texas when the only changes to the landscape were the fields cleared for planting by the Caddos of East Texas and the hunting and trading trails that crisscrossed the region? What was the Texas animal kingdom experienced by seventeenth- and eighteenth-century pioneers, royal officials, and frontier missionaries? Those are the questions I address in "'A Fine Country with Broad Plains—The Most Beautiful in New Spain': Views of Land and Nature in Colonial San Antonio," employing the many expedition journals, official reports, and diaries that tell us what Texas was like at the dawn of the modern age.

"Forgotten Founders: The Military Settlers of Eighteenth-Century San Antonio de Béxar" represents one of my earliest published works on one of the central themes driving my research of Texas history. Invited in 1988 to participate in an Institute of Texan Studies conference on the Tejano origins of San Antonio, I was tasked with exploring the beginnings of the community, a subject on which organizers Jerry Poyo and Gilberto Hinojosa knew I had a fresh perspective. The more I delved into the historical record, the more it became evident that despite the celebrated importance of the Canary Islanders to San Antonio and early Texas history, there was a whole other story to tell. That other story was the importance of Spanish colonial frontiersmen from what is today Mexico. In fact, the placement of the handful of Canary Islander families who arrived in San Antonio in 1731 next to the presidio was a calculated action on the part of the presidio's commander to help them survive. As this chapter demonstrates, the Canary Islanders, although they received preferential treatment, were dependent on the work and support of the military settlers who had previously started construction of irrigation ditches, cleared fields, and put up the first dwellings in the community over the course of the previous decade.

Consequently, the story of San Antonio is really the story of a military community, the subject of "'To the Last Drop of Our Blood': Defending King and Empire in San Antonio." This was another essay that was a special request. In this case it came from Alfred Hurley, organizer of the program for the 2004 Philosophical Society of Texas meeting that took place at the University of North Texas. Long known for its important military history program, the theme for the annual meeting was the military experience in Texas. My job was to provide a paper on some aspect of the Spanish colonial background, and the event afforded me an opportunity to do a bit of experimenting. The first half of the essay takes the story backwards in time, from one major event back to a previous one approximately a decade apart, while the second part emphasizes that, above all, San Antonio in the eighteenth century was a military community, something that remains true to a significant degree to this day.

At the same time that I was completing work on "'To the Last Drop of Our Blood,'" I was at work on yet another commission, this one from Arnoldo De León, who was bringing together a group of scholars to produce a collection of essays, *Tejano Epic: Essays in Honor of Félix D. Almaráz, Jr.* Appearing in 2005, "The Saltillo Fair and Its San Antonio Connections" links Spanish Texas to its neighboring Coahuila in social and economic terms. I had first become interested in the fair during my doctoral research. Having repeatedly come across references to Saltillo and the fair, I went looking for scholarly literature that would shed light on this obviously important event. To my surprise, little had been written on the subject of the fair, and Texas historians had entirely ignored the state's ties to it. Thus, my essay disputes outdated notions of Bexareños' lack of industry by showing efforts at entrepreneurship even under extremely difficult frontier conditions.

Exploration of the military, economic, and social aspects of life in early San Antonio has brought me into contact with sometimes fascinating documents revealing the lives of people often reduced to simple statistics or limited examples in broad socioeconomic studies. Such was the case with a marriage opposition pitting a mission Indian from San Antonio de Valero and a young woman from one of the families that had transferred to San Antonio from Los Adaes. "Why Urbano and María Trinidad Can't Get Married: Social Relations in Late Colonial San Antonio," which served as my presidential address at the 2008 meeting of the Texas State Historical Association, appeared in the October 2008 issue of *Southwestern Historical Quarterly*. In tracing the course of the proceedings, which involve efforts by Urbano and the friar at Mission Valero to overcome the opposition of María Trinidad's male relatives to a marriage agreed to by her mother, I explore the racial, ethnic, gender, and status roles present even in such a remote corner of the empire as Texas. Texas historiography, tending to be written from the American history perspective, often overlooks the subtleties and complexities of the Spanish-Mexican experience. This case offered me an opportunity to detail the workings of a seemingly highly racialized and patriarchal society whose members sought not to overthrow it but to manipulate it for personal and family advantage.

Another often neglected aspect of San Antonio society is frontier culture. When Jorge Iber, a sports historian who was putting together a special issue of *International Journal of the History of Sport* on Mexican Americans and sports, asked me for an article on early Texas, I was intrigued by the challenge. Although over the years I had collected fragments of information regarding ball games, horse racing, dancing, and even bullfights, I had never thought enough existed to tell a history of sports in early San Antonio. It was, however, possible to tell a broader story of recreational and entertainment activities. Thus, "'Buena gana tenía de ir a jugar': The Recreational World of Early San Antonio, Texas, 1718–1845" introduces the reader to a wide variety of activities that kept Bexareños from leading lives of unrelenting danger and misery. By looking elsewhere in the Spanish world for clues about what ball and card games were being played, what types of songs were being sung at the frequent dances, and what bullfights looked like, I have reconstructed an aspect of early Texas history that has gone entirely unexamined.

My interest in some aspects of San Antonio's cultural dimensions stretched well back to shortly after I finished my dissertation. Although I decided against expanding the scope of work when I transformed my doctoral thesis into *San Antonio de Béxar*, mostly because the evidence I was coming across dealt largely with the Mexican and Republic eras, I began thinking about a stand-alone piece that would cover some of these subjects. In addition, I was becoming increasingly convinced that the frontier experience of Anglo Americans did not differ all that much in archetypes from those of Tejanos. Corn was the staff of life to both frontier populations, animal husbandry was central to their ways of life, housing was equally simple and rustic, the vices and entertainments of both groups followed similar trajectories. In 1994 I had an opportunity to present some of my early ruminations on the matter at a symposium at the University of Texas at Arlington, and the paper was further refined when I was invited by Charles Cutter to participate in a session on "Community and Culture in the Borderlands" at the 1997 meeting of the Society for Historians of the Early Republic. The result was "Discovering the Tejano Community in 'Early' Texas," which, although not strictly speaking a work on San Antonio, has a great deal to say about how Bexareños lived not all that differently from their Texian neighbors. Although examples from other parts of Texas are included, it is the reaction of visitors and residents of San Antonio that make up the bulk of the examples I deploy to argue that had Anglo Americans not been saddled by such an extremely racialized view of the world, the commonalities between Texians and Tejanos would have made for a different story. As James Ronda concluded regarding the essay, "Drawing on both travelers' accounts and a series of revealing contemporary illustrations, de la Teja charts a country of shared place and yet increasingly divided space."[5]

My attention to social and cultural matters has not prevented me from continuing to consider certain basic issues of identity and self-determination. *San Antonio de Béxar* did not cross the chronological divide into the nineteenth century mostly because key aspects of the Texas story change with Spain's loss of Louisiana. The turbulence of the first decade of the nineteenth century was followed by the destruction of the Mexican War of Independence in the second decade. That was followed by a little over another decade of turmoil during the Mexican period, when Tejanos began the long slide into minority status. Finally, the 1830s brought a revolt against Mexican authority, in which Tejanos attempted to be full partners with Texians. It was a failed experiment that remains stubbornly resistant to a clear explanation.

Those decades and processes are the topic of the last two essays in this collection, "Rebellion on the Frontier: San Antonio Texas in the Mexican War for Independence" and "The Colonization and Independence of Texas: A Tejano Perspective." The former essay arose out of a conference in 1993 organized by Jerry Poyo exploring "Tejano Identity, Resistance and Accommodation, 1770–1860." The main concern for my essay was to look at the

Bexareño side of the story. Much of what had been and continues to be written about the Mexican War of Independence in Texas is about outside forces and personalities. For all his importance, Bernardo Gutiérrez de Lara was an outsider to the San Antonio community; his stay in Texas was eventful but brief. Likewise, Royalist General Joaquín Arredondo is a larger-than-life figure in events, particularly in what is commonly understood to be the bloodiest clash ever fought on Texas soil, the Battle of Medina on August 18, 1813. But what do we know of the motives of the local population for participating on either side of the struggle?[6] It is a subject for which I continue to collect evidence in hopes of returning to it at a future date. In the meantime, we have the first fruits of my efforts to understand the Mexican independence process in Texas from the perspective of the people it most affected—San Antonio Tejanos.

And, as I argued in *A Revolution Remembered: The Memoirs and Selected Correspondence of Juan N. Seguín*, it is impossible to understand the motivations of Tejano leaders in the 1820s and 1830s without making sense of their previous experiences during the disastrous decade of the 1810s. Texas historians have tended to relegate Tejano elites to the back of the Texas Revolution bus. Eugene C. Barker once gave a talk in which he claimed that a number of Mexican Texan leaders deserved attention but that sources were lacking. Similarly, Mexican historians have tended to ignore the Tejano part in the story. Well, the collection of essays on Tejano leaders that I edited in 2010, *Tejano Leadership in Mexican and Revolutionary Texas*, served to dispel that decades-old notion. My work on Juan Seguín had previously led me to debates with Mexican historian Josefina Zoraida Vázquez about Mexico's loss of Texas, and so she invited me to balance her account of Mexico's loss of Texas with one presenting a Texas perspective for a collection of essays on Mexico–United States relations.[7] The argument in my essay "The Colonization and Independence of Texas," a theme that I have been pursuing ever since my work on Seguín, is that Tejanos had their own reasons for pursuing an alliance with the Anglo Americans. They certainly could not have foreseen just how badly they were miscalculating the interest of the immigrants from the United States in making them full partners. Physical isolation, their mixed-blood heritage, their Catholicism, and their steep decline as a percentage of the Texas population doomed the vast majority of Tejanos to second-class citizenship in the course of the late-nineteenth and early-twentieth centuries.

It would seem that this collection ends on a down note, at least as far as Tejanos are concerned. Yet the very existence of this work and of the growing body of Tejano studies offers a different conclusion, a more upbeat one. First, despite the loss of status and the prevalence of racial, religious, and cultural

INTRODUCTION

discrimination, Tejanos have not only survived but thrived. Reinforced first by the creation of new Tejanos with the annexation of far South and West Texas in 1848, then by succeeding waves of migration, Texas Mexican Americans will soon constitute a plurality of the state's population. As they ascend the ranks of socioeconomic status, as they participate more fully in the educational, political, and social life of the state, they acquire the means to join their fellow Texans in search of their personal and ethnic roots, and increasingly they demand that those roots be part of the school curriculum and the public memory of Texas. I hope this volume speaks to the richness and complexity of the Tejano experience and feeds the demand for that knowledge.

Second, the variety of themes and periods treated in this volume, broad as it is, should make clear that much remains to be done. Recent interest in the more immediate past—the twentieth century—has produced a historiography that challenges the received truths of generations of Lone Star historians who ignored, marginalized, or misrepresented the Tejano building blocks of Texas history. But, the "deeper" history represented in my work and that of the small group of scholars working on that more distant past is just as critical because it forms the foundation of the story of Texas. For those who seek to explore that early history, I hope this volume serves as a worthwhile introduction.

NOTES

1. Andrés Tijerina, "Constructing Tejano Memory," in *Lone Star Pasts: Memory and History in Texas*, ed. Gregg Cantrell and Elizabeth Hayes Turner (College Station: Texas A&M University Press, 2007), 179.

2. See the difference in definition of "Tejano" between Armando Alonzo, *Tejano Legacy: Rancheros and Settlers in South Texas, 1734–1900* (Albuquerque: University of New Mexico Press, 1998), 5, and Daniel D. Arreola, *Tejano South Texas: A Mexican American Cultural Province* (Austin: University of Texas Press, 2002), 8, 44–45.

3. David J. Weber, *The Spanish Frontier in North America* (New Haven: Yale University Press, 1992).

4. Oakah L. Jones, *Los Paisanos: Spanish Settlers on the Northern Frontier of New Spain* (Norman: University of Oklahoma Press, 1979).

5. James Ronda, "Other Countries, Other Maps," *Journal of the Early Republic* 18, no. 1 (Spring 1998): 136.

6. On the continued absence of Tejanos from the Mexican War of Independence story of Texas see, for instance, Raúl Coronado, *A World Not to Come: A History of Latino Writing and Print Culture* (Cambridge, MA: Harvard University Press, 2013).

7. Barker's speech in McAllen is contained in his article "Native Latin American Contribution to the Colonization and Independence of Texas," *Southwestern Historical Quarterly* 46, no. 4 (April 1943): 317–335; Jesús F. de la Teja, *Tejano Leadership in Mexican and Revolutionary Texas* (College Station: Texas A&M University Press, 2010); Jaime E. Rodríguez O. and Kathryn Vincent, eds., *Myths, Misdeeds, and Misunderstandings: The Roots of Conflict in U.S.-Mexican Relations* (Wilmington, DE: Scholarly Resources, 1997).

Theodore Gentilz, *Mexican Market, Pay Day, Coal Miners, San Felipe, Coahuila, Mexico*. Throughout the Spanish colonial period, Texas could boast of only three areas of Hispanic settlement, San Antonio, La Bahía (today's Goliad), and Los Adaes-Nacogdoches. Soon, San Antonio emerged as the largest and most successful of the settlements and by the 1780s supported a merchant community that provided a variety of wares, some imported from far-away Europe and Asia. "Downtown" San Antonio would have looked very much like this at the turn of the nineteenth century. Courtesy of the Witte Museum, San Antonio, Texas.

Spanish Colonial Texas*

Until the early eighteenth century Texas was an almost completely neglected region, the very remoteness of which served as protection against foreign encroachment. The Gulf Coast and parts of the interior had been explored during the first half of the sixteenth century. Seaborne explorations in 1519 and 1558 vaguely outlined the coast. Álvar Núñez Cabeza de Vaca and the three other survivors of the Pánfilo de Narváez expedition to Florida, which wrecked on the Texas coast in 1528, traversed parts of Texas on their way to Mexico. A decade later, the De Soto-Moscoso expedition entered East Texas in a similar effort to reach Spanish-occupied territory. To the west at the same time, Francisco Vázquez de Coronado led his men in search of the mythical Gran Quivira.[1] Finding no great Indian kingdoms to conquer nor precious metals to exploit, the Spanish lost interest in these parts until the threat of foreign encroachment materialized a century and a half later.

THE FIRST TEXANS

These sixteenth-century Spanish intrusions into the geographic space of modern-day Texas resulted in contact with all the major native peoples that inhabited the region.[2] From the time he shipwrecked on one of Texas' barrier islands in 1528 until he entered Spanish-occupied northwestern Mexico in 1536, Cabeza de Vaca made the most observations. He met and lived among hunter-gatherer peoples, the Karankawas of the lower Galveston Bay area and various Coahuiltecan bands of southern Texas. If his claims of years as a trader and slave among these people are accepted, then he also had contact with the Caddo-speaking people of eastern Texas,

---

*First published in *New Views of Borderlands History*, ed. Robert H. Jackson (Albuquerque: University of New Mexico Press, 1998).

western Louisiana, and southwestern Arkansas. Finally, out beyond the Big Bend country of the Rio Grande, he met and described the elusive semi-sedentary Jumanos, whom he called Cow People because of their buffalo-hunting practices. On the southern plains of eastern New Mexico and the Texas Panhandle, the Coronado expedition encountered the Querechos and Teyas, ancestors of the eastern Apaches, who apparently were part-time agriculturists before the introduction of the horse among them. In their abortive effort to reach New Spain overland from the Mississippi River following De Soto's death, Luis de Moscoso penetrated the Caddo country of East Texas, encountering numerous groups of well-organized, village-dwelling agriculturists. Unfortunately, the paucity and confusing nature of archival records has prevented scholars from venturing any guesses of population size at first contact.

Although acceptable population estimates have not been made, scholars have developed a clear picture of which Indian groups were present in Texas in the course of the next three centuries. Aside from the contact-period groups noted above, numerous Indian peoples made their way into Texas, at least in some degree owing to the impact of European expansion into the interior of North America. As Plains Indians acquired Spanish horses and French and English firearms and trade goods in the seventeenth century, a series of territorial adjustments took place that pushed the less-advantaged groups into contact with the northward-expanding Spanish. The eastern Apaches, specifically the Lipan, found themselves under increasing pressure from the more bellicose Comanches and by the 1720s had been pushed southward into the Texas Hill Country. The pressure, both from Comanches and Wichita-related groups, would continue, and by the early nineteenth century the Lipan Apaches were living southwest of San Antonio. The Comanches, who replaced the Lipan Apaches, established themselves as lords of the Southern Plains by the 1740s, when they are first mentioned in Spanish colonial records. Various Wichita groups, themselves under pressure from the Osages and Comanches by the late seventeenth century, settled in the Red River region at the beginning of the eighteenth. By the end of that century they had spread southward to the middle Brazos Valley.

At the turn of the nineteenth century, another period of Indian migration into Texas occurred following the transfer of Louisiana to the United States and the pursuit of Indian-removal policies in the US South and Midwest. In part, this new settlement was possible because of the demographic collapse of East Texas Caddo population. Members of the Five Civilized Tribes, Shawnees, Cherokees, and Creeks (Seminoles), as well as Delawares,

Alabamas, Coushattas, and Kikapoos, established themselves in Texas and sought protection from Spanish and, later, Mexican authorities, who found these predominantly sedentary peoples attractive residents. Their stay in the area after Texas independence was to be marked by increasing violence, so that by the Civil War only the Alabama-Coushatta (by now banding together for protection) survived in Texas at a small reservation in Polk County.

It is not necessary to have initial population figures for Texas Indian groups to note the devastating demographic collapse that followed Spanish occupation of the region. Only the Comanches and Wichita, with access to rich buffalo hunting grounds, European trade goods, and Spanish equine stock both in New Mexico and Texas, seem to have escaped decline until after the passing of Mexican sovereignty. To the contrary, the Comanches reached their heyday during the Mexican period. The Lipan Apaches also managed to survive as independent agents until the end of Mexican rule, but in much-reduced numbers. The Jumanos, who had prospered during the first three-quarters of the seventeenth century as traders between the Pueblo Indians of New Mexico and the Caddos, quickly declined following the Pueblo revolt of 1680 and encroachment of their hunting grounds by southward-moving Apaches. By the mid-eighteenth century the Jumanos incorporated themselves into the southward-moving Apache bands. These tribes remained beyond effective Spanish control, although individuals were incorporated into Spanish society and all adopted some Hispanic cultural practices.

It was among missionized Indians that the most severe demographic collapse occurred, in almost every case resulting in cultural extinction. Shortly after the first missions were established among Caddo groups in East Texas, in 1690–91, an epidemic broke out that killed one missionary, approximately three hundred mission Indians, and untold numbers of nearby villagers. Epidemic fever, which engulfed all of New Spain in the 1730s, reached Texas in 1739 and killed over one thousand Indians at the San Antonio missions. Between 1749 and 1757, the first decade of Spanish settlement along the lower Rio Grande Valley, epidemics severely reduced local Coahuiltecan populations both within and outside missions. At the two missions established for the Lipan Apaches on the upper Nueces River in 1762, a smallpox epidemic in 1764 claimed the lives of seventy-four baptized natives and an unknown number of others. One of the most devastating epidemics occurred in 1777–78, when large numbers of Caddos and Bidais succumbed to a disease that also affected the non-Indian populations of San Antonio, Bucareli, and nearby Natchitoches, Louisiana.[3]

In his *History of Texas*, written in part from personal observations made as a member of Cmdt. Gen. Teodoro de Croix's inspection tour to the northern frontier in 1777–78, Fray Agustín Morfi noted the impact of disease, missionary activity, and intertribal warfare on Texas Indians. After discussing the most important Indian groups, he concludes:

> There are many other nations besides those already mentioned. Some of these were congregated in the missions; others do not deserve to be noted because of their idleness; still others disappeared or died out during the various epidemics; while some were absorbed by the nations described, such as the Nasones, Tatases, Quitseis, Yscanis, Yojuanes, Deadose, and Xanas [Xaraname].[4]

THE MISSION EXPERIENCE

The role of the missions in this disappearance or die-out of various Indian cultures is well documented, although it is as unquantifiable as the size of contact populations. Missionaries worked at not only training the Indians in the arts of agriculture and animal husbandry, but also at replacing their native cultural norms with Spanish colonial ones. Working with these goals in mind in mission fields in which the target groups were often small independent bands of people speaking distinct dialects or altogether different languages, Texas' Franciscan missionaries early gave up on learning the Indian languages and concentrated on using Spanish or, at the very least, using a standardized version of Coahuiltecan as a lingua franca.[5] The entire missionary program therefore contributed to the reduction in the number of native culture groups and their eventual disappearance altogether. After all, the product of a successful missionary endeavor *was* the transformation of natives into Spanish subjects.

A number of circumstances, some beyond the control of Spanish religious and secular authorities, combined to restrict and frustrate the missionary enterprise in Texas. Geographically, the province was so remote from the central parts of the viceroyalty that complete integration of the missions into the colonial economic system proved impossible. On the other hand, nearby French-influenced Louisiana offered many Texas Indians an attractive alternative to Spanish goods and services without the need to alter their lifeways. Not only the agricultural Caddos, but many of the hunter-gatherer cultures had easy access to the necessary subsistence resources, making mission life unattractive. The few colonials sent to Texas, both secular and religious, could not hope to control a territory of continental breadth, in which the natives effectively lost themselves when convenient. Too, European goods and horses, once introduced among the Indians who occupied North America between the Rockies and the Mississippi, set in motion a centuries-long rearrangement of the cultural landscape of Native Americans in which the Spanish were often only a marginal element. Many Indian groups quickly learned to set European rivals against each other, tell Spanish religious and secular authorities what they wanted to hear, and selectively submit to acculturation. Consequently, Texas Franciscans had only limited and spotty success.

In East Texas, missions for the Caddo were attempted in 1690–93 and 1716–73. Franciscan efforts among these sedentary agriculturists must be considered among the most sustained failures in Spanish colonial history. The 1690 epidemic that killed hundreds shortly after the first missionaries arrived was enough to convince the Caddos that baptism brought on death. When supplies failed to arrive in a timely manner and the villagers received no gifts, they lost interest in a continued relationship with the missionaries. By 1692 they were demanding that the Franciscans leave, which they did the following year. Returning in greater numbers a score years later to form a barrier against French penetration of Spanish territory, the Franciscans found a population indifferent to their ministry and still fearful of the deadly effect of baptism. Consequently, the ambitious field of six missions founded in 1716–17 was reduced by half in 1730, and the remaining missions made only individual proselytes, most of them deathbed conversions when there was nothing to be lost. The failure of this mission field was acknowledged by the Franciscans themselves. Fray Morfi asserts in his *History of Texas*: "At the same time the useless missions of Nacogdoches, Aix, and others that had been maintained under the protection of the said presidios without Indians and *against the will of the missionaries* in charge of them, were to be abolished."[6] Although this statement does not square with the historical record entirely (apparently the missionaries did want to stay), the ineffectiveness of the East Texas missions is beyond dispute.[7]

The most graphic illustration of the deleterious effects of combined epidemic disease, missionary settlement, and intertribal conflict can be found in a decade-long struggle to operate a cluster of missions on the San Gabriel River. Between 1746 and 1751 three missions and a presidio were established to serve various Central Texas tribes. During that time, the missions suffered attack from Lipan Apaches, a smallpox epidemic, and supply shortages that led to wholesale abandonment of the missions. The following four years saw more of the same: smallpox and measles epidemics, drought, summer outbreaks of typhoid, and Indian desertions to pursue foraging, self-defense, and campaigns against the Apaches. By the summer of 1755 the Spanish gave up on the mission-presidio complex that had been permanently abandoned by most of the Indians for whom it had been intended.[8] The missionaries and soldiers were then assigned to a mission for the Apaches, but that effort proved even more disastrous. The first mission, on the San Saba River near present-day Menard, was destroyed in 1758, within months of its founding, by a large force of Plains and Caddo Indians hostile to the Lipans. A subsequent effort, an Apache mission on the upper Nueces that lasted from 1762 to 1769, proved equally ineffective, although the Lipans found it a useful haven from their enemies and some individual conversions were made.[9]

The most successful missions, judged by physical infrastructure and peak agricultural output, turned out to be those located along the San Antonio River Valley from San Antonio down to present-day Goliad. In the vicinity of the presidio founded at the headwaters of the river in 1718, five missions were active by 1731. Near the coast, Mission Espíritu Santo followed Presidio La Bahía as it was moved from Matagorda Bay (hence the name) to the Guadalupe River, and in 1749 to its present location. There, the missionaries established a sister mission, Rosario, for Karankawa bands in 1754.

Activity at these missions concentrated on the seemingly most pliable and defenseless hunter-gatherers, the Coahuiltecans and some Karankawa bands. Pulled to the missions by trinkets and food offerings from the Franciscans and pushed there by pressure from aggressive Apaches, the Coahuiltecans and Karankawas nevertheless accepted acculturation on their own terms. Witnesses called to attest to the progress of the San Antonio missions in 1745 declared that "the tribes that are unconverted have been gradually brought under the influence of the missionaries, replacing from these [Indians] many of those who have died in the mission." They went on to state that

> although these missions have reached the flourishing state of development which is known to everyone, they do not believe they are ready to be turned over to the secular [priest] because new converts are brought daily, and even among those who have been in the missions a long time, there are many who frequently run away, making it necessary for the missionaries to go after them and start their labors anew to bring them back to the bosom of our Holy Mother the Church.[10]

The above statement is only one piece of evidence indicating the inherent instability of mission populations. Evidence from the sacramental records indicates that the initial mission populations were unviable over the long term, as death rates consistently exceeded birthrates. This conclusion is further supported by the steady decline in mission populations as the sources for new recruits disappeared. Additional instability arose from the behavioral patterns of the would-be converts. The refusal of many Indians to accept the regimentation of the sedentary-agricultural life the missionaries preached along with the Gospel led to periodic and prolonged absenteeism. Indians also abandoned missions upon the outbreak of epidemics, which were sometimes occasioned by poor sanitary and living conditions and inadequate diets. The approach of Indian enemies likewise provoked flight. Among the Karankawas, and likely too among the Coahuiltecans, the missions represented little more than one stop among the various ones that made up their seasonal migrations. Consequently, the missions were often occupied only by the infirm, the elderly, some of the very young who were under the direct supervision of the missionaries, and small core groups of converts that had accepted the new way of life.[11]

That Spanish secular and religious authorities did not learn important lessons from their seventy-five years of work with South Texas hunter-gatherers is best illustrated in the experience of Mission Nuestra Señora del Refugio, the last mission founded in Spanish Texas. Established in 1793 for the Karankawas proper, one of whose chiefs had solicited a mission the previous year, the authorities considered this the best opportunity yet to civilize one of the most recalcitrant tribes in the province. The Karankawas had their own agenda, however, and the relationship soon soured as the supplies of cattle and other victuals did not turn out as bountiful as the Indians expected, and sickness spread among those residing in the mission. Chief Frezada Pinta and his followers, who had asked for the mission, refused to enter it, and a group of Indians vandalized the mission compound and its ranch. By the middle of June 1794 most of the Karankawas had abandoned Mission Refugio. The friar in charge then moved the mission to the present-day location of Refugio, where, employing paid labor from the province's settler population, permanent buildings and a farm were established. There, the mission attracted Karankawas from the older Mission Rosario, probably because it placed them closer to their coastal home range. From 43 Indians at this time, the mission grew to 224 in December 1804, and then down to 21 when the mission was secularized in 1830.[12]

By the time the various missions were secularized, the transfer of chattels and real property was most often made to settlers, some of whom had always been present at the missions. Although the Franciscans feared the corrupting influences of mixed-blood settlers, they required the presence of Hispanics in order to properly train the neophytes in the crafts and skills of Spanish colonial life. The small "Spanish" population that always resided at the missions, whether military or civilian, was augmented in the 1770s and 1780s by increasing numbers of civilians, on whom the missionaries came to rely as a dependable workforce. Some intermarriage necessarily took place between mission Indians and settlers, contributing to the small stable population at the missions.[13]

THE HISPANIC TEXANS

Throughout the Spanish colonial period Texas never generated a successful economy. This important handicap, when combined with the chronic state of Indian depredations, created a considerable disincentive for settlement. A letter from Texas governor Domingo Cabello to Louisiana governor Bernardo de Gálvez in July 1779 puts Texas' problems in perspective more than sixty years after the province had been occupied. In it, Cabello asks that the Louisiana official use the proceeds from the sale of two hundred head of cattle he is sending to Louisiana to purchase a male slave cook or female slave cook who can also sew, wash, and iron,

> because here all that is lacking, and particularly a cook, for a very good one that I employed in Cadiz in 1763, when I went to serve in the government of Nicaragua, was told so many things about this place as soon as we arrived in Mexico City last year, that he came to believe that the Indians would eat him, for which reason he resigned from my service. And the same thing happened with my manservant and a secretary, so that I am reduced to the most deplorable state. Although I recognize that they did right, because this [place] is worse than Siberia and Lapland.[14]

Throughout the eighteenth century the Spanish population remained small and heavily dependent on military settlers. The initial expeditions that served to occupy the province, those of Domingo Ramón in 1716 and Martín de Alarcón in 1718, brought the first two hundred or so settlers. In 1721–22 the Marqués de San Miguel de Aguayo reinforced the existing presidios and established two additional ones, leaving another two hundred soldiers in the province, many of them with families. In 1731 the population of San Antonio was augmented by the arrival of fifty-five Canary Island colonists sent to Texas at royal expense. Twenty years later a number of recruits, perhaps twenty, and their families were brought to Texas as part of the new presidio at San Xavier, where they were joined by another twenty or so families of volunteers from San Antonio. In 1756, when the garrison was transferred to the San Saba River, it was augmented to one hundred men, mostly by reducing San Antonio's garrison and recruiting among the civilian population.[15]

Despite the unattractiveness of frontier Texas, there was a small but steady stream of incoming settlers who contributed significantly to what little demographic growth the province experienced in the last fifty years of Spanish rule. Lax control of the border with Louisiana and the dire need for settlers meant that official regulations against frontier settlement by foreigners were ignored. At Nacogdoches in 1793, among a total population of about 460 there lived 24 foreigners, including 5 European Frenchmen, 8 Louisianans, 5 French Canadians, 2 Englishmen, 2 Irishmen, 1 Italian, and 1 Guinean black.[16] Most of the late-colonial immigrants to Texas came from other parts of northern New Spain, however. Coahuila, Nuevo León, and Nuevo Santander were the provinces of origin for most of them, with the one supplying the largest number being Saltillo, the oldest population center in the northeastern corner of the viceroyalty. The 1793 census of San Antonio, for instance, indicates that over 12 percent of the town's residents were from other parts of New Spain, and that 130 of these 164 Mexicans came from the three above-named provinces.[17]

If this remote province's population had disparate national origins, it also had a very mixed racial background. As early as 1718 the missionaries with the Alarcón expedition complained that the colonists the governor had recruited belonged to the baser castes—mestizos and mulattos. Other outside observers throughout the colonial period, from governors to visitors, also commented on the mixed racial characteristics, and the parish registers and census reports support their conclusion of widespread miscegenation.[18] The fluidity of racial boundaries on the frontier, and especially in isolated Texas, was helped by royal requirements that soldiers in the service of His Catholic Majesty be Spaniards. Hence, no matter what their baptismal records indicated or the way they were described in their enlistment papers, company commanders routinely listed their men as "Spaniards." Also contributing to racial mixing was the limited availability of marriage partners for the predominantly male immigrants. The evidence is clear that whatever their true racial composition, about half of Texas and Laredo settlers considered themselves "Spanish," with mestizo and other mixed-blood groups making up most of the rest, and Indians within the civil settlements accounting for between 10 and 15 percent of the population.[19] Following the transfer of Louisiana to the United States in 1803, the crown stationed in Texas hundreds of additional troops from the militias of neighboring provinces, reaching a high of 1,368 in 1806.[20] This population boom proved transitory, however, as the disruptions of the Mexican War of Independence led to the transfer of troops, the rebellions in the province, the death of hundreds of Tejano insurgents, and the flight of hundreds of others to Louisiana. Although the numbers available are very problematical, it is certain that Texas had a smaller Hispanic population on the eve of Mexican independence—fewer than twenty-five hundred men, women, and children—than it did at the turn of the century.

SETTLEMENT PATTERNS ON THE TEXAS FRONTIER

Throughout the colonial period Texas' small population was concentrated at three geographic centers. The most stable center of settlement was located in the upper San Antonio River Valley, at present-day San Antonio, where Spanish occupation began in 1718 with a presidio and Mission San Antonio de Valero (the Alamo). In 1720 a second Franciscan mission, San José y San Miguel de Aguayo, opened its doors some miles downstream. In 1731 three other missions, Nuestra Señora de la Concepción, San Juan Capistrano, and San Francisco de la Espada, which had failed to take root in East Texas, relocated along alternating sides of the river below the older settlements. That same year, the fifty-five Canary Islander immigrants founded the only chartered civil settlement in the province, San Fernando de Béxar. Located adjacent to the presidio for protection, the two entities merged so thoroughly that by the late colonial period the entire settlement was commonly referred to as Béxar. Because of its location on the road from the interior of New Spain to the other Texas settlements, Béxar quickly grew into the largest and most diversified settlement. In recognition of its strategic importance, in 1773 Béxar became the provincial capital.

East of San Antonio, in the coastal region near Matagorda Bay, was located the second population center of the province, the presidio-mission complex known as La Bahía. Originally established at the site of La Salle's Fort St. Louis by the Marqués de San Miguel de Aguayo in 1722, the presidio and mission were removed some thirty miles inland to a more healthful location in 1726. In an effort to give José de Escandón's plans for settling the coastal region between the Rio Grande and the Texas border a northern anchor, the complex was moved once again in 1749 to its present location on the San Antonio River at Goliad. Here the original mission, Espíritu Santo de Zúñiga, was joined by Nuestra Señora del Rosario in 1754. At the end of the century, just when the other missions were moribund and about to begin the secularization process, the last Texas mission, Nuestra Señora del Refugio, was established about twenty miles south of La Bahía for nearby Karankawa bands. Although a sizable civilian settlement grew around the presidio from an early date, La Bahía remained under the administrative jurisdiction of the military commander until 1820, when the settlement was raised to the status of villa and established a town council.

The third area of permanent settlement in the province was in eastern Texas. In 1716 the Domingo Ramón expedition established a short-lived presidio and four missions on the Neches and Angelina rivers near present-day Nacogdoches. The following year two more missions were founded, including San Miguel de los Adaes, which was located near the French settlement at Natchitoches. In his effort to reinforce the frontier against French encroachments, the Marqués de San Miguel de Aguayo established another presidio, Nuestra Señora del Pilar de los Adaes, between Mission San Miguel and Natchitoches. The presence of this border military post and the moribund status of most of the missions of the Neches-Angelina area brought about the closure of the presidio protecting them in 1729 and the transfer of three of the missions to Central Texas in 1730. Between that year and 1773, when the area was abandoned on the recommendation of the Marqués de Rubí, Spanish East Texas consisted of the Presidio de los Adaes, its companion mission of San Miguel, and missions Nuestra Señora de los Dolores de los Ais and Nuestra Señora de Guadalupe de los Nacogdoches.

As in the case of La Bahía, the East Texas presidio became the hub of a considerable civil settlement with substantial ties to the neighboring French colony. Not surprisingly, many of the residents resented being moved to the San Antonio area when Los Adaes was disbanded as no longer necessary in light of Louisiana's transfer to Spain following the Seven Years War. A large group of Adaesanos successfully petitioned for permission to return to East Texas and in 1774 founded the short-lived pueblo of Bucareli on the Trinity River crossing of the Camino Real. Indian depredations and floods led to the abandonment of this site in 1779 for the vicinity of the abandoned mission of Nacogdoches, where the settlers established a town by that name. Although it had its roots in the military settlement of Los Adaes, Nacogdoches was a civil settlement governed by a lieutenant governor appointed by the governor. Following United States acquisition of Louisiana, Nacogdoches was garrisoned by royal troops beginning in 1795, and during the Mexican War of Independence became the target of filibustering expeditions, which left it almost totally abandoned until 1821.[21]

Aside from the above-described settlement areas, Spanish officials undertook a number of abortive efforts to expand the province's area of settlement. The failed effort to establish the San Xavier Mission-Presidio complex in Central Texas in the early 1750s gave way to the disastrous Apache mission experiment at San Saba. Although the accompanying presidio remained in that location for more than a decade, and two new Apache missions were opened on the upper reaches of the Nueces River, by 1772 the crown recognized the uselessness of such a remote post and ordered the area's abandonment. As San Saba was failing to the west, the presidio-mission complex known as Orcoquisac was meeting a similar fate to the east. It was established in 1755 at the northern end of Galveston Bay for the Christianization of the Akokisa Indians and the defense of Spanish territory against French and English intruders. The location proved unhealthful, the Indians uncooperative, and the garrison querulous. Unable to attract settlers, and its garrison in greater demand at Béxar and La Bahía, the post was often undermanned. It too was closed at the time Los Adaes was abandoned, although the garrison had been removed sometime before.[22]

With the exception of the Adaesanos' efforts to relocate themselves at Bucareli and, finally, at Nacogdoches, no other settlement efforts were made until after the turn of the century. The Louisiana Purchase by the United States drew that expansion-minded country much closer to the rich mining regions of northern New Spain than Spanish officials felt comfortable with. The debate between those officials who wanted to accept French- and Anglo-American émigrés as settlers in Texas and those who did not want any foreigners so close to the border was won by the former. The commandant general gave permission for settlements on the Trinity, Brazos, Colorado, San Marcos, and Guadalupe rivers. But only two of these were actually realized, Santísima Trinidad de Salcedo (1806) and San Marcos de Neve (1807). Salcedo, as the former was known, was settled with a few families from Béxar and a larger number of émigrés from Louisiana. San Marcos, on the other hand, was founded by a group of colonists from Nuevo Santander. Both succumbed to the disruptions of the Mexican War of Independence. In 1810 Governor Cordero, using his authority as governor of Coahuila, established one last settlement in the territory of present-day Texas. The town of Palafox, located on the east bank of the Rio Grande halfway between Laredo and San Juan Bautista, went untouched by the insurrections in Texas, but fell prey to repeated Indian assaults, which brought about its abandonment by the mid-1820s.[23]

Another town with civilian origins was Laredo, which, although part of present-day Texas, was until the Treaty of Guadalupe Hidalgo part of Tamaulipas. Laredo was the northwestern-most of the Rio Grande settlements founded by José de Escandón, the colonizer of Nuevo Santander (renamed Tamaulipas after Mexican independence); it was also the only one on the east bank of the river. Founded in 1755 with a handful of ranching families from the downstream Hacienda de Dolores, the settlement was quickly augmented by families from another Rio Grande settlement, Revilla, and in 1767 Laredo received a royal charter as a villa and was granted a local government. Indian depredations in these years proved too much for the local militia, and in 1775 the governor stationed a small garrison there, although from the available evidence it is clear that it did not play an important role in community development.[24]

TEXAS COLONIAL SOCIETY

The social structure of colonial Texas was a simpler and more fluid version of broader Mexican colonial norms. Outside the governor and presidio commanders, there were no governmental representatives of the crown. The only members of the ecclesiastical hierarchy present were the missionaries, who also served the needs of the Hispanic residents at La Bahía and Los Adaes/Nacogdoches, and the lone diocesan priest in the province, who served at Béxar. Because the province had no mines or well-developed estates, there were no rich residents.[25] A limited number of the most successful rancher-farmers (many of them one-time soldiers) and merchants constituted the local elites of the various settlements, although even these would have been recognized as little more than poverty-stricken yokels in the central parts of the empire.

Within the confines of the limited economic and social world that Tejanos constructed for themselves, there was room for mobility, however. The reality of miscegenation, combined with the demands of a hierarchical social system that emphasized the primacy of Spaniards, produced widespread "passing." Mulattos and Indians tried to pass as mestizos, and mestizos tried to pass as Spaniards. As mentioned above, military service, which tended to "whiten" individuals socially, provided an additional avenue of mobility through promotion. Because the frontier presidio system was separate from the regular Spanish army and relied on men with knowledge of Indian warfare, competent frontiersmen could and did rise to command.[26]

In the case of San Antonio there was an important additional element that contributed to social status: descent from the Canary Island settlers who arrived in 1731. Because the king had granted them privileges as original settlers (*primeros pobladores*), the original Isleño group and its descendants took pains to point out their social rank, although it did not necessarily correspond to economic or political status. In the course of time the Canary Islanders had to seek spouses among the much larger Mexican population, so that by the latter part of the eighteenth century many second- and third-generation Bexareños could claim Isleño status.[27]

As a military-agricultural society, property ownership was the most important measure of social status. Limited access to farmland—irrigated fields were only available at Béxar—and the financial requirements for obtaining ranch land divided society into the few haves and the many have-nots. Although anyone showing a little industry and the intent of establishing and maintaining a family could gain access to a town lot and, therefore, the status of *vecino*, participation in local affairs was limited to individuals of substance. The few merchants and craftsmen who braved the frontier did not, by their mere presence, gain status within their communities. They too had to acquire landed property and, if possible, marry into an established family in order to climb the local social ladder.[28]

As in the greater colonial society, the trappings of social status were many and readily evident in colonial Texas. Length of family residence in the community, for example; claim to Isleño descent; location of one's residence in proximity to the town's plaza; participation in local government; undertaking some form of conspicuous consumption, like sending a son to train for the priesthood or assuming the expenses of religious celebrations; and having one's name prefaced by the honorific *don* or *doña* were all symbols of rank within one's community. Because of the limited financial means of all members of local society, manual labor consisting of farming and ranching did not reduce one's status. In colonial Texas everyone had to work.[29]

COLONIAL TEXAS: AN ECONOMIC BACKWATER

Unlike other parts of the frontier, where mining or large-scale sheep and cattle operations extended the zones of Spanish control, in Texas the military served that function. It is not surprising that at the end of the colonial period the surviving pre-independence settlements (including the almost abandoned Nacogdoches) had military origins. What little market economy existed in colonial Texas relied heavily on meeting presidial needs. Not only did the presidios serve as markets for foodstuffs produced by both the missions and civilian settlers, they also supported tailors, blacksmiths, carpenters, shoe makers, and other artisans. After economic control over the garrisons was wrested away from governors and presidio commanders in the latter part of the eighteenth century, a handful of petty merchants made a meager livelihood supplying soldiers and their families with second-grade goods from central Mexico and a few imported luxuries. The military payrolls proved to be the only consistent, if inadequate, source of money supply in the province. Of the colonial settlements within present-day Texas, only Laredo had a history of independence from this military economy.

Outside of military service, economic opportunity was by and large limited to farming and ranching. Most farming took place near the towns and, of course, at the missions. Farming at La Bahía and in East Texas seems to have been a strictly subsistence practice, which at the former often did not meet local needs. In San Antonio, where the terrain lent itself to irrigation, Mission San Antonio de Valero and the presidio both opened *acequias* in 1718. It was the presidio's *acequia* and farm that the Canary Islanders appropriated when they arrived in 1731. Another farm for the town opened in 1778, with the construction of a second public *acequia* spanning the San Antonio River and San Pedro Creek. By the 1750s all five Béxar missions had sophisticated irrigation works that, in the case of San Francisco de la Espada, included an aqueduct that has remained in service to this day. The productivity of the San Antonio farms was such that they regularly supplied other Texas communities with agricultural products, mostly maize, and sometimes sold crops as far away as the Rio Grande and Coahuila. But the limited range of Texas agriculture is evinced in the absence of gristmills until the beginning of the nineteenth century at all establishments except Mission San José.[30]

Not surprisingly, the limited markets available to Béxar farmers contributed to periodic disputes between settlers and missionaries. Soon after the Canary Islanders arrived, they complained to the viceroy that the presidio commanders and missionaries were conspiring to prevent the sale of Isleño corn to the garrisons. Throughout the rest of the colonial period, the town's civilian farmers used the viceregal order that resulted from the complaint to force the presidios to purchase their crops in preference to that of the missions. The townspeople did not get everything they wanted, however, for the missionaries were successful in preventing the settlers from gaining access to neophyte labor.[31]

Disputes between missions and civilians extended to ranching as well. The ranching practiced by Tejanos also remained at a rudimentary level. Because of chronic Indian hostilities, operations during the colonial period remained limited in size and in ranching methods. Prior to their decline in the 1780s, the missions developed the earliest ranches and owned the largest herds. Overall, there were few standing herds, however, most branded animals being allowed to roam at will until roundup time. Until the late 1780s missionaries protested that settlers raided mission pastures, indiscriminately slaughtering cattle that clearly belonged to the Indians. Civilian ranchers, for their part, complained that the missions had not only appropriated excessive amounts of land in order to prevent settlers from establishing viable ranches, but that they claimed the descendants of animals originally brought to the province by the colonists.[32]

Notwithstanding the continual disputes, ranching proved, overall, the most lucrative economic pursuit available from the Rio Grande to the Louisiana border. In the first decades following Spanish settlement, animals were slaughtered at temporary work sites, where vaqueros dried the meat and extracted useful byproducts. Hides, tallow, and dried beef made their way out of the province in mule trains organized both by local settler and mission ranchers and by outsiders who had brought in merchandise. For a quarter century beginning in 1770, economic conditions in New Spain and Louisiana combined with impressive growth in the wild cattle population to create a market for live-cattle exports. Tejanos made cattle drives to New Orleans in the east and Coahuila, Nuevo León, and Nuevo Santander to the south. One favorite destination was the annual trade fair at Saltillo, where ranchers could exchange cattle for goods that they brought back to Texas for sale. As the wild cattle population succumbed to unbridled exploitation, Tejanos turned to horse and mule trading at the end of the eighteenth century.[33]

Trade in colonial Texas was limited not only by the geographic isolation of the region, but also by imperial regulations aimed at preventing foreign access to colonial markets. Commerce with Natchitoches was officially proscribed, even during the decades when it was a Spanish possession. Bernardo de Gálvez's efforts to acquire Texas cattle for Spanish military efforts against the British during the United States War of Independence required special dispensation from viceregal officials. Contraband, nonetheless, was widespread, particularly in East Texas, but its overall economic importance remains the subject of debate.[34]

The possibilities for trade with the Indians were likewise limited by official Spanish policy. Until late in the eighteenth century it was illegal for Spanish subjects to trade in firearms with the Indians. Even after it became permissible, many limitations were placed on it, as at Béxar, where the governor refused the settlers permission to trade in firearms with the

Lipan Apaches. European trade goods, also in demand by the Indians, were expensive for would-be Spanish traders because of the costs of bringing them overland from Veracruz. Another obstacle to trade was that the Spanish never acquired the interest in pelts and furs that other Europeans did. Consequently, French, English, and (after the turn of the nineteenth century) American traders held the upper hand in dealing with the Indians. Nevertheless, some commerce between Indians and settlers did take place, especially in locally produced agricultural goods and services (for example, in smithing) in return for buffalo hides, deerskins, horses (often taken from other Spanish settlements), and, on occasion, human captives. In the absence of any account books documenting such transactions, any estimate of the scope of this activity is impossible.[35]

The economic development of Texas during the colonial period was largely limited to these incipient, rudimentary activities. Outside the mission textile shops, with their looms and spinning wheels, Texas contained no intensively organized economic enterprises. Activities such as soap and candle making made up small cottage industries that sometimes produced enough surplus to provide export quantities, but most often only served local needs. *Piloncillo* (brown-sugar cones) and *chinguirito* (a crude rum) were also manufactured for local consumption, although production of the latter was illegal until the mid-1790s.[36]

There are indications that conditions improved in the first decade of the nineteenth century. The arrival of additional troops to defend the new border with the United States, efforts on the part of the governor and other royal officials to foster the province's development by establishing new settlements, and a lull in Indian depredations all contributed to expanding economic opportunities. But this period was short lived. The outbreak of the Mexican War of Independence brought an end to government subsidies for Indian gifts, and the disgruntled tribes increased their raids on Spanish settlements and ranches. Rebellion and filibustering threw provincial government into disorder, led to the abandonment of Nacogdoches and the new settlements, and resulted in the flight of hundreds of settlers.[37] Governor Martínez, the last Spanish colonial governor of Texas, documented the deplorable state of the province on the eve of Mexican independence. About Béxar he had the following to say:

> This citizenry has no other occupation than farming, and he who cannot practice it employs himself in hunting bear and deer. The crops that they work are reduced to maize, wheat, and sugarcane. There is no manufacturing at all nor any freighting, nor are there any miners.

The number of livestock upon which this citizenry can count at this time is small, and cannot be detailed because it has fled from its respective pastures; there being no wool-bearing livestock left now, with the exception of some sixty head of sheep and about thirty goats. There are also no breeding mares and the number of tame horses reaches sixty.[38]

SOCIAL MOBILITY ON THE FRONTIER: A FAMILY CASE STUDY

The various characteristics of social and economic development in colonial Texas can be seen at work in numerous families whose Texas roots stretch from the earliest days of settlement to the present. One such family is the Seguíns, among whose colonial ancestors can be counted soldiers, artisans, town councilmen, farmers, ranchers, and legislators.[39]

The first Seguín in Texas was linked to the early military history of the province. Santiago Seguín was in San Antonio by 1722, as a member of the presidio company, most probably having been recruited for the Marqués de San Miguel de Aguayo's expedition to drive the French out of East Texas. His son, José Miguel, had the distinction of being one of three Bexareños who, in 1756, accompanied Bernardo de Miranda y Flores on his search for the fabled silver mines of Los Almagres.[40]

In the 1740s Santiago was joined by Bartolomé, who was probably his nephew. Bartolomé did not enter military service, for he was a carpenter. He did marry the daughter of a Béxar alderman, who himself had been a local soldier in the 1720s. Also unlike his kinsman, Bartolomé prospered in Béxar. Aside from his extensive carpentry work, which included providing estate appraisals and led to a grant of land on which to build a shop, he did some farming. In 1776 he received a grant for an irrigated field in the town's new farm. Other signs of his rise in local society included his purchase of an expensive plot of land near the military plaza, his service as an officer for one of the town's religious feasts, and his three-time election to the town council. Bartolomé died in 1791 at about age seventy, leaving behind children and grandchildren by his first two wives, and having buried his third wife some time before.

The vagaries of achieving and maintaining social status on the frontier are illustrated in the fortunes of two of Bartolomé's sons. His only child by his first wife, Santiago, inherited his maternal grandfather's farming and ranching interests and parlayed them into enough wealth to join the ranks of San Antonio's prosperous. In contrast, Bartolomé's son by his second wife, Esmeregildo, remained a landless farmhand throughout his later life after a brief military career in the 1780s. Béxar's census of 1793 makes the distinctions between the two clear.[41] Santiago is listed as a *labrador* (farmer) and bears the title of *don*. Esmeregildo, meanwhile, appears simply as a *jornalero* (farmhand) with no honorific preceding his name.

As was the case with most other successful colonial Texans, Santiago had his hand in a number of different economic activities. He farmed, hauled stone, and perhaps even served as a mule skinner. It was in ranching that Santiago found the most success, however. From the late 1770s onward, he was one of the town's most prominent cattle ranchers, driving a number of herds to Coahuila during the period. Although his herds consistently numbered in the hundreds, he, like a number of other ranchers, did not own his own ranch land, instead keeping his cattle with those of relatives. Santiago's prospects were good enough that in 1778 he married María Guadalupe Fuentes, sister of the parish priest. In 1784, at age thirty, he was already serving as a member of the town council.

As he grew older, Santiago also grew more unsettled, however. Trouble with the authorities over compensation for construction work, beginning in 1790, at least in part contributed to Governor Manuel Muñoz rejecting his selection to the town council in 1795. The following year, he was found guilty of assaulting one of the town's aldermen. By the end of the century Santiago had moved his family to Saltillo, although in 1803 he was living in Béxar because his brother-in-law, Father Pedro Fuentes, asked the governor to order his return to his family in Saltillo.

At least two of Santiago's sons decided to make Texas their home after Santiago's family moved away. Juan made his way to Nacogdoches, where he got into trouble with the authorities in 1805 for displaying an anticlerical poster. Despite the disruptions of the Mexican War of Independence, Juan remained attached to the Nacogdoches area and served as *alcalde* during the mid-1820s. He died there in August 1836.[42]

Juan's older brother Erasmo led a longer and more influential life as one of San Antonio's leading citizens during the first four decades of the nineteenth century. In 1807 the twenty-five-year-old Erasmo, already described as a merchant, became Béxar's postmaster. The post proved profitable enough that, despite two or three interruptions, he occupied it for almost thirty years. Of course he also worked the fields he had inherited from his father's family and by 1810 managed to acquire a considerable amount of ranch land that had belonged to the now secularized Mission San Antonio de Valero. The invasion of Texas by the Gutiérrez-Magee expedition of 1812–13 brought a sharp but temporary decline in Erasmo's fortunes. Accused of treason, his property was confiscated. He refused to participate in a general amnesty, however, and sought to prove his innocence. Although he was cleared of the charges by 1818 and his house and ranch were restored to him, Erasmo never recovered approximately eight-thousand-dollars' worth of other property that he claimed.

A man of considerable talents, Erasmo quickly rebuilt his position in the community. In 1820 he served as *alcalde* of San Antonio—the first of a number of municipal posts he was to hold throughout the next decade. The following year he was selected by Governor Antonio Martínez as his emissary to Moses Austin, to carry word that the Anglo-American's colonization plan had been approved. And his protestations of loyalty to the crown did not prevent his early emergence as one of the town's post-independence political leaders. In 1822 he recovered the postmastership and in 1825 added that of quartermaster. Having been selected as backup representative to Mexico's first constitutional congress, he was elected as the Texas delegate to the second and helped draft the Federal Constitution of 1824. A strong proponent of Anglo-American settlement, he would eventually side with the Texans in the Texas War of Independence. His son, Juan Nepomuceno, not only served as an officer in the Texas army, but went on to have a colorful political-military career in the border region.

CONCLUSION

Under such circumstances, it should not surprise us that Tejanos supported liberal immigration and economic policies throughout the Mexican period. A few Tejanos even managed to prosper through their dealings with the new Anglo-American settlers, but most of the Mexican population did not benefit from the growing population. Anglo-Americans directed their commercial and productive activities toward markets in the United States, New Orleans in particular. Most were yeomen farmers who produced the very types of goods Tejanos would have been in a position to sell them—agricultural products. Those Anglo-American immigrants who came as cotton farmers tended to bring their own labor with them—slaves—and, therefore, had little need of Mexican agricultural workers. Consequently, by the end of the Mexican period, Texas was well on the way to the kind of economic development that had eluded the region during the colonial period. But the beneficiaries of that development were by and large the new arrivals. Having attained economic and demographic predominance within fifteen years of their initial legal arrival in 1821, Anglo-Americans were ready by 1835 to wrest political control from Mexico and from a Tejano population that had come to be looked upon as alien to Texas.

Spanish Colonial Texas

Estimated Population of Texas Settlements and Laredo

	1740	1747	1754	1757	1789	1790	1793	1794	1830
Bexar Presidio & Civilian	400					1,383			
Mission Valero	238					48			
Mission San José	249					144			
Mission Concepción	210					47			
Mission Capistrano	169					21			
Mission Espada	121					93			
La Bahía Presidio & Civilian	200					633			
Mission Espíritu Santo		400						125	
Mission Rosario			500			67			
Mission Refugio							138		21
East Texas	300					524			
Laredo				85	708				

SOURCES

Peter Gerhard, *The North Frontier of New Spain* (rev. ed., Norman: University of Oklahoma Press, 1993), 341.

Gilberto M. Hinojosa, *A Borderlands Town in Transition: Laredo, 1755–1870* (College Station: Texas A&M University Press, 1983), 9–19.

Robert H. Jackson, "Congregation and Population Change in the Mission Communities of Northern New Spain: Cases from California and Texas," *New Mexico Historical Review* 69, 2 (1994): 174, 176.

Alicia V. Tjarks, "Comparative Demographic Analysis of Texas, 1777–1793," *Southwestern Historical Quarterly* 77, 3 (1974): 303.

NOTES

1. For the Pineda and Lavazares expeditions, see Robert S. Weddle, *Spanish Sea: The Gulf of Mexico in North American Discovery, 1500–1685* (College Station, 1985), 99–101, 257–58. Narratives of the Cabeza de Vaca and De Soto journeys are collected in Frederick W. Hodge and Theodore H. Lewis, eds., *Spanish Explorers in the Southern United States, 1528–1543* (repr., 1907; Austin, 1984). The best monograph on the Coronado expedition is Herbert E. Bolton, *Coronado: Knight of the Pueblos and Plains* (repr., 1949; Albuquerque, 1964).

2. The following discussion of the region's Indian cultural landscape is based on W. W. Newcomb Jr., *The Indians of Texas: From Prehistoric to Modern Times* (Austin, 1961). An excellent brief account can be found in Donald E. Chipman, *Spanish Texas, 1519–1821* (Austin, 1992).

3. Peter Gerhard, *The North Frontier of New Spain*, rev. ed. (Norman, 1993), 340; Elizabeth A. H. John, *Storms Brewed in Other Men's Worlds: The Confrontation of Indians, Spanish, and French in the Southwest, 1540–1795* (Lincoln, 1981), 189, 369, 498–99; Martín Salinas, *Indians of the Rio Grande Delta: Their Role in the History of Southern Texas and Northeastern Mexico* (Austin, 1990), 140.

4. Agustín Morfi, *The History of Texas*, 2 vols. (Albuquerque, 1935), 1:92.

5. Gilberto M. Hinojosa, "The Religious-Indian Communities: The Goals of the Friars," in Gerald E. Poyo and Gilberto M. Hinojosa, eds., *Tejano Origins in Eighteenth-Century San Antonio* (Austin, 1991), 71.

6. Morfi, *History of Texas*, 2:421; italics in original. The other missions to which Morfi refers include Nuestra Señora del Pilar de los Adaes, near the Red River and the Louisiana settlement of Natchitoches, and Nuestra Señora de la Luz del Orcoquisac, on the Trinity River just above Galveston Bay.

7. Carlos E. Castañeda, *Our Catholic Heritage in Texas, 1519–1936*, repr. ed. (New York, 1976), 2:225–26, 237–38, 4:33; Hinojosa, "Religious-Indian Communities," 74.

8. Bolton, *Coronado*, 137–278; John, *Storms Brewed in Other Men's Worlds*, 279–92.

9. The most detailed account of the San Saba Mission is Robert S. Weddle, *The San Sabá Mission: Spanish Pivot in Texas* (Austin, 1964).

10. Castañeda, *Our Catholic Heritage in Texas*, 3:121.

11. Robert H. Jackson, "Congregation and Population Change in the Mission Communities of Northern New Spain: Cases from the Californias and Texas," *New Mexico Historical Review* 69:2 (1994), 171–75; Hinojosa, "Religious-Indian Communities," 74–78.

12. Castañeda, *Our Catholic Heritage in Texas*, 5:67–109, 6:126, 324–26; Jackson, "Congregation and Population Change," table 6, p. 177.

13. Hinojosa, "Religious-Indian Communities," 79–80; Castañeda, *Our Catholic Heritage*, 5:96–108.

14. Domingo Cabello to Bernardo de Gálvez, July 25, 1779, Papeles de Cuba, leg. 70, Archivo General de Indias, transcripts at the Texas State Archives, Austin.

15. Oakah L. Jones, *Los Paisanos: Spanish Settlers on the Northern Frontier of New Spain* (Norman, 1979), 46–47; Herbert E. Bolton, *Texas in the Middle Eighteenth Century: Studies in Spanish Colonial History and Administration*, repr. ed. (Austin, 1970), 84–85, 246–47.

16. Alicia V. Tjarks, "Comparative Demographic Analysis of Texas, 1777–1793," *Southwestern Historical Quarterly* 77 (Jan. 1974), table 23, note a.

17. Tjarks, "Comparative Demographic Analysis," table 21.

18. Castañeda, *Our Catholic Heritage*, 2:87; Jesús F. de la Teja, "Indians, Soldiers, and Canary Islanders: The Making of a Texas Frontier Community," *Locus* 3 (Fall 1990), 88.

19. Tjarks, "Comparative Demographic Analysis," 322–28; Gilberto M. Hinojosa, *A Borderlands Town in Transition: Laredo, 1755–1870* (College Station, 1983), 17.

20. Odie B. Faulk, *The Last Years of Spanish Texas, 1778–1821* (The Hague, 1964), 124; Mattie Austin Hatcher, *The Opening of Texas to Foreign Settlement, 1801–1821*, repr. ed. (Philadelphia, 1976), 61–62, 70–71.

21. Bolton, *Texas in the Middle Eighteenth Century*, 377–446; Chipman, *Spanish Texas*, 240–41; James M. McReynolds, "Family Life in a Borderland Community: Nacogdoches, Texas, 1779–1861" (PhD diss., Texas Tech University, 1978), 7–25.

22. Chipman, *Spanish Texas*, 147–66; Weddle, *San Saba Mission*, 156–83.

23. Hatcher, *Opening of Texas*, 94–105, 124–26, 202, 224–25, 230.

24. Hinojosa, *Borderlands Town*, 5–16.

25. A good contemporary description of the little progress Texas had made by the beginning of the nineteenth century is a report by Juan Bautista Elguézabal, governor of Texas, to the commandant general of the Interior Provinces in 1803. See Hatcher, *Opening of Texas*, appendix 5.

26. Tjarks, "Comparative Demographic Analysis," 322–30.

27. De la Teja, "Indians, Soldiers, and Canary Islanders," 93–94.

28. McReynolds, "Family Life in a Borderland Community," 243–47; De la Teja, "Indians, Soldiers, and Canary Islanders," 86–87, 92.

29. Jesús F. de la Teja, "The Structure of Society: The Spanish Borderlands," in *Encyclopedia of the North American Colonies*, Jacob Cooke, ed. (New York, 1993), 379–80.

30. Jesús F. de la Teja, *San Antonio de Béxar: A Community on New Spain's Northern Frontier* (Albuquerque, 1995), chap. 4; McReynolds, "Family Life in a Borderland Community," 243–45. Scattered throughout vols. 2–6 of Castañeda's *Our Catholic Heritage in Texas* are descriptions of the economic activities of all the Texas missions; see, for example, 4:22–39. A good compact survey of the San Antonio missions that gives considerable attention to material development is

Marion A. Habig, *The Alamo Chain of Missions: A History of San Antonio's Five Old Missions*, rev. ed. (Chicago, 1968).

31. Castañeda, *Our Catholic Heritage in Texas*, 3:103–4; De la Teja, *San Antonio de Béxar*, chap. 4.

32. De la Teja, *San Antonio de Béxar*, chap. 5; Jack Jackson, *Los Mesteños: Spanish Ranching in Texas, 1721–1821* (College Station, 1986), 33–41, 53–54.

33. De la Teja, *San Antonio de Béxar*, chap. 5; Jackson, *Los Mesteños*, 503–4.

34. Jackson, *Los Mesteños*, 250–51, 508–10; McReynolds, "Family Life in a Borderland Community," 14; Robert S. Weddle and Robert H. Thonhoff, *Drama and Conflict: The Texas Saga of 1776* (Austin, 1976), 170–71.

35. Ordinances of Governor Muñoz, Oct. 24, 1793, Bexar Archives (hereafter cited as BA); McReynolds, "Family Life in a Borderland Community," 19–21.

36. Nava to Muñoz, Dec. 27, 1796, BA.

37. Castañeda, *Our Catholic Heritage in Texas*, 6:56, n8, 121–26; Chipman, *Spanish Texas*, 238; McReynolds, "Family Life in a Borderland Community," 15, 23.

38. Ciudad de Béxar, Jurisdicción de la Provincia de los Texas, Jan. 1, 1820, BA.

39. Unless otherwise stated, the following paragraphs are based on Jesús F. de la Teja, ed., *A Revolution Remembered: The Memoirs and Selected Correspondence of Juan N. Seguín* (Austin, 1991), 1–56; and Frederick C. Chabot, *With the Makers of San Antonio* (San Antonio, 1937), 118–29.

40. Roderick B. Patten, trans. and ed., "Miranda's Inspection of Los Almagres: His Journal, Report, and Petition," *Southwestern Historical Quarterly* 74:2 (1970), 229.

41. Padrón de las almas que hay en esta villa de San Fernando de Austria [*sic*], Dec. 31, 1793, BA.

42. Nettie Lee Benson, "Bishop Marín de Porras and Texas," *Southwestern Historical Quarterly* 51:1 (1947), 23–24; Anthony R. Clarke to Austin, May 22, 1824, Eugene C. Barker, ed., *The Austin Papers*, vol. 2, part 10f, *Annual Report of the American Historical Association for the Year 1919* (Washington, DC, 1924), 797; Columbia *Telegraph and Texas Register*, Sept. 21, 1836.

Theodore Gentilz, *Ojo de Agua San Pedro*. The clean and plentiful springs that created San Pedro Creek and the San Antonio River boasted fish, eels, and waterfowl that, combined with low banks that were conducive to the opening of irrigation works, made the area an ideal location for settlement. Well into the nineteenth century, San Pedro Springs was the source for the water of San Antonio's Acequia Madre, or Main Ditch, which supplied irrigation water not only to the city's first farm but also to the orchards, gardens, and households that lined its banks. Courtesy of Mr. Larry Sheerin, San Antonio, Texas.

2

"A Fine Country with Broad Plains —The Most Beautiful in New Spain"

VIEWS OF LAND AND NATURE IN COLONIAL SAN ANTONIO*

As in most fields, study of the Texas environment tends to begin with the advent of large-scale Anglo-American immigration in the 1820s.[1] The premise that Texas was "a howling wilderness" redeemed by intrepid, westward-moving pioneers leads to the conclusion that environmental change, significant change in any case, started with them. In the second of his two books on the state's environmental history, *At Home in Texas: Early Views of the Land*, Robin Doughty asserts that "Native American and Hispanic views of the environment are beyond the scope of this book." Although he quickly qualifies the statement with "this is not because they are unimportant," he never quite explains just why they are left out. At the beginning of chapter two it is quite clear that for Doughty—his protest to the contrary—the Hispanic experience is of little relevance to the story of Texas settlement.[2] A stagnant subsistence economy at the turn of the century remained so twenty years later, when Stephen F. Austin arrived. This portrayal is, nonetheless, an improvement over Doughty's first book, *Wildlife and Man in Texas: Environmental Change and Conservation*, in which the possibility that the preexisting population of Texas when the Anglo Americans arrived might have had something to contribute on these issues is not addressed at all.[3]

Limited as the Hispanic presence in Texas might have been before 1820, it left a rich record of observations about the natural world and interactions with it that challenges most evaluations of the significance of the interaction with the South Texas environment. Even if the impact of this population on the region's fauna and flora was limited, it went beyond

---

*First published in *On the Border: An Environmental History of San Antonio*, ed. Char Miller (Pittsburgh: University of Pittsburgh Press, 2001), 41–55.

the introduction of European livestock. The evidence makes clear that the Hispanic frontiersmen who came into the region in the eighteenth century made themselves as much "at home" as the Anglo- and African-American and European immigrants who followed. In expedition journals, administrative reports, and a miscellany of other documents, the Spanish colonial population of Texas has left us its impression of the challenge and potential that was Texas.

The land they knew as Texas, from just south of San Antonio to western Louisiana, was a well-watered region of rolling prairies and forests with much promise for civilization.[4] It is this much smaller Spanish Texas, and how Spanish colonials dealt with it, that is the subject of this chapter. The emphasis on San Antonio, the largest center of Hispanic settlement and provincial capital after 1773, is natural because its record of human interaction with the natural world is the richest. Founded in 1718 as a way station between the Rio Grande outpost of San Juan Bautista and the Louisiana border region, San Antonio quickly became colonial Texas' most successful settlement. Even during the fifty years before San Antonio became capital of Texas in 1773, governors often resided there for long stretches. In the last fifty years of the Spanish colonial period, it contained about half of the province's population. Consequently, it was at San Antonio that Spanish colonials had the greatest impact on the Texas environment.

Texas offered a variety of landscapes that compared favorably with the rest of New Spain. The vast grasslands of the region from the Medina River to the East Texas forests evoked the word "beautiful" to describe their appearance. This judgement, by Gen. Domingo Terán de los Ríos, governor of Texas between 1691 and 1693, was echoed by subsequent travelers through the region. Father Juan Antonio de la Peña, chronicler of the Marqués de San Miguel de Aguayo's 1721–22 expedition, described the Colorado River area downstream from Austin as composed of "some beautiful plains."[5] Spanish appreciation for the aesthetic quality of the landscape is no more clearly evident than in the following passage regarding the New Braunfels area from Fray Isidro Espinosa's diary of the 1716 expedition:

> May 18 ... The waters of the Guadalupe [Comal River][6] are clear, crystal and so abundant that it seemed almost incredible to us that its source arose so near. Composing this river are three principal springs of water which, together with other smaller ones, unite as soon as they begin to flow. There the growth of the walnut trees competes with the poplars. All are crowned by the wild grapevines, which climb up their trunks. They gave promise already in their blossom for the good prospect of their fruit. The white

and the black mulberry trees, whose leaves were more than eight inches in length, showed in their sprouts how sharp were the frosts. Willow trees beautified the region of this river with their luxuriant foliage and there was a great variety of plants. It makes a delightful grove for recreation, and the enjoyment of the melodious songs of different birds.[7]

Aside from the region's plentiful and impressive prairies, explorers and later travelers could also appreciate more rugged terrain—for better and worse. Domingo Ramón, leader of the 1716 *entrada* that established a permanent Spanish presence in East Texas, spoke of the country in present Dimmit County as containing "beautiful canyons." At the other end of the province, where missions, Indian villages, and Spanish Texas' first capital, Los Adaes, occupied clearings in the region's dense forests, Fray José de Solís described the site of the Nacogdoches mission as "situated in a small plain, surrounded by a great number of beautiful and shady trees."[8]

Travel through the dense forests of eastern Texas and along the coast was not necessarily a pleasant experience, however. The Marqués de Rubí, during his 1767 inspection of the region, named part of the route between Los Adaes and Orcoquisac "Purgatory" because it went "through a more dense forest of oaks, live oaks, and underbrush, with frequent hills, vales, and marshes, which made the going most vexing. Winter travel through this region of "ice, snow, and wind" led an exasperated Terán de los Ríos to comment "I will not describe the character of the country, for no rational person has ever seen a worse one." In the coastal prairies it was not the terrain, but the summer climate that provoked travelers' ire. Francisco Alvarez Barreiro, engineer for Pedro de Rivera's 1727 inspection tour, was among the earliest commentators on the Texas summer. "In that season [the heat] is particularly oppressive on the coast which the province has on the Gulf of Mexico; and to this is added the plague of mosquitoes that is experienced greatly at that time."[9]

Despite the weather's ability to cause periodic discomfort or distress, the overall judgement of the province's climate was overwhelmingly favorable. Fray Morfi, exercising a considerable degree of hyperbole, addressed the issue as the second point in his general description of the province, commenting:

> Its climate is excellent, neither too cold nor too warm. Seldom is the sky covered with clouds for a whole day, though it rains abundantly at times. The heavy dews contribute to the fertility of the land, but it is not necessary to take precautions against their evil effect. In winter, snow and frosts are

frequent, but neither one nor the other is so severe as to hinder the cultivation of the soil or molest the settlers. Storms and earthquakes have never been known in this country, and epidemics are very rare. The inhabitants are blessed with sound health and live to a ripe old age without suffering the infirmities of declining years.[10]

The vast variety of animals and plants that travelers encountered in Texas only served to highlight for them the prodigious fertility of the region.[11] Lions (cougar), and tigers (jaguar), and bears are mentioned prominently in expedition accounts, as are wolves and coyotes, foxes and badgers, beavers and otters. Alligators inhabited many Texas streams as far as the foot of the Balcones Escarpment. Although birds are mentioned less frequently and more generically, the presence of song birds is noted, along with raptors and migratory species. The wild turkey stood out because it made good eating. Travelers also seemed impressed with the large assortment of fish to be found in Texas waters. Trout, bass, catfish, and some unidentified species are mentioned in numerous reports as providing good inland fishing. Along the coasts, shrimp, oysters, and other shellfish abounded.

Of all the animals to be found in Texas, none drew more comment than the American buffalo. Found from the Rio Grande northward in the late seventeenth century, the animal roamed both plains and forests. In July 1691 the Terán de los Ríos expedition encountered them in the woods in the Fayette County area, "covered with ticks, red bugs and other vermin."[12] The *cíbolo*, as the bison was called throughout the colonial period, drew forth the most inspired descriptions from travelers. The best effort to capture the animal's uniqueness comes from the pen of Fray Peña:

> It is a monstrous animal; its horns are crooked, its back humped as that of a camel, its flanks lean, its tail short, and hairless as that of the pig, except the tip, which is covered with long hair. The entire skin, which is of a dark tanned color, resembling that of the bear, though not so fine, is also covered with long hair. It has a beard like that of a goat and, as the lion, its neck and forehead have hair a foot and a half long, that almost covers the big black eyes. Its feet are cloven, and its forehead is armed [with horns] as that of the bull, which it imitates in ferocity, although it is much more powerful and swift. Its meat is as savory as that of the best cow.[13]

Except for its meat and its athletic ability, Domingo Ramón was less impressed with the animal, calling it "ugly." Among its shortcomings he counted the bison's "ill-shaped" forehead, long hair that obstructed its view, and that "the animal is very malodorous, does not hear well, and sees less on account of the mane of hair." The importance of the animal to the Indians was not overlooked, and Fray Morfi's description of the bison focuses on the varied uses the native peoples made of it: brains to soften leather; horns to make household items; shoulder blades for plowing; ligaments as bowstrings; hoofs ground down for glue; wool and hair to make rope, belts, and other ornaments; and the skin for all manner of leather goods and for blankets.[14]

The flora of Texas was no less outstanding. Diarists commented on the variety of useful plants to be found in seemingly limitless bounty. Aside from various species of oak (live and deciduous), pine, elm, and juniper (including cedar and cypress), willows, cottonwoods, and mesquite are reported throughout the province. As far as nut trees are concerned, use of the words *nogal* and *nuez* make clear identification difficult, but pecans, hickory, and walnut are all native to Texas. So too is the chinquapin, which the diarists referred to as *castaño* (chestnut). During the 1709 *entrada*, Fray Espinosa commented that "the nuts are so abundant that throughout the land the natives gather them, using them for food the greater part of the year.... Not all the nuts are of the same quality, for there are different sizes and the shells of some are softer than others, but all of them are more tasty and palatable than those of Castile."[15]

As for useful plants, Texas offered an abundance of species with dietary and manufacturing properties. Observers noted the abundance of wild grapes throughout Texas. Even the taciturn Alonso de León, whose diary contains few references other than to direction, character of the landscape, and streams crossed, notes in his entry for May 21, 1690 the presence of fruit-bearing grapevines in the area of Houston County. During the 1716 expedition Domingo Ramón claimed to have "gathered some grapes as large as eggs." Blackberry (*zarzamora*), mulberry (*mora*), persimmon (*chapote*), and plum (*ciruela*) grew in much of the province. Other plants also showed dietary potential. For instance, Fray Solís wrote of finding "plants that looked like lettuce, and also some wild onions," in the Guadalupe River country. "These plants, prepared with vinegar and oil, make very fine salad."[16] Two staples of the Mexican diet, prickly pear (*nopal*) and wild sweet potato (*camote*), were so ubiquitous as to go almost without mention.

Texas also contained plants with commercial potential. By the time the Spanish entered Texas in a meaningful way in the late-seventeenth and early-eighteenth centuries, they had become acquainted with species of North American plants that had useful applications. The lechugilla root, for instance, provided a substitute for soap. Spanish moss, in reality a member of the bromeliad family, served as fodder in the absence of grass. Numerous expeditions mentioned flax and hemp growing wild in Texas. Regarding the latter, Espinosa stated in his 1709 diary that it "was so flourishing that it seemed to be cultivated though it had received no other care than that of the liberal hand [of nature] that beautifies everything."[17]

The consensus among travelers was that Texas was prime agricultural country. Pedro de Rivera, who inspected the province in 1727, commented that "corn, vegetables, and other crops can be grown everywhere in the province. Even without the benefit of irrigation the land demonstrates its fertility and utility to the pagan Indians who cultivate it." Later in the century, Fray Morfi's observations, based on the accomplishments of the small Hispanic population, were even more enthusiastic: "The fertility of the soil exceeds all exaggeration. Wheat, barley, corn, beans, chick-peas, pepper, melons, watermelons, excellent potatoes, cotton, cane, all kinds of vegetables, and, in a word, whatever is planted yields abundantly."[18]

Spanish colonials, then, had a clear and deep understanding of the Texas environment. They recognized its variety, its potential, and the limitations of what they could do with it given the technology at their disposal. In humid East Texas for instance, they did not try to build with adobe or stone, the traditional building materials of northern Mexico, but made use of the region's abundant timber resources. Fray Solís found the buildings of Los Adaes "suitable structures and well put together. The walls are of wood and the roofs are shingled."[19] The region's abundant rainfall and the presence of a large agricultural Indian population ensured the region's settlers an adequate food supply. Still, with the intervening country between Los Adaes/Nacogdoches[20] and San Antonio essentially unoccupied during the colonial period, East Texas remained an isolated and small establishment until it began to flourish as a center of Anglo-American settlement under Mexican rule.

The coastal plains, on the other hand, challenged Spanish colonial agricultural practices. At the three different locations where the mission-presidio complex of La Bahía was located before 1750, gravity-flow irrigation was made impossible by the high banks of adjoining streams and the sandiness of the soil. As late as 1791, an experienced surveyor from San Antonio was sent to La Bahía to investigate the possibilities for irrigation, but he found neither the river nor five nearby streams suitable.[21] Consequently, agriculture at La Bahía frequently suffered from prolonged periods of little rainfall and high temperatures. An environmentally less attractive area, the Spanish colonial settlement of the vicinity remained limited to the presidio and a couple of neighboring missions.

From the very beginning of permanent settlement, what is today South-Central Texas received the lion's share of attention as the most environmentally promising part of the province. Here the San Antonio River was fit for irrigation; there was plentiful timber and rock for construction and abundant grazing land nearby. In 1709 Fray Espinosa had described the San Antonio River as capable of supplying "not only a village but a city, which could easily be founded here because of the good ground and the many conveniences, and because of the shallowness of said river."[22] On his return visit in 1716 Fray Espinosa was even more descriptive of the area's natural environment: "It is surrounded by very tall nopals [sic], poplars, elms, grapevines, black mulberry trees, laurels, strawberry vines and genuine fan-palms. There is a great deal of flax and wild hemp, an abundance of maiden-hair fern and many medicinal herbs." The missionary was no less encouraging regarding "its copious waters, which are clear, crystal and sweet. In these are found catfish, sea fish, *piltonte, catan* and alligators. Undoubtedly there are also various other kinds of fish that are most savory."[23] Consequently, San Antonio de Béxar quickly became the largest of Texas' Spanish colonial settlements.

By the 1770s a presidio, small town, and five missions hugged both banks of the river. Fray Morfi's description of the settlement leaves no doubt of the continued fertility of the area, even after forty to fifty years of use:

> The trail is flat, with good footing and comfortable, and for the most part follows the margin of the San Antonio River and along a very thick wood of corpulent mesquite, pecan, live oak, oak, mulberry, wild grapevine, and many other trees and different plants. It is populated by various handsome birds, although owing to the inappropriateness of the season we found very few. The wild turkeys go about in flocks of 100 and 200. There are different species of squirrels, the prettiest being very blond with a red belly. On both sides of the trail can be found the missions' fields, and never in my life have I seen such a multitude of ducks, geese, and cranes as I admired on this sown land, which had just been harvested, for I do not exaggerate if I say that they covered the entire plain. These fields are crisscrossed by ditches through which the water of the river is abundantly carried to irrigate an immense portion of the country. In them, when they are dried out in order to clean them, much fish is taken, and the eels are especially delicious.[24]

The very size and diversity of the agricultural enterprise at San Antonio allowed for a regular annual cycle to emerge in the course of the century.

The census report of 1778 mentioned that very little wheat was cultivated in the San Antonio area, which was planted in October or November and harvested in May and June. More important, the conditions allowed for two corn crops, an early one planted along with cotton, beans, and chiles in February or March and harvested from July to September, and a late corn crop planted with beans in late May and throughout June, with the corn harvested in December and January and the beans in October and November. January and early February were the months devoted to mending fences, cleaning irrigation ditches, and preparing the fields.[25]

San Antonio was well suited not only to crop agriculture but to horticulture as well. At the settlement's founding in 1718, Martín de Alarcón provided for "grapevines and fig trees and diverse fruit seeds, melon and watermelon as well as squash [and] peppers."[26] Vegetable gardens and orchards soon sprouted, both in the neighborhood of the presidio and at the missions, benefitting from the *acequias* (irrigation ditches) that were also made to run through the center of each population center. By the 1740s, the presence of fruit trees on a lot was worthy of mention in land sales at San Antonio and added to the value of property.[27] Sugarcane did well enough to warrant the considerable investment that Francisco Delgado, one of the Canary Island immigrants, made in a sugar mill and associated processing equipment. Fray Solís claimed that the peaches of Mission San José, "which are grown in large quantities, weigh about a pound each."[28]

For the most part, farming and gardening in and around San Antonio provided for the subsistence needs of the population as a whole and the commercial aspirations of a few. The irrigation system normally mitigated the effects of droughts and other natural disasters to which the area was regularly subject, but there is evidence that at times the limited technological means available were inadequate. A year-long drought broke in April 1776, just in time to supply the needs of a plague of locusts and cause additional damage to new crops, "the said locust adding to the hunger that afflicts these inhabitants owing to the meager harvest of last year."[29]

During the 1780s conditions became particularly severe, not only causing damage to pastures, but to the irrigated farms of the settlement. At the end of June 1787, Governor Rafael Martínez Pacheco reported that a severe drought and harsh winter had finally broken in mid-March with abundant rains that had lasted until the middle of June and allowed for adequate corn, bean, chile, and cane crops to be harvested. Drought conditions soon returned, however, and reached such severity that in January 1789 Martínez Pacheco tried to institute price controls on corn and ban its export from the settlement. In March he had to inform visiting Comanches that he could not give them the usual gifts because the drought had kept the shipment from arriving.[30] The drought continued for another year, leading the governor to explain in June 1790 that "we have suffered from hunger to this day for lack of having harvested enough grain last year, so that in order to plant it [the farmers] have not eaten it." He went on to add that the quartermaster, being unable to purchase enough corn to satisfy the troop, resorted to giving the troopers their corn ration in cash so that they might buy what they could from the mission Indians.[31]

While the level, well-watered land in the immediate vicinity of the settlement's presidio, town, and missions provided ample opportunity for agriculture, similar conditions in the rest of the San Antonio River basin made attractive ranch land.[32] After all, throughout this part of Texas immense bison herds roamed when the Spanish first arrived. On reaching the San Antonio area in June 1691, the Terán de los Ríos expedition encountered "so many buffaloes that the horses stampeded and forty head ran away."[33] Soon after missions San Antonio de Valero (1718) and San José y San Miguel de Aguayo (1720) were founded, the friars started herds of cattle, sheep, and goats. In the early 1730s the other missions, which had relocated from East Texas, followed suit, and the first of the civilian ranches was claimed. By the 1770s, the area between Ecleto Creek to the east and Hondo Creek in the west was almost entirely taken up with ranch claims.

Although Bexareños (residents of San Antonio de Béxar) and the missions established herds of cattle and flocks of sheep, the former dominated the commercial landscape throughout the eighteenth century.[34] Environmental conditions, which residents were well aware of, prevented colonial Texas from becoming an important sheep-raising region. As a 1789 report on the Texas missions by the Franciscan in charge, Fray José Francisco López, makes clear, "sheep increase very slowly in this country for many reasons, but especially because the land, being thickly wooded, abounds in wild animals that destroy them. Also many are lost in the brush." Fray López also went on to blame the carelessness and laziness of the Indian shepherds, but the available numbers suggest that the civilian population had little better luck.[35]

Cattle and horses stood a much better chance of successfully adapting to frontier conditions. Heavily wooded stream banks, patches of oak and mesquite wood, and a sparse population combined to give cattle the run of the country. One hint at the success that large stock had in going feral can be found in Fray Solís's comment that "in the woods between La Bahía and San Antonio there are a few lions and a great number of cattle, horses, deer, wolves, coyotes, rabbits, wildcats and boars." A decade later, Fray Morfi's observations led him to conclude, "Nothing proves the fertility of the land and the richness of the soil more than the incredible number of wild horses and cattle found everywhere."[36]

Given the open range situation, much of the cattle in the San Antonio region came to be treated as simply another product of the land. Until the 1770s harvesting of wild cattle most often took the form of slaughters, resulting in the production of dried beef and tallow. In the 1770s, roundups of large numbers of feral as well as branded cattle and drives to the interior of New Spain and north to Louisiana became common. The fecundity of the stock suggested to Bexareños that there was an inexhaustible supply. Although the arguments over ownership of this unbranded stock are beyond the scope of this chapter, it needs to be pointed out that missionaries and civilians both laid claim to the feral stock. For instance, in 1777 Francisco Xavier Rodríguez claimed that since his father, one of the settlement's founders, had lost cattle in the brush, he was entitled to collect unbranded stock. Some Bexareños with no rural property at all also participated in illegal cattle harvests, despite the efforts of officials.[37]

The supply of cattle was not, of course, inexhaustible. The indiscriminate slaughter of cattle by both raiding Indians and Bexareños, failure to control or improve pastures, and the latter's driving of large numbers to market constituted a real threat to the viability of the cattle population. Warnings regarding poor pastoral practices are evident as early as late 1758. In a letter complaining of the behavior of the townspeople, Fray Mariano Francisco de los Dolores stated that as soon as they set up ranches next to those of the missions, the latter's herds suffered dramatic reductions. "The cause being the continuous slaughters that they practice at their ranches, from which they not only supply themselves, but also send loads of lard, tallow, and meat to the presidio and town; the large number of cattle they scare away in their roundups being most deplorable." In regard to cattle, a comment in the census of 1778 presents a more ominous problem: "In the last few years there has been a considerable extraction of cattle, very disproportionate to the reduced means of the inhabitants.... And, extracting of it many females, it will become extinct, to which the Apache nation effectively contributes."[38]

The result of these practices was implementation of the first environmental legislation in Texas history. Cmdt. Gen. Teodoro de Croix, on his 1778 visit to San Antonio, heard the complaints of Bexareños, missionaries, and the governor regarding ownership, depletion, and jurisdictional questions. He quickly instituted a licensing system for cattle exports, imposed a tax on the capture of unbranded stock, and issued a ban on the slaughter of wild stock "in order to stop the abuses committed in the field against the wild cattle, which is property of the king, because they are killed in the field and left there, only the tallow used for soap being taken." In 1780 Governor Domingo Cabello imposed a further restriction, banning the export of breeding cows. These and other measures met with the ire of Bexareños, who launched a seventeen-year litigation effort to claim ownership of all unbranded stock. In 1795 the royal government issued its final decision: while all taxes due since 1778 were forgiven, stockmen had one year to round-up whatever cattle they could manage, after which time unbranded stock belonged to the crown and became subject to taxation.[39]

Reckless slaughter was not the only threat to the feral cattle population; the weather played a crucial role in the late-eighteenth-century decline. During the drought of 1775–76 Governor Ripperdá reported that he had had to move the presidio's horse herd to La Bahía, where the grazing was better. At Béxar, he commented, the pastures were so bad "that even the cattle have left the area, so that this year the branding could not be made." The droughts of the late 1780s did even more damage. In 1787 Governor Martínez Pacheco explained that local stockmen paid cowboys one peso per day for more than a month, sometimes without catching any. Two years later, Martínez Pacheco was forced to defend himself from the commandant general's order for five hundred head of cattle and other cattle products for a campaign against the Lipan Apache by seeking an affidavit from San Antonio residents that "the strong snows and ices which fell on those making the dried beef resulted in the loss of much of their horse stock," and whether "the drought which has lasted to this month has not impeded the collection of cattle and beef."[40] Even the return of regular rainfall in the 1790s could not undo over two decades of damage. Governor Manuel Muñoz reissued a ban on the slaughter of breeding cows in 1794:

> Keeping in mind the reports of *vecinos* on the great shortage of livestock, which is evidenced by the inability to provision this garrison with meat from December 9 to this date, or to provide for the visiting Indians, or the inability of *vecinos* to capture many livestock in spite of the many licenses issued, [for] what does exist is in the brush and canyons, making roundups impossible and forcing the *vecinos* to shoot what they can, which is much effort spent on very little.[41]

In 1796 Manuel Delgado asked for permission for himself and others to go as far as the Colorado River "in search of cattle."[42] Owing to continued

Indian depredations, and hostilities during the second decade of the nineteenth century, conditions would not markedly improve for cattle until the period following Mexican independence.

The extractive nature of the Texas livestock economy points out the significant degree to which Bexareños depended directly on nature's bounty. Béxar's town council put it well in a 1772 complaint to the viceroy, when it declared that it was "impossible to live in this province without going into the country."[43] Just what they got in the countryside, aside from cattle and horses, Bexareños made clear in a 1788 complaint against the tithe collector, who demanded that wild livestock captured by Bexareños be tithed: "buffalo, bear, deer, turkey, and the other wild animals and fruits of the fields."[44] There is considerable evidence in the colonial records that as the eighteenth century progressed, San Antonio's population went farther afield to obtain food stuffs and building materials. The evidence also makes clear that in carving out their home in the wilderness, Bexareños had a significant impact on the regional environment.

The buffalo, on which some of the population had a dietary dependence in the late-eighteenth century, is a good example of the effect of even such a small-scale settlement as Béxar on the landscape. Cíbolo Creek, named for the bison, when the animal was so abundant in the region in the late-seventeenth century, was no longer its home by the mid-eighteenth century. Instead, as cattle and horses became the dominant grazers throughout the San Antonio River watershed, those seeking to hunt bison had to go farther afield. Evidence from the 1770s suggests buffalo had to be sought on the Guadalupe and San Marcos rivers and even the Colorado River, more than seventy miles north of San Antonio.[45] In the 1790s the Pedernales was among the destinations mentioned in petitions for buffalo hunts.[46] By this time a pattern of semi-annual bison hunts had become the norm and, according to Governor Juan Bautista Elguézabal in 1803, if these slaughters that took "place in the months of May and October did not in a measure relieve the misery, the majority of the families would no doubt starve."[47] Not that Bexareños exterminated the buffalo in the San Antonio area, for there is no evidence for the export of such large numbers of hides as would indicate the kind of wholesale slaughter seen on the Great Plains the following century. Rather, it seems that the native grazer was displaced by "weed species"—cattle and horses.

Evidence also makes clear that Bexareños exhausted the better timber resources around San Antonio fairly quickly. As early as 1744 Governor Tomás Felipe de Winthuisen reported to the viceroy that the failure to finish construction of the presidio was not for lack of stone, but for a shortage of timber, which was located "far away, and its cutting and transport requiring an escort" because of the presence of enemy Indians.[48] By the late decades of the century it had become "customary" in January or February of every year for a group of Bexareños to make carts and cut timber at the Guadalupe or San Marcos rivers.[49]

Another product harvested by Bexareños for sale outside the province was pecans. The quality of the Texas nuts had been admired by members of some of the early expeditions, and as Indian populations in the region collapsed, the potential harvest increased. Among the goods of petty merchant Tomás Travieso confiscated in 1777 were "some San Antonio nuts."[50] In 1791 Antonio Baca took sixteen mule loads of pecans out of San Antonio for sale in neighboring provinces.[51]

Baca and the handful of fellow Bexareños who fancied themselves merchants and businessmen also dealt in other commodities that had their origins in the wild. Some, no doubt, were the product of the hunting and gathering activities of Bexareños themselves, and others were acquired from the Indian peoples who came to San Antonio to trade and receive government gifts. The most important of these products, buffalo hides and deer skins, were transported to the interior of Mexico in mule trains that also carried dried beef, cowhides, tallow, soap, pecans, and, on occasion, corn. Much work remains to be done to discover the range and size of this trade, however.

At the end of the colonial period, San Antonio and Texas as a whole remained a land of promise. Spanish colonials themselves realized that in almost a century of Hispanic occupation and settlement, the region's rich potential had yet to be fully tapped. Miguel Ramos Arizpe, native of Coahuila and deputy to the revolutionary Cortes in 1811–12, reported on Texas that

> it was previously covered with millions of undomesticated bovine and equine stock, or as they are called there, *mesteño*. For lack of regulation, which allowed its disorderly extraction and slaughter in the paltry interest of a half-peso per head, today it does not have enough cattle for the basic needs of its own small population, and there is little domesticated horse stock. It has very abundant populations of deer, tiger, bear, bison, beaver, otter, and also abounds in all manner of fish in its rivers, lakes, and bays on the Gulf of Mexico. The Spanish are but mere spectators to these prodigious and very interesting products, of which the native Indians make a great commerce with the Anglo Americans.[52]

What Ramos Arizpe and other critics of the colonial Texas frontier failed to notice was that the land itself contained obstacles to development. Efficient communication between Texas and the rest of New Spain was often impeded by both climate and topography. All the rivers ran perpendicularly to the line of travel, and the Texas coast was considered unhealthful and treacherous. Periodic droughts and catastrophic floods often disrupted travel, ruined crops, and endangered lives. In the absence of precious metals, the one natural resource that could have made the Spanish colonials interested in overcoming all obstacles, there was little incentive to undertake the taming of Texas. Even the most effusively positive descriptions of the province failed to overcome these handicaps during the colonial period.

Bexareños did alter the natural environment in their settlement's vicinity, although they did not have the means to fully exploit their natural world. To the extent that their limited numbers and economic circumstances allowed, they could and did harvest Texas' natural bounty. In promoting the growth of extensive herds of domesticated livestock, cattle and horses in particular, they started the long-term withdrawal of the American bison from the Texas landscape. In constructing sophisticated and extensive irrigation works, they mitigated some of the harsh effects of the region's semi-dry environment and created a successful, if limited, agricultural economy. In the end, they thrived in the Texas wilderness and made it their own.

NOTES

1. *Anglo American* is here defined as the English-speaking population that began to immigrate into Texas early in the Mexican post-independence period.

2. *Hispanic* is defined in this chapter as the Spanish-speaking population of New Spain, including acculturated Indians and people of African ancestry.

3. First and second quotes, Robin W. Doughty, *At Home in Texas: Early Views of the Land* (College Station: Texas A&M University Press, 1987), 6; see also pp. 14–15, Doughty, *Wildlife and Man in Texas Environmental Change and Conservation* (College Station: Texas A&M University Press, 1983).

4. In December 1836 the congress of the nascent Republic of Texas declared its borders to stretch from the mouth of the Rio Grande to its source thence to the Adams-Onís Treaty line in present-day southern Wyoming, thus including the eastern half of New Mexico, and parts of Colorado, Kansas, and Oklahoma in its boundaries.

5. "The Expedition of Don Domingo Terán de los Rios into Texas (1691–1692)," trans. Mattie Austin Hatcher, *Preliminary Studies of the Texas Catholic Historical Society* 2, no. 1 (January 1932): 14; Juan Antonio de la Peña, "Peña's Diary of the Aguayo Expedition," trans. Rev. Peter P. Forrestal, *Preliminary Studies of the Texas Catholic Historical Society* 2, no. 7 (January 1935): 24.

6. The early expeditions, from the 1680s to the 1720s, following different routes during different seasons, often confused the names of streams. The modern names of those Texas streams with Spanish names were established by the end of the eighteenth century.

7. Fray Isidro Félix Espinosa, "Ramón Expedition: Espinosa's Diary of 1716," trans. Rev. Gabriel Tous, *Prepaing the Way: Preliminary Studies of the Texas Catholic Historical Society* 1 (*Studies in Southwestern Catholic History*) 1 (Austin: Texas Catholic Historical Society, 1997), 75–76.

8. Domingo Ramón, "Captain Don Domingo Ramón's Diary of His Expedition into Texas in 1716," trans. Rev. Paul J. Foik, *Preliminary Studies of the Texas Catholic Historical Society* 2, no. 5 (April 1933): 11; Fray José de Solís, "The Solís Diary of 1767," trans. Rev. Peter P. Forrestal, in *Preparing the Way*, 140.

9. Cayetano María Pignatelli Rubí Corbera y San Clement, "Itinerary of Señor Marqués de Rubí, Field Marshal of His Majesty's Armies, in the Inspection of the Interior Presidios that by Royal Order He Conducted in this New Spain, 1766–1768," trans. David McDonald, in *Imaginary Kingdom: Texas as Seen by the Rivera and Rubí Military Expeditions, 1727 and 1767*, ed. Jack Jackson (Austin: Texas State Historical Association, 1995), 132; "Expedition of Don Domingo de Terán," 43; "Barreiro Provincial Descriptions of Coahuila-Nuevo León and Texas, 1727–1728," trans. Ned F. Brierley, in *Imaginary Kingdom*, ed. Jackson, 58.

10. Juan Agustín Morfi, *History of Texas, 1673–1779*, trans., intro., annotations Carlos E. Castañeda, 2 parts (Albuquerque: The Quivira Society, 1935), 1:48.

11. William C. Foster, in his *Spanish Expeditions into Texas, 1689–1768* (Austin: University of Texas Press, 1995), has cataloged the fauna and flora mentioned in the diaries, journals, and reports on eleven different expeditions to Texas. The two appendixes are an invaluable tool for anyone wishing to begin the process of studying biological distribution in early Texas. Two other appendixes list the documented epidemic diseases in northern New Spain from the late sixteenth to mid-eighteenth centuries and Indian groups reported by the expeditions discussed in the book. Discussion of the fauna and flora in this and the following paragraphs is based on Foster unless otherwise noted.

12. "Expedition of Don Domingo de Terán," 17.

13. "Peña's Diary," 24.

14. "Domingo Ramón's Diary," 14; Morfi, *History of Texas*, 1:67.

15. Fray Isidro Félix Espinosa, "The Espinosa-Olivares-Aguirre Expedition of 1709," trans. Rev. Gabriel Tous, in *Preparing the Way*, 61.

16. Juan Bautista Chapa, *Texas & Northeastern Mexico, 1630–1690: The First Official History of Texas*, ed. and intro. William C. Foster (Austin: University of Texas Press, 1997), 165; "Domingo Ramón Diary," 20; "Solís Diary of 1767," 125.

17. "Espinosa-Olivares-Aguirre Expedition," 61.

18. Jackson, ed., *Imaginary Kingdom*, 42; Morfi, *History of Texas*, 1:49.

19. "Solís Diary of 1767," 135.

20. Los Adaes, which is located near present-day Robeline, Louisiana, was abandoned in 1773, following the advice of frontier inspector the Marqués de Rubí. Hispanic residents were removed to San Antonio, but many of them returned to East Texas the following year, settling first at the Camino Real crossing of the Trinity River, and in 1779 at the former mission site of Nacogdoches.

21. Carlos E. Castañeda, *The Mission Era: The End of the Spanish Regime, 1780–1810*, vol. 5 of *Our Catholic Heritage in Texas, 1519–1836*. (Austin: Von Boeckmann-Jones Co., 1942), 177.

22. "Espinosa-Olivares-Aguirre Expedition," 55.

23. "Ramón Expedition," 74.

24. Juan Agustín de Morfi, *Viaje de indios y diario del Nuevo México*, annotations by Vito Alessio Robles (Mexico: Manuel Porrúa, 1980), 357–58.

25. Padrón de Texas, September 26, 1778, Archivo San Francisco del Grande, Biblioteca Nacional de México, transcript in Spanish Material from Various Sources, vol. 32, Center for American History, University of Texas at Austin (hereafter cited as ASFG). For further discussion see Jesús F. de la Teja, *San Antonio de Béxar: A Community on New Spain's Northern Frontier* (Albuquerque: University of New Mexico Press, 1995), 92.

26. "Diario de la conquista y entrada a los Thejas," *Universidad de México* 5 (1933): 233.

27. José Padrón v. Juan Leal Goraz, June 25, 1733, Bexar Archives, Center for American History, University of Texas at Austin (hereafter cited as BA); Notary protocols, March 22, 1738, and September 15, 1747, ibid; Testamentary proceedings for Francisco Hernández, October 5, 1751, ibid. See also De la Teja, *San Antonio de Béxar*, 46–47.

28. Testament of Francisco Delgado, February 7, 1764, Spanish Archives of Bexar County, Bexar County Clerk's Office, San Antonio, Texas; "Solís Diary of 1767," 122.

29. Gov. Ripperdá to viceroy, April 20, 1776, in Correspondencia con el Gobernador de Texas, Barón de Ripperdá, en los años de 1774 hasta 1777 inclusive, Carpeta 2a., ramo Provincias Internas vol. 99, Archivo General de la Nación de México, microfilm reel 93, Benson Latin American Collection, University of Texas at Austin (hereafter cited as AGN:PI).

30. Noticia que el Capitán D. Rafael Martínez Pacheco, gobernador Interino, y Comte. de las armas de dha. Proa. manifiesta del tpo. que se ha experimentado en ella, June 30, 1787, BA; Martínez Pacheco to Ugalde, January 30, 1789, ibid; Martínez Pacheco to Ugalde, March 30, 1789, ibid.

31. Martínez to Viceroy Revilla Gigedo, June 6, 1790, BA.

32. Except where otherwise noted, the following discussion on ranching is based on De la Teja, *San Antonio de Béxar*, 97–117. For a narrative political history of Spanish ranching, see Jack Jackson, *Los Mesteños: Spanish Ranching in Texas, 1721–1821* (College Station: Texas A&M University Press, 1986).

33. "Expedition of Don Domingo de Terán," 55.

34. *Bexareños* refers to Hispanic residents of the jurisdiction of San Antonio de Béxar.

35. "The Texas Missions in 1785," trans. J. Autrey Dabbs, in *Preliminary Studies of the Texas Catholic Historical Society* 3, no. 6 (January 1940): 18; De la Teja, *San Antonio de Béxar*, 113–14.

36. "Solís Diary of 1767," 120; Morfi, *History of Texas*, 1:49.

37. Causa formada pr. el Govr. de esta provincia Barón de Ripperdá, contra Francisco Xavier Rodríguez, Juan José Flores, y Nepomuceno Travieso, vecinos de la villa de Sn. Fernando, sobre extracción de reses orejanas, March 7, 1777, BA.

38. Carta de Fray Mariano Francisco de los Dolores, respecto a quejas de los indios contra los habitantes de San Fernando de Béxar, 1758, legajo 95, no. 28 ASFG; Padrón de Texas, September 26, 1778, ibid.

39. Bando de buen gobierno expedido por el Sñr. Come. Gral de estas Proas. Internas, January 11, 1778, BA; De la Teja, *San Antonio de Béxar*, 109.

40. Gov. Ripperdá to viceroy, December 19, 1775, Carpeta 2a; Martínez Pacheco to Juan de Ugalde, November 11, 1787, BA; Questionnaire concerning the commandant general's order, May 21, 1789, BA.

41. Contiene tres vandos sobre el buen régimen que deven observar estos vezinos en las corridas del ganado orejano, February 15, 1794, BA.

42. Petition of Manuel Delgado, April 3, 1796, BA.

43. Cabildo to viceroy, August 4, 1772, in Correspondencia con el ayuntamiento de la Villa de San Fernando y con varios individuos en distintos años desde el de 1771 hasta el de 1793, incluyéndose un informe sobre la Prova. del Gobernador que fue de ella D. Jacinto de Barrios, Carpeta 8a, microfilm reel 93, AGN:PI.

44. Petition of citizenry, January 29, 1788, BA.

45. Gov. Ripperdá to viceroy, February 8, 1773, vol. 100, microfilm reel 94, AGN:PI.

46. Petition of Francisco Bueno, April 16, 1796, BA.

47. Quoted in De la Teja, *San Antonio de Béxar*, 112.

48. Tomás Felipe de Winthuisen to [viceroy], August 19, 1744, BA.

49. Gov. Ripperdá to viceroy, April 5, 1775, Carpeta 2a; Causa criminal contra soldado Juan Chirinos por dar muerte a el soldado Cristóbal Carabajal, January 16, 1772, BA; Bernardo Fernández to Gov. Muñoz, January 6, 1791, ibid.; Petition of Manuel de Arocha, et al., February 8, 1792, ibid.

50. Appeal of Tomás Travieso of murder conviction, Guadalajara [1777], BA.

51. Manuel Espadas to Martínez, May 6, 1790, BA; Petition of Antonio Baca, March 30, 1791, ibid.; Petition of Manuel Rodríguez, November 7, 1792, ibid; License by Muñoz, January 2, 1793, ibid.

52. Quoted in Vito Alessio Robles, *Coahuila y Texas en la época colonial*, 2nd ed. (Mexico: Editorial Porrúa, 1978), 608.

Theodore Gentilz, *On the Trail*. For Tejanos there was little difference between civilian and military life throughout the Spanish colonial period. The military settlers who came to Texas in the early eighteenth century were horsemen and Indian fighters by tradition. Most of them were recruited in frontier regions to the south, in Coahuila, Nuevo León, and Nueva Vizcaya. They would continue handing these skills down the generations through the end of the nineteenth century. Courtesy of the Witte Museum, San Antonio, Texas.

3

Forgotten Founders

THE MILITARY SETTLERS OF EIGHTEENTH-CENTURY
SAN ANTONIO DE BÉXAR*

INTRODUCTION

Historians have generally looked upon the foundation of the formal villa of San Fernando de Béxar on March 9, 1731, by a group of Canary Islands immigrants as the beginning of San Antonio. But shrouded in the mists of meager documentary evidence that has largely escaped the attention of scholars is Béxar's earliest history. Indeed, the more familiar story of the Canary Islanders, or Isleños, could not be told if a determined and resourceful group of military settlers had not established a small but thriving community despite dangers and isolation. Without the protection and instruction of these Mexican frontiersmen, the band of Old World immigrants who came to the Texas wilderness would not have survived long. The Isleños' arrival in Béxar marked the end of an initial flourishing based on military settlement by frontiersmen from Coahuila and Nuevo León. The emerging community's simple and united society, which was centered on the presidio, gave way to social and political cleavages between existing and new settlers. Yet the Crown's creation of a villa (town) and grant of privileges to the new arrivals did not alter the endurance of the settlement's frontier character. Béxar's garrison continued to protect civilians from Indian attack, served as a market for local goods, and provided impetus for population growth. Without the fort, the town's existence would have been tenuous at best. Scholars must therefore look to the early military settlement and its population in order to trace the development of community in San Antonio de Béxar.

---

*First published in *Tejano Origins in Eighteenth-Century San Antonio*, edited by Gerald E. Poyo and Gilberto M. Hinojosa (Austin: University of Texas Press, 1991) for the University of Texas Institute of Texan Cultures at San Antonio.

BÉXAR'S SETTLEMENT

Settling an intermediate location between the Tejas missions of East Texas and the Rio Grande was essential to the successful occupation of the province, a task Crown authorities considered critical to protecting New Spain's rich northern mining districts from French encroachment. On the edge of Mexico's advancing frontier, Texas and Béxar began as imperial outposts, first against a rival European power and later against Apaches and Comanches. They continued in this role throughout the eighteenth century and well into the nineteenth.

Interest in the San Antonio region arose early. A plan drawn up in 1689 by Coahuila governor Alonso de León called for a presidio on the Guadalupe River to discourage French advances. Explorer Domingo Terán de los Ríos in 1691 considered the upper San Antonio River valley, with its abundant water supply, woods, and agricultural land, the ideal site for missions and towns.[1] The same vicinity made a deep impression on Fray Antonio San Buenaventura Olivares, who, according to historian Carlos Castañeda, "had nursed a hidden desire to found a mission at the headwaters of the San Antonio River" ever since his visit to the region in 1709.[2] Fray Olivares advocated Spanish settlement of the area, "for an entire province will fit in the said river [valley]."[3]

The viceroy's orders to Martín de Alarcón, named governor of Texas in 1714, reflected these recommendations. In addition to establishing missions between the San Antonio and Colorado rivers, the viceroy envisioned the founding of two towns or cities. One town was to be established on the San Antonio River by at least thirty families, who would receive all the rights and privileges granted by royal laws.[4] And to partially offset the obvious hazards associated with occupying hostile Indian country, each settler was to receive a salary of 450 pesos, livestock, and other supplies.[5]

Despite the incentives, recruitment proved troublesome because of the small number of available settlers in the sparsely populated provinces of Coahuila and Nuevo León.[6] Nevertheless, a small expedition that included artisans and a group of women and children arrived at San Antonio in late April 1718. On May 1 Alarcón designated a spot on the west bank of the river for Mission San Antonio de Valero. Approximately three-quarters of a league from the mission near San Pedro Springs he selected a site for the "Villa de Béxar" and performed the act of possession on May 5.[7]

NEW SPAIN'S NORTHERN ADVANCE AND BÉXAR'S FOUNDERS

People accustomed to frontier life built, protected, and fostered what became Texas' most successful colonial settlement. These people included soldiers, friars, and settlers who worked together at San Antonio (as they had on countless occasions throughout the Mexican north) to defend Spain's claims to the region through the incorporation of Indians and land into the colonial system.

The settlers from Coahuila who moved north to found the settlement of San Antonio followed a pattern that was well established by the early eighteenth century. Throughout the colonial period, pioneers from the most recently settled areas usually spearheaded the further extension of the frontier. Sinaloans settled Sonora, and these two provinces furnished the people for California's settlement. Nueva Vizcayans settled New Mexico and southern Coahuila. With the exception of a few Canary Islanders, pioneers from Coahuila, Saltillo, and Nuevo León settled Béxar. As the prominent Spanish Borderlands historian Oakah Jones observes: "In all cases, therefore, most of the colonists either had passed through the frontier experience themselves recently or were still in that stage."[8]

Béxar's frontiersmen brought elements of northern Mexico's distinctive society to Texas. The inhabitants of the northern regions made their living primarily in mining and ranching. The sparse population and long distances between urban centers mitigated against a manufacturing economy. Indeed, local investments centered on mines, mule trains, and land. Commerce involved the export of raw materials (wood, hides, livestock, and a little cotton) to the central provinces of New Spain in return for manufactured goods and tropical agricultural products.[9] The vast, open rangelands of South-Central Texas fit snugly this land-oriented economy.

Alarcón's expeditionaries founded Béxar not only in their capacity as military personnel but also as settlers. Since the colonial Mexican presidio companies were not regular army units, they relied on inhabitants of the frontier who willingly defended presidio outposts in return for the opportunity to participate in the establishment of a permanent settlement. Soldiers took families to their new posts and together provided a small but viable market for merchants, artisans, ranchers, and farmers who congregated around the presidios. After retiring from service, soldiers often obtained land grants near their frontier posts, swelling the civilian population. Friendly Indians also frequently sought security and integrated into the presidio communities.[10]

Though isolated and harsh, life in the northern presidios offered large numbers of frontiersmen opportunities for social and economic advancement. Usually of mixed-blood heritage, frontier soldiers could hope to rise through the ranks to become noncommissioned and commissioned officers and even acquire the title of "don." Such mobility was less feasible for persons of mixed-blood backgrounds in the more-established areas of New Spain. If young soldiers remained in a particular company for some time, they could expect to marry into a family of the neighboring civilian settlement, acquire land and livestock, and even become socially influential in the community.[11]

BÉXAR'S POPULATION IN THE 1720s

The Béxar presidio provided the most important demographic foundation for the permanent settlement of Texas. While the presidio's original population is not known, it grew steadily throughout the 1720s. Alarcón's expedition had seventy-two persons, including thirty-four soldiers (seven with their families) and several muleteers, but the number that settled permanently in Béxar is unclear. In all probability, not all remained, since conditions on the frontier were very difficult. In fact, during 1724 Governor Fernando Pérez de Almazán reported on the shortage of recruits and the difficulties of attracting settlers. "It is necessary to seek [recruits] outside this province because here there is no population whatever," Almazán complained. He suggested that some inducements be given to potential recruits "besides their salaries, because of the resignation with which they all come to this country."[12]

On the other hand, Béxar benefited from the political instability on the border with French Louisiana. When the French invaded Spanish East Texas in 1719, many settlers retreated to San Antonio. Subsequent efforts by the Marqués de San Miguel de Aguayo, governor of Coahuila and Texas, to reestablish Spanish authority in that area in 1721 likewise brought increased numbers to San Antonio.[13] When the Marqués left Texas in 1722 he increased Béxar's garrison to fifty-four men, of whom approximately twenty were members of Alarcón's original military contingent.[14] Four years later, in 1726, Governor Pérez de Almazán calculated a total of two hundred inhabitants distributed among fifty-four presidial families plus four civilian residents.[15]

Consistent with the soldier-settler philosophy of frontier development implemented in the Mexican north, the Presidio de San Antonio de Béxar also had a civilian character almost from the start. To ensure the establishment of a permanent civilian settlement, Alarcón's original instructions called for granting the first *pobladores* (settlers) all the privileges and concessions allowed by the law, including "the lands, pastures, water, and proportionate woods, with the sole reservation that there be left vacant enough lands for one hundred families who will be introduced in time."[16] Furthermore, the act of possession in May 1718 gave the new settlement a civilian title, "Villa de Béxar."[17]

The civilian contingent of four residents cited by Pérez de Almazán in 1726 grew considerably during the next five years, increasing to an estimated twenty to twenty-five male heads of household. This growth is explained by two factors. First, as a result of a frontier inspection that found things quiet at Béxar, the government reduced the garrison by ten soldiers. At least some of the retired soldiers remained and joined the civilian community. Second, the families that came to Texas with the soldiers in the 1720s probably included individuals who did not join the presidio but instead established their own civilian households.

The arrival of these families ensured that Béxar, like other parts of New Spain's non-mining north, would develop as a balanced and stable community with real possibilities of growth. Many of the soldiers' families arriving in Béxar included children of marrying age.[18] Two of Cristóbal Carvajal's daughters, for example, married soldiers in Béxar between 1721 and 1723.[19] Overall, eight daughters of the first Bexareños (who arrived in 1718) married soldiers in the period 1720–24. Another four marriages involved widowed women and local soldiers. There were, by 1730, approximately forty married couples in the settlement, at least half of whom were wed at San Antonio.[20]

In Béxar, as in the north of New Spain generally, commonality of purpose, isolation, and a small population resulted in relatively unrestricted racial boundaries. On the frontier, and in San Antonio, many passed as "Spanish" despite their dark skin. The ethnically mixed were the rule rather than the exception.[21] Despite the desire of Fray Antonio de Olivares of San Antonio de Valero mission that "pure-blooded" Spanish families settle the area, virtually all of Alarcón's recruits were "mulattoes, lobos, coyotes, and mestizos." These were, according to the priest, "people of the lowest order, whose customs are worse than those of the Indians."[22] Nevertheless, San Antonio's missionaries generally collaborated with obscuring their racial "shortcomings." In registering the civilian population for baptisms, marriages, and deaths, the friars did not indicate an individual's ethnic status unless he or she was considered Spanish. For instance, only one interracial marriage is registered in San Antonio during this time—between a Spanish settler and the commander's Indian servant.[23] And, as in another case, even when the groom is identified as the son of a Spaniard and an Indian, he is listed in the marriage register as Spanish, not mestizo.[24] Such obfuscation permitted descendants of racially mixed individuals to "pass" as Spanish, the preferred social status in the larger colonial society.

LIFE IN EARLY SAN ANTONIO

Throughout the 1720s life in Béxar revolved around the presidio and its obligations. The soldiers' military functions were numerous. They protected supply convoys and travelers between the presidio at Rio Grande and East Texas; two or three soldiers stood guard at Missions Valero and San José, a second mission founded in 1720, and acted as overseers and teachers to the Indians; they protected the horse herd from continual Indian thefts; and, of course, they stood guard duty and scouted.

As a military outpost Béxar faced the test of Indian hostility almost at once. In 1720 Lipan Apaches attacked supply trains and killed soldiers, civilians, and mission Indians in their efforts to obtain horses. Three years later Apaches made a direct assault on the presidio horse herd, absconding with eighty animals. After the raid Capt. Nicolás Flores led a force of thirty soldiers and an equal number of mission Indians over three hundred miles in pursuit of the raiders. Flores achieved a decisive victory, capturing hostages and a large Apache horse herd, but this failed to stop depredations. Despite his military successes, Flores could not obtain permission for a major campaign two years later, and Bexareños had to content themselves with short pursuits of raiders after each attack.[25] By 1727 the garrison had become proficient in pursuing raiders, as witnessed by Brigadier Rivera during an inspection of San Antonio. He observed that "these Indians have learned by experience what the soldiers can do in the exercise of their duty when the occasion arises[;] they observe a certain restraint which minimizes the need for vigilance." While "it is a habit of the Indians to steal, and they do not fail to indulge in thefts, robbing the soldiers of their horses when not watchful," Rivera continued, "they are generally chastised by the troops for their daring."[26] As a result of his observations during this visit to Béxar, Rivera recommended a reduction of the presidial company by ten men. In fact, the lull in Apache activity was not solely attributable to the military effectiveness of the soldiers, and Béxar's security was seriously endangered by the reduced presidio contingent.

The military system also served to supply the settlement with food and manufactured goods. Until 1728 the governor controlled the settlement's provisioning, providing seed, farm implements, oxen, and even some Indian labor. Through his connection with Mexico City merchants, the governor arranged for the collection of the garrison's payroll and its use to purchase provisions, armaments, clothes, and even luxury items. After Rivera's inspection in 1721, Béxar's captain became solely responsible for supplies but under a similar arrangement.[27]

At the same time, the settlement worked to become self-sufficient. Soldiers and Indians opened *acequias* (irrigation ditches) for the presidio-villa and mission at the time of the settlement's founding. They also cleared land and planted maize and *huertas* (vegetable gardens). Pobladores opened another acequia when the presidio was relocated in 1722 as a result of its exposure to Indian attack. The acequia was described as "capable of irrigating the two leagues of fertile land found within the angle formed by the San Pedro and San Antonio, taking the water from the former for the benefit of the presidio troops and settlers that might join them."[28] The new acequia allowed settlers to utilize lands south of the presidio for crops and gardens.

The community's social structure was simple, even after the increase in the civilian population toward the end of the 1720s. Béxar's social hierarchy consisted of a usually "well-bred" governor (when he was present), the captain, the troops and their families, and the civilian settlers. Soldiers and former soldiers alike worked the presidio's irrigated fields, which belonged to all. They also possessed at least rudimentary blacksmithing, carpentry, and other skills which were used in the presidio and community.[29] Friars from Missions Valero and San José tended to the settlement's spiritual needs. While some soldiers had homesteads some distance away, most of the population lived around the military plaza. Civilians and military lived side by side, and those soldiers with families did not live in the barracks but in their own dwellings.[30]

As would be expected in a young frontier community, Béxar's physical appearance was not impressive in the 1720s. Most structures consisted of simple *jacales*, constructed of upright wooden poles plastered with mud or clay, that were easy to build and abandon. While suitable to this frontier situation, the thatch-roofed jacales caught fire easily. Late in 1721, for instance, sixteen jacales and a similarly built granary burned, affording the governor an opportunity to move the settlement to a more favorable location.[31] After 1722, jacales and adobe buildings began to give way to some stone structures.[32] The actual presidio was also modest. In fact, during his inspection of the presidio in 1727, Brigadier Rivera found no formal presidio fortification at all; instead, he noted a few stone houses "constructed by Don Fernando Pérez de Almazán in the year 1726." The presidio also included "an as yet unfinished chapel" and a barracks "in which the soldiers live . . . made of the same material [i.e., sticks and mud] as those of the Presidio de Texas."[33] Isolated and concerned with matters of survival, the pobladores did not build more than they absolutely needed nor seek title to the plots they worked, a decision they would soon regret.

THE OLD SETTLERS BECOME NEW RESIDENTS

By 1731 San Antonio de Béxar had consolidated its position as a permanent settlement. A community routine and tradition was clearly emerging, but the town's trajectory was altered by the arrival of a new group of settlers from the Canary Islands. The community changed in many ways, but the immediate impact on the soldier-settlers was the loss of their lands. The Isleños arrived at the critical spring planting season, preventing presidio Capt. Pérez de Almazán from sufficiently reflecting upon his instructions for settling the new arrivals. One immediate problem was that the land designated in his instructions for the Isleños' town site and farmlands had no irrigation facilities. Concluding that it would be too expensive and time-consuming to open up a new irrigation ditch, the captain distributed the irrigated fields south of the presidio among the recent immigrants.[34]

Furthermore, Pérez de Almazán apparently believed that his orders required him to maintain the presidio as a separate jurisdiction from the new villa to be established by the Isleños. He excluded the garrison's civilian population from any participation in the new town's creation and distributed town lots only to Islanders.[35] The captain also named an all-Islander town council, thus excluding non-Islanders from participation in local government. Until now the presidio commander exercised civil jurisdiction as chief magistrate (*justicia mayor*), hearing all civil and criminal cases in the region. When the town magistrate elections began under the Canary Islanders, the commander's jurisdiction was considerably reduced.[36] Furthermore, apparently without much thought to the consequences, Pérez de Almazán gave the immigrants general privileges as original settlers (*primeros pobladores*) to an area occupied by the military settlers for over a decade.

In several short months the military settlers were dispossessed, but they did not remain passive. While some sought permission to leave the province altogether, noting that "having observed the Islander families' behavior, it has not appeared good to them, and they do not wish to be neighbors with [Canary Islanders]," most were determined to stay and demand their rights.[37] Demonstrating their unity and sense of community, they protested their treatment as a group, submitted formal petitions for land to replace what they had lost, and demanded participation in the municipal government.

Initially the results were mixed. By 1734 only three non-Islander residents, former soldiers Alberto López and José Martínez and the blacksmith Juan Banul, had received town lot grants. Another four individuals received lots from Governor Manuel de Sandoval shortly after he took up his post in 1732. None received water rights with their grants, but this was the least of their problems, for Sandoval's farmland grants to six of these settlers met with so much opposition from the Isleños that, despite viceregal support, none of the grants were actually sustained locally.[38]

Despite the reverses, some pobladores managed to gain access to irrigated farmland in the Islanders' *labor*, or farmlands. As some Isleños found less profit in farming than in other activities, including military service, they found buyers among the military settlers. Retired soldiers Francisco Hernández, Gerónimo Flores, and Pedro Ocón y Trillo, as well as Capt. Toribio de Urrutia, all bought farmland from Isleños in 1739–41.[39] The ability of these men to pay for land they had once freely used attests to their influence and strength in the community and dispels the myth of monolithic Islander control over the settlement and its resources.

The military settlers also succeeded in breaking the Isleños' monopoly over local administration. During San Fernando's first decade they petitioned Mexico City on more than one occasion to be made participants in the town's council. The settlers demanded that one of the two *alcaldes* (magistrates) be a non-Islander and that half of the *regidores* (aldermen) be appointed from their group as the original incumbents died.[40] These petitions received a favorable response from viceregal officials in the capital, but the Islanders objected. Not until 1741 did the Isleño council give in to pressure from the majority population and begin selecting an alcalde from among the military settlers. Death, departure, incapacity, and intermarriage also forced the dwindling Isleño male population to grant the pobladores posts as regidores. In 1745 three military settlers served as regidores on the town council.[41]

CONCLUSION

In the summer of 1730, before the Islanders even left Veracruz on their long trip to San Antonio, the viceroy (on the advice of Brigadier Rivera) recommended to the king that he discontinue the recruitment of Canary

Islanders for settlement in Texas. The prohibitive costs of transportation and equipment made the program impractical, but in addition it soon became apparent that such immigrants were ill-prepared for settlement on that far-off frontier. Soon after their arrival in Béxar, for example, Capt. Pérez de Almazán observed that the Islanders did not know how to tend to their livestock or even fire weapons, making them useless for watch duty.[42] Obviously, Mexican families accustomed to frontier life were preferable and could be recruited far less expensively.

No further recruitment efforts were launched, however, even among Mexican families. After the Isleño experiment, migration to Texas once again depended on the voluntary movement of frontiersmen. The presidio continued to act as a magnet for population as new soldiers brought their families to San Antonio or settled down with one of the local daughters. In time, most families in Béxar, presidiales and Isleños alike, could trace their San Antonio roots to these settlers of the 1720s. Such terms as *primeros* and *principales pobladores* came to mean both the early military settlers and the Isleños they mixed with to form one of the most successful Spanish colonial communities in the American Southwest.

NOTES

1. Mexico, Archivo General de la Nación, *Boletín* 28:1 (1957), 64; 28:2 (1957), 357–58 (hereafter AGN, *Boletín*).

2. Carlos E. Castañeda, *Our Catholic Heritage in Texas* (reprint; New York: Arno, 1976), II, 71.

3. AGN, *Boletín* 29, no. 2 (1958): 305.

4. The viceroy's fiscal wrote that, in his opinion, "If possible, all the sixty soldiers should be Spaniards, not mulattoes, coyotes, or mestizos, so that the occurrences of 1693, will not be repeated." AGN, *Boletín* 29, no. 2 (1958): 339. The missionaries had previously complained of the ill effects the behavior of low-caste soldiers toward the Indians had on the first occupation.

5. "Título de gobernador e instrucciones a Don Martín de Alarcón para su expedición a Texas," AGN, *Boletín* 6, no. 4 (1935): 537.

6. Olivares to viceroy, June 22, 1718, Archivo General de la Nación, Ramo Provincias Internas (hereafter PI), vol. 181.

7. *Universidad de México* 5, nos. 25–26 (1933): 62–63; Castañeda, *Our Catholic Heritage*, II: 94.

8. Oakah L. Jones, *Los Paisanos: Spanish Settlers on the Frontier of New Spain* (Norman: University of Oklahoma Press, 1979), 247.

9. David A. Brading, *Mineros y comerciantes en el México borbónico (1763–1810)* (Mexico: Fondo de Cultura Económica, 1975), 37–38.

10. Max L. Moorhead, *The Presidio: Bastion of the Spanish Borderlands* (Norman: University of Oklahoma Press, 1975), 4; Herbert E. Bolton, "Defensive Spanish Expansion and the Significance of the Borderlands," in John Francis Bannon, ed., *Bolton and the Spanish Borderlands* (Norman: University of Oklahoma Press, 1964), 50–51.

11. Moorhead, *The Presidio*, 25–26, 182–84, 200.

12. Governor Pérez de Almazán to viceroy, March 24, 1724, AGN PI, vol. 183.

13. Richard G. Santos, ed. and trans., *Aguayo Expedition into Texas, 1721: An Annotated Translation of the Five Versions of the Diary Kept by Br. Juan Antonio de la Peña* (Austin: Jenkins

Publishing, 1981), 25, 30–31, 79; Fr. Isidro Félix Espinosa, Chrónica apostólica de todos los colegios de propaganda fide de esta Nueva España (Madrid, 1746), 452–57; Castañeda, *Our Catholic Heritage*, II: 115–19.

14. Comparison of the list made of those present in 1718 with the list of officers and soldiers of the Presidio of San Antonio de Béxar, Apr. 25, 1722, in "Autos a consulta hecha del Pe. Fr. Joseph González, Misionero del Presidio de San Antonio Balero Contra el Capitan Don Nicolás Flores por los motivos que expresa," AGN PI, vol. 32.

15. Fernando Pérez de Almazán to viceroy, July 11, 1726, in "Carpeta de correspondencia de ls. Proas. Internas por los años de 1726 a 1731 con los Exmos. Sres. Marqués de Casa y Fuerte, y Conde Fuenclara, ...," AGN PI, vol. 236.

16. "Título de gobernador," AGN, *Boletín* 6, no. 4 (1935): 537.

17. "Diario de la conquista y entrada a los Thejas," *Universidad de México* 5, nos. 27–28 (Jan.–Feb. 1933).

18. Ibid., 58. See also "Autos sobre diferentes noticias que se han participado a su Exa. De las entradas que en estos dominios hacen los Franceses por la parte de Coahuila… 1715," AGN PI, vol. 181; Espinosa, *Chrónica apostólica*, 449.

19. Marriage of Joseph Martínez to Juana de Carbajal, May 8, 1721, no. 31, San Fernando Parish Records, transcribed and translated by John O. Leal, "Mission San Antonio de Valero Marriages" (hereafter SF:VM); marriage of Cristóbal Basques to Ana de Carbajal, Feb. 20, 1722, no. 32, SF:VM; marriage of Diego Camacho to Juana Antonia de Carbajal, June 24, 1723, no. 50, SF:VM.

20. Estimate based on the appearance of married couples as witnesses or participants in San Antonio de Valero Mission marriages and baptisms between 1719 and 1730.

21. Castañeda, *Our Catholic Heritage*, II: 86–87.

22. "Autos sobre diferentes noticias… 1715," AGN PI, vol. 181.

23. Marriage of Juan Pais to Margarita, Sept. 24, 1724, no. 56, SF:VM.

24. Marriage of Joseph de la Fuente to Clara Gonález, Jan. 3, 1724, no. 52, SF:VM.

25. Castañeda, *Our Catholic Heritage*, II: 73, 190–91; Elizabeth A. H. John, *Storms Brewed in Other Men's Worlds: The Confrontation of Indians, Spanish, and French in the Southwest, 1540–1795* (College Station: Texas A&M University Press, 1975), 258–61; William Edward Dunn, "Apache Relations in Texas, 1718–1750" *Quarterly of the Texas State Historical Association* 14, no. 3 (Jan. 1911): 205.

26. Quoted in Carlos E. Castañeda, ed. and trans., *History of Texas, 1673–1779, by Fray Juan Agustín Morfi* (Albuquerque: Quivira Society, 1935), II: 257.

27. Governor Pérez de Almazán to viceroy, Oct. 24 and 25, 1724, AGN PI, vol. 183; Moorhead, *The Presidio*, 42.

28. Castañeda, *History of Texas*, I: 225.

29. Autos concerning distribution of lands in Béxar, July 31, 1731, AGN PI, vol. 163; Mardith K. Schuetz, "The People of San Antonio, Part I," in *San Antonio in the Eighteenth Century*, ed. San Antonio Bicentennial Heritage Committee (San Antonio: Clarke Printing), 81; Frederick C. Chabot, *With Makers of San Antonio* (San Antonio: Artes Gráficas), 56, 67, 137.

30. Case against Felipe de Avila for the murder of Nicolás Pasqual, Apr. 12, 1730, AGN PI, vol. 32.

31. Arnoldo De León, *The Tejano Community, 1836–1900* (Albuquerque: University of New Mexico Press, 1982), 2–3; Jones, *Los Paisanos*, 248; Santos, *Aguayo Expedition into Texas*, 74–75.

32. "Diario de la conquista"; "Auto de posesión," July 10, 1731, in autos concerning the distribution of lands in Béxar, July 31, 1731, AGN PI, vol. 163; Governor Fernando Pérez de Almazán to viceroy, Oct. 24, 1724, AGN PI, vol. 183; "Relación de los méritos y servicios de Don Fernando Pérez de Almazán" (Madrid, 1729).

33. "Testimonio de los Austos en virtud de Rl. Cédula sobre que pasen 400 familias para que pueblen la Bahía de Sn. Antonio, misiones de los Adais y los Texas," Feb. 14, 1729, Sevilla, Archivo General de Indias (hereafter AGI), Audiencia de Guadalajara (hereafter AG), legajo 67-4-38, transcription in *Spanish Material from Various Sources*, vol. 23, BTHC.

34. Castañeda, *Our Catholic Heritage*, II: 301–302.

35. Ibid., 302–308.

36. "Ordenanzas q. han de observer y guarder todos los Governadores y Comandtes, de los Presidios y Provins. Internas pa. El mejor Govo. De ellas, (1729), art. 50," AGI Audiencia de México, legajo 62-1-41, transcription in *Spanish Material from Various Sources*, vol. 81, BTHC; Toribio de Urrutia to [viceroy], Dec. 17, 1740, in "Autos a consulta de dn. Thoribio de Urrutia Capn. del Presidio de Sn. Antonio de Véjar, . . ." AGN PI, vol. 32; cabildo meeting, Aug. 25, 1745, BA, BTHC; Order of Colonel D. Angel de Martos y Navarrete, June 25, 1759, in Order of Viceroy D. Agustín Ahumada Villalon, Marqués de las Amarillas, Apr. 7, 1758, BA; Lt. Gov. Ramírez de la Piszinca to cabildo, Nov. 21, 1760, BA.

37. Almazán to viceroy, Dec. 1, 1731, AGN PI, vol. 32.

38. Petition of land by Juan Banul, Jan 12, 1734, in "Testimonio del decreto de su Exca. En qaue contiene varos puntos pertenecientes a los vecinos pobladores de esta Villa de S. Fernando sacado a pedimiento de dos. Vecinos para los efectos qaue les combenga" (1734). This expediente has inadvertently been filed within the following: "Testimonio de las disposiciones del Viery respecto a los vecinos y pobladores de la Villa de San Fernando y del Real Presidio de San Antonio de Béjar en las Provincias de las Nuevas Filipinas," 1735, AGN PI, vol 163; Auto of Governor, Jan. 29, 1734, AGN PI, vol. 163; "venta de solar y casa por Matías de la Zerda a favor de José Salinas," July 26, 1761, San Antonio, Bexar County Archives (hereafter BCA), Land Grant Series, no. 67 (hereafter LGS-67).

39. Antonio Rodríguez Mederos to Francisco Hernández, Apr. 10, 1739; José Cabrera to Antonio Rodríguez Mederos, Jan. 2, 1740; José Padrón to Gerónimo Flores, Oct. 7, 1740; Manuel de Niz to Pedro Ocón y Trillo, May 26, 1741; Juan Leal Alvarez to Toribio de Urrutia, No. 25, 1741, in Notary protocol, Mar 22, 1738, BA.

40. Petition by the residents of the presidio, Feb. 3, 1733, "Dictamen de Juan de Rebolledo," March 24, 1733, and viceroy's decree, Apr. 8, 1733, in "Autos sobre las providencias dadas por su ex. Al gobernador de la provincia de Texas para la pacificación de los Indios Apaches y sus aliados," 1731, AGN PI, vol. 32.

41. See "Appendix D: Composition of Béxar's Town Council," in Jesús Francisco de la Teja, "Land and Society in 18th Century San Antonio de Béxar" (PhD diss, University of Texas at Austin, 1988), 407–28.

42. Castañeda, *Our Catholic Heritage*, II: 275–76, 283–84; "Auto en que se da razón de haver ospedado a los Ysleños y otras providencias," March 10, 1731, AGN PI, vol. 32.

Theodore Gentilz, *Comanches on the War Path*. Comanches first appeared in the San Antonio area in the late 1740s and soon formed the most formidable challenge to Spanish interests in Texas. Throughout the mid-eighteenth century, San Antonio's presidio was hard pressed to defend the community against the Comanches and their allies, who retreated into the vastness of northwestern prairies and plains beyond the military's reach. Even after a general peace came in the late 1780s, young warriors eager to test their mettle proved an ongoing headache to San Antonio military and civilian authorities. Courtesy of the Witte Museum, San Antonio, Texas.

4

"To the Last Drop of Our Blood"

Defending King and Empire in San Antonio*

On May 8, 1791 the citizens of San Fernando de Béxar, as the chartered town we now call San Antonio was then known, addressed a petition to the commandant general of the Interior Provinces, the military-political jurisdiction of which Texas was a unit. Governor Manuel Muñoz had issued an order calling for the removal of the civilians' horses from the company herd. Not only was this a break in tradition, but it exposed the impoverished citizenry to great hardship. They asked to be relieved of the burden of guarding their horse herd, except for those times when the company went on campaigns, scouting expeditions, and other royal business. The reasons they gave for their request were familiar to every governor and other royal official who had had the misfortune of dealing with Bexareños for over a half century. They were a miserable lot of wretched unfortunates, who had little on which to maintain themselves other than their limited plantings and personal labor, the result of the many years "that the enemy Indians have pursued and harassed us, for which reason we have not been able to raise our heads above water." The request did not mean, however, that they were not willing to undertake other services "to the last drop of our blood."[1] The commandant general, sympathetic to their plight, granted them their request and ordered Governor Muñoz to allow the integration of the civilian herd, including tame mares, into the military *caballada* (horse herd).

Ten years earlier, in his monthly military report, then-governor Domingo Cabello wrote an account of an event—one of many over the decades—that supported the truthfulness of the citizens' petition noted above. The lone survivor of a Comanche ambush of a patrol out of the Fuerte del Cíbolo, a post on the road between San Antonio and La Bahía,

---

*Presented at the 2004 annual meeting of the Philosophical Society of Texas and published in vol. 68 of the Proceedings of the Society.

led a rescue party to the site of the skirmish. There, according to Cabello, they found the troop "leaning against trees, their scalps missing and their fingers and noses cut off. But they must have put up a good fight, for fifty spent cartridges were found and the lips and teeth of the soldiers were black with powder, and from the evidence it seems they must have killed some Indians."[2] Shortly after, Cabello received a summons for help from Ensign Valdez, who while out on patrol from the Cíbolo post felt threatened by a superior force of Indians. Retired ensign Baltasar de los Reyes Pérez offered to lead the rescue party, which consisted of thirty-seven soldiers and forty-five citizens. They set out at 11 p.m. and managed to join up with Valdez early the next morning, but could not catch the Indians. On the way back they found the bodies of José Flores and Melchor Ximénez, who had stayed behind hunting for a cow when Valdez left Cíbolo.

The Cíbolo post had been established ten years earlier, in March 1771, as a result of increased hostilities in the countryside. A temporary respite from Comanche, Apache, and Norteño raiding in the late 1760s had led to the reoccupation of a number of civilian ranches in the valleys of the San Antonio and its tributaries east of town. Renewed hostilities as far as La Bahía had brought the rancheros to request of Governor Barón de Ripperdá that he provide a guard so that the ranchers could plant their fields. The result was the construction of a stockade at the site of Vicente Alvarez Travieso's Rancho Las Mulas, where, "because of the great danger, only one horse per man should be taken." The arrangement was to last until it was once again safe for each ranchero to return to his lands and fields.[3]

A decade before that, in June 1762, the townspeople of San Antonio joined the missionary at Espíritu Santo in complaining about Apache depredations to the new governor, Angel Martos y Navarrete. "The Apaches are stealing our horses and slaughtering our cattle and oxen in the vicinity of the presidio and town with such audacity that they almost take no precautions. If a group from the town goes to the *rancherías* (Indian villages) and spots livestock with known brands, not only do the Indians not return them, but they laugh at us since our forces are so weak."[4]

The correlation between Indians and presidio and the survival of San Antonio had been made clear yet another ten years earlier, in June 1750, during an investigation on the desirability of moving the presidio to a site on the Pedernales River in support of a new mission for the Apaches. Although Fray Mariano Francisco de los Dolores of Mission Valero agreed that the transfer would result in the ability of the citizenry to move into the countryside to farm and raise cattle, conditions in town did not permit the move. The citizenry was poor, lazy, and dependent on the supplies provided to the presidio for their sustenance. Béxar's town council agreed, stating that the town counted no more than fifty or sixty *vecinos* (citizens), not all of them armed. "If the presidio were moved, not one-half the citizenry would remain, because of all who would follow it, because it is the only commerce this country has."[5]

Talk of bringing the Apaches to the light of salvation and civilization had been going around among missionaries for over a decade by the time the Pedernales plan was proposed. In fact, much of the debate centered on whether Béxar's settlers were not making things tough on themselves because of their treatment of the Indians. Lipan attacks in the late 1730s finally drove Capt. Joseph Urrutia to organize the first of three campaigns into Apache territory in the winter of 1739. The expedition was roundly condemned by Fray Benito Fernández de Santa Ana, who claimed that the time of year and the lack of discipline among the soldiery only served to increase the hostility of the Indians. Moreover, "it is ridiculous that these same persons should claim certificates as servants of the King our Lord, when they were interested in what I have stated, and had greater hopes of a considerable prize of horses, hides, and Indian men and women to serve them."[6]

Horses, settlers, and soldiers—they had been part of the mix from the very beginning of San Fernando, a decade before Urrutia's campaign. Having taken stock of the Canary Islanders who had just arrived in Béxar after more than a year-long journey from their homeland, Capt. Juan Antonio Pérez de Almazán could only scratch his head in wonderment. He provided lodgings for the settlers in the most comfortable dwellings available in the presidio, despite the hardship caused to the soldiers' families. Then, signaling his disapproval of the whole affair, and "considering the exhausted condition of the settlers, their inexperience with the weapons used against the Indians, and their lack of horsemanship to hinder their usefulness on the watch, I therefore placed the horses of the settlers with those of the company."[7] Thus were presidio and town joined, a tradition started, and San Antonio's career as a military town cemented.

One last decade-long step back in time brings us to the beginning of our story in the earliest days of San Antonio, when it was a fledgling community not yet completely settled into its permanent site. In 1721 the Marqués de San Miguel de Aguayo was in the midst of his reorganization of the province, making sure that it was sufficiently strong to hold off further French incursions from Louisiana and Indian depredations from the interior. A year earlier, the first documented Apache attack on the settlement had taken place—the killing of two men out searching for missing horses.

Aguayo felt the Lipan Apache menace so strong that he increased the garrison by over twenty enlisted men, bringing troop strength to fifty-four officers and men.[8]

It was the failure of the 1690–93 religious occupation of Texas, which had been based on the Franciscans' exaggerated hopes of converting the Hasinais into loyal Christian Spanish subjects, which served as a good lesson for the 1716–18 permanent settlement of the province. Texas would no doubt be a religious province, but it would also be a military district. The mission and the presidio would work hand in hand, just as they had come to do throughout the colonial Mexican far north. It was from that religious-military tradition that San Antonio was born. It was the tradition on which the occupation of California would take place fifty years later.

The upper reaches of the San Antonio River held a number of natural advantages as a site for a missionary-military complex to serve as a way-station between presidios San Juan Bautista del Río Grande and Nuestra Señora del Pilar de Los Adaes. To a greater degree than other Texas streams, the San Antonio River was fit for irrigation. The area held plentiful supplies of timber and rock for construction, and nearby prairies offered an abundance of grazing land. During a 1709 exploration Fray Isidro Espinosa was effusive in his praise for the area; returning to the site in 1716 as part of the expedition headed for the occupation of East Texas, he sounded even more like a real estate agent in his description of the locale's potential, praising the abundance of useful plants, animals, and fish. A veteran of northern Mexico's arid environment, he was laudatory of the aquatic resources: "its copious waters . . . are clear, crystal, and sweet."[9]

Finding a location for the military-religious complex was the easy part. It would prove much more difficult to turn the post into a flourishing settlement. Governor Martín de Alarcón founded Mission San Antonio de Valero and Villa de Béxar at the beginning of May 1718, but the *villa*, or town, never developed. Working alongside mission Indians and the few retirees who stayed on after fulfilling their enlistments, soldiers cleared fields, dug *acequias* (irrigation canals), and erected homes and other buildings. Some of the younger men married from among the daughters of the older soldiers, or found spouses among the presidio families at Los Adaes or La Bahía, but others had to go in search of their wives outside the province. Although the thirty or so soldier-settlers of the Alarcón expedition were joined by those recruited by Aguayo, and later in the 1720s by a few more, it soon became clear that Texas offered no incentives to civilian colonization.

When Inspector General Pedro de Rivera inspected the company late in 1727 he was generally satisfied with the military community: the garrison was well armed and disciplined, although the prices charged by the commander to his men were high; the Apaches, he believed, had been chastised to the point of submission. The soldiers may well have boasted to him of the successful 1723 campaign in which they had killed over thirty braves and captured many horses along with women and children. With the appearance of the regulations of 1729, based on Rivera's recommendations for cost savings, Presidio de Béxar experienced a reduction in troop strength by ten billets, ironically producing the first substantial boost in the settlement's civilian population.

Two other Rivera recommendations conspired to turn San Antonio into the center of Spanish activity in Texas. One had to do with the largely moribund missions of East Texas, which soaked up scarce financial resources. Rivera recommended reducing their number because the Hasinais were peaceful Indians who seemed willing to deal with the Spaniards without the intervention of missionaries. After a few months' stay at what is now Barton Springs in Austin, three missions found a permanent location along the San Antonio River south of the existing communities. In early March 1731 missions Concepción, San Juan Capistrano, and San Francisco de la Espada joined the original San Antonio mission, Valero (now the Alamo), and another founded in 1720, San José y San Miguel de Aguayo, to form the Alamo chain of missions.

Rivera's second recommendation echoed one that had been made by the Marqués de Aguayo upon his return to Coahuila: to foster the civilian settlement of the province, families from Spain or the Canary Islands should be encouraged to migrate. The king eventually approved the plan for the transfer of four hundred families, but of these only fifteen eventually reached San Antonio. Seeing what he had to work with, Captain Almazán thought unworkable the order that the Canary Islands be settled in their own separate community. Instead, as stated earlier, he housed the new arrivals among the presidio families while he prepared the area immediately east of the presidio as the site of San Fernando de Béxar.[10]

The small garrison had its hands full. The garrison provided each mission with a guard of about three men. The community's horse herd, as we have seen, itself required a substantial guard. Escort service—of the mail, of visitors entering or leaving the province, of civilians going to cut timber or to hunt—also reduced the number of troopers available at the garrison itself. When not otherwise occupied, the soldiers performed construction work around the presidio. Of the forty-three men in the company, the commander could rarely count on more than a handful to be on hand, and these were usually the infirm or injured. Not surprisingly, Béxar's commanders came to rely on civilians and mission Indians to supplement presidio troops. In the summer of 1745, following Capt. Toribio de Urrutia's campaign against the Apaches, the Indians mounted one of their most determined attacks on the settlement, which was saved only through the timely arrival of a militia composed of Mission Valero Indians.

A temporary peace with the Apaches was reached in 1749, following another campaign by Captain Urrutia, the main purpose of which was to take captives for negotiation. In one of the most spectacular events to have taken place in the frontier community to that time, Apaches and Spanish colonials gathered around a large pit dug in the center of the military plaza, where the symbols of war—a horse, hatchet, lance, and arrows—were buried while settlers, Indians, and dignitaries danced to seal the peace.

The years of relative peace that followed led royal officials to repeat the mistake that General Rivera had made in 1727, the erroneous assumption that peace with the Indians was at hand and that the garrison could be reduced. Always short of funds, royal officials decided to populate the garrison being created to protect a new mission for the Apaches in part with twenty-two men from the Béxar company. The reduction of the garrison to twenty-one effectives, not counting the captain, not only posed a setback to the community's growth, but it forced the civilian population to take on a greater share of the defensive burden. It is during this time that an organized militia emerged, although, as might be expected, the citizenry always played down its ability to contribute to the community's defense in order to restore the company's fighting strength.

In the punitive expedition that followed the Comanche-Norteño attack on Mission San Sabá in 1758, a few soldiers and numerous civilians and mission Indians from San Antonio participated. The expedition proved a miserable failure and only served to make Béxar the target of the Apaches' enemies, who now considered San Antonio's population allies of their Apache enemy. The result was an increasing level of violence that required the posting of temporary detachments from other presidios at Béxar to help manage the situation. The twenty-two men that Béxar had provided for the San Sabá presidio returned in 1769 when the viceroy approved their temporary posting. By 1773 San Antonio's garrison could count on a permanent troop strength of eighty men, led by none other than the provincial governor, whose capital the viceroy officially moved to Béxar that year.

What happened? From its beginnings until the late 1760s the presidio had been a virtual fiefdom. Presidio commanders had almost complete autonomy in running their companies. They recruited their own men for enlistments of ten years, controlled the payrolls, faced only infrequent inspections, and meted out justice as *justicia mayor* in the jurisdiction—in San Antonio this last prerogative became a major bone of contention between the commander and the town council, which claimed that the king had granted its civilian authorities jurisdictional autonomy. In sum, the presidio system had evolved as an ad-hoc response to local circumstances in New Spain and was neither part of the regular army nor a distinct unified command. Presidios came in all shapes and sizes, and while some were under the direct jurisdiction of the viceroy, others were under the authority of the provincial governor.[11]

In Béxar's case, command had actually become a family legacy. After the terms of the first two commanders, Juan Pérez de Almazán and Nicolás Flores de Abrego, the captaincy had passed to Joseph de Urrutia, an old frontier hand with personal knowledge of Texas' Indians going back to the early 1690s. Following his death his son Toribio took command, and upon his retirement Luis Antonio Menchaca, Toribio's nephew, assumed the post. It was Toribio who had built what is now called the Governor's Palace, a building that served as both home and general store for the town until an independent civilian commercial sector developed in the 1770s. Because they controlled the payrolls, and because the payroll was converted into goods for issuance at elevated prices, the captains were the wealthiest men in town and ran stores that supplied the rest of the community. This state of affairs was so normal that when Toribio de Urrutia asked for retirement at full pay after thirty years of service, the viceroy's advisor replied that although the law did not allow it without the king's permission, he and his successor could split the salary since "the advantages of the post will surely make someone take it up even under these conditions."[12]

The 1760s marked a turning point in San Antonio's military history. Increased hostilities from Comanches and the Nations of the North created a need to address its long-term survivability. Viceregal authorities and the governor attempted to deal with the growing crisis by shuffling available resources around, with detachments from as far away as Nuevo Santander and Coahuila stationed at San Antonio for limited periods of time, but that was no solution. In 1766 Captain Menchaca found an opportunity to press the case for reinforcing San Antonio when Governor Navarrete instructed him to supply ten soldiers and thirty-five mission Indians to an exploratory expedition to the coast. Menchaca refused to supply the soldiers and was unable to convince the missionaries to do likewise. His reasons reveal the state of defenses at Béxar in the face of growing Indian hostilities. He was not responsible for the missionaries' unwillingness to supply Indians—they argued that the Indians made their living from doing daily manual work and should be compensated for being drawn away from their labor for such a mission—and he went on to state that he had only six men on hand, three of whom were on guard duty over the horse herd, and the other three on watch over the artillery. Although the company was composed of twenty-one men, with three stationed at each mission, and with no instructions to remove them, he could not see how he could carry out the order. Furthermore, the presidio, town, and missions were subject to constant Indian attack about which he could do nothing. The solution lay in increasing the garrison and having soldiers from La Bahía and Los Adaes temporarily stationed at San Antonio. The worst was yet to come, he warned, as Indians had stolen about one thousand animals, and although the detachments he had sent out to track them down had failed, a group of mission Indians from San José had met up with four Comanches, whom they managed to kill. "So it is certain that the war with the Comanche will only grow worse."[13]

From the king on down there was a growing realization that the entire frontier defense structure needed a serious overhaul, especially Texas, which had been the border province with French Louisiana, but the strategic importance of which had changed now that Spain had acquired the territory west of the Mississippi River. The man charged with evaluating New Spain's northern frontier defenses was the Marqués de Rubí, a Spanish officer trained in the latest military techniques. His inspection took him from the Gulf of California to the Gulf of Mexico over a two-year span, at the end of which he presented a bold plan that had major consequences for Texas, particularly San Antonio. Although he recommended that a presidio line be established at 30° north latitude, with all territory above that line abandoned to the Indians, he also recommended that because of their importance Santa Fe and San Antonio be allowed to remain. Béxar came in for special attention, as Rubí recommended an increase in the size of the garrison, something that townspeople and commanders had been lobbying for since the removal of half the command in 1757. The additional troops would come from closure of East Texas presidios Los Adaes and Orcoquisac. The expanded garrison would be commanded by the provincial governor, who would now have his capital at San Antonio.

The changes officially took effect in 1773. Governor Juan María, Barón de Ripperdá, oversaw the permanent expansion of the company to eighty men and the establishment of the Cíbolo post. Rubí's recommendations, incorporated into the *Reglamento* of 1772 and other decrees, for the first time addressed the presidios of New Spain as a system rather than as an ad hoc collection of semi-autonomous posts. The *Reglamento* called for each company to have a quartermaster, elected from among the officers of the company by the entire garrison. That officer would hold fiduciary responsibility for handling the payroll of the garrison, from which provisions and supplies were to be bought. By taking the payroll and supply functions away from the company commander, higher officials sought to end the rampant corruption and inefficiencies that ill-served royal interests. Each soldier was to receive part of his pay (which was reduced under the logic that given the reforms, less would be more) in cash in an effort to boost the local economy and to encourage him to keep his uniform, equipment, and mounts, which in the past had often been sold to cover personal expenses. The regulations also called for regular drilling, including target practice, and inspections. On the bureaucratic side, company commanders were to make monthly reports of all military activities within their jurisdiction and maintain a monthly muster book stating the detail to which each member of the unit was assigned.

The reordering of the presidios was followed up by the creation of a new administrative unit for the frontier that would make communications and decision making more efficient. The Comandancia General de las Provincias Internas, although never the fix-all that the king's ministers thought it would be, at least created a chain of command at the top of which sat an individual with intimate knowledge of frontier conditions and a zeal for the royal service. In the first decade of its existence, the *comandante general*'s most important actions were to plan a new strategy for dealing with the various autonomous tribes, particularly the multiple bands of Apaches that carried out depredations from the Sonora-Arizona border region to San Antonio and La Bahía.

For Presidio de Béxar the changes were profound. Although Ripperdá's successor, Colonel Domingo Cabello, abolished the Cíbolo post, the challenges he faced in his administration, between 1778 and 1786, contributed to the further expansion of the presidio company. By 1781 the garrison had increased to one hundred men and had been divided into two companies, one light cavalry and one heavy cavalry. The citizens' militia was reorganized and supplied with standard weapons. And San Antonio became the center of negotiations with the various Comanche and Norteño bands. Campaigns from San Antonio and Santa Fe against the Apaches brought most of these bands under general control by the end of the decade.

The last decade of the eighteenth century was one of relative stability on San Antonio's Indian frontier. Still, the presidio represented the settlement's most important institution. Most members of the garrison were locals, some of them third or fourth generation soldiers of the company. Thus, the presidio was Béxar's most important employer, as it was the most important market. While in the early years the captain's store, stocked from the profits the commander gained from managing the company payrolls, served the rest of the community, by late decades a number of full-time shopkeepers and artisans had the garrison and its dependents for regular customers. Recruits had always seen the presidio as an opportunity to escape the general poverty of Texas; enlistment protected soldiers and families from the instability of the local agricultural economy and most presidio work called for skills that young men already possessed—horseback riding, herding, reading Indian signs, construction. With a little luck and moderate habits, a soldier could stay relatively out of debt, yet know that in case of need the company served as an economic safety net.

The early nineteenth century takes us into a complicated set of political and military transformations that would require an additional paper to explain. The Louisiana Purchase reestablished Texas as a border province with an acquisitive neighbor willing to work through area Indians to undermine Spanish authority. United States' claims of Texas as part of Louisiana required a massive reinforcement of the province that brought hundreds of troops from throughout northeastern Mexico to Texas. In the midst of this, the Mexican War of Independence erupted and Texas' military establishment blew with the winds of change, fighting both against and for royalist interests. By the time of Mexican independence in 1821, the progress that had been made in creating a sustainable society based on a relatively well-equipped military force and strategic consideration of Indian interests was in shambles.[14] Independent Mexico was never equipped to properly restore the presidio system to its required strength and vitality, and its feeble attempts to do so in the early 1830s made up one of the contributing factors leading to the struggle for Texas independence.

NOTES

1. Representación hecha por el vecindario de esta villa solicitando la reunión de sus caballerías al situado de la tropa, Año de 1791, May 8, 1791, Bexar Archives, Center for American History, the University of Texas at Austin (hereafter cited as BA).
2. Estado de la fuerza efectiba. Feb. 28, 1781, BA.
3. Auto of Gov. Ripperdá, Feb. 24, 1771, BA.
4. Petition of Fr. Pedro Ramírez, June 6, 1762, BA.
5. Testimonio de los autos fechos sobre la reducción de los indios gentiles de la nación Apache a las misiones de los ríos de San Xavier de la provincia de Texas. Nov. 29, 1749, Audiencia de Mexico 92-6-22, Archivo General de la Nación de México, in Spanish Materials from Various

Sources, vol. 90, Center for American History, the University of Texas at Austin (hereafter cited as SM).

6. Carlos E. Castañeda, *Our Catholic Heritage in Texas* 7 vols. (reprint; New York: Arno, 1976) 3:47.

7. Auto en que se da razón de haber hospedado a los isleños y otras providencias. Mar. 10, 1731, Provincias Internas vol. 32, pt. 2, SM vol. 727.

8. Unless otherwise cited, this paper is based on Jesús F. de la Teja, *San Antonio de Béxar: A Community on New Spain's Northern Frontier* (Albuquerque: University of New Mexico Press, 1995).

9. Jesús F. de la Teja, "'A Fine Country with Broad Plains—the Most Beautiful in New Spain': Colonial Views of Land and Nature," in Char Miller, ed., *On the Border: An Environmental History of San Antonio* (Pittsburgh: University of Pittsburgh Press, 2001), 48.

10. Spanish jurisdictional nomenclature is rather confusing, which no doubt contributed to the modern names of city and county. The district to which the city, presidio, missions, and outlying ranches belonged was called San Antonio de Béxar, as was the presidio. The chartered town, named in honor of the heir to the Spanish throne and the medieval saint-king, was San Fernando de Béxar. Each mission had its individual name, as did each ranch. For the sake of clarity, I will refer to the settlement as Béxar or San Antonio, identifying the specific entity—town, presidio—when necessary.

11. On the history of the presidio system see Max L. Moorhead, *The Presidio: Bastion of the Spanish Borderlands* (Norman: University of Oklahoma Press, 1975).

12. El virrey de Na. España da quenta con Testimonio de haver concedido reforma a D. Toribio Urrutia Capitán del Presidio de Béjar y nombrado a D. Luis Menchaca. Aug. 11, 1763, Audiencia de Guadalajara 104-6-13, Archivo General de Indias, SM vol. 42.

13. Diligencias que en virtud de no haber contribuido don Luis Menchaca los diez hombres y 35 indios que se le pidieron para el reconocimiento de las islas blancas que se cometió al coronel Parrilla, tubo a bien de practicar el gobernador de Texas con lo demás que en ellas se expresa. June 30, 1766, BA.

14. For the Texas War of Independence period see Jesús F. de la Teja, "Rebellion on the Frontier," in Gerald E. Poyo, ed., *Tejano Journey, 1770–1850* (Austin: University of Texas Press, 1996), 15–30; for Mexican-period San Antonio see Jesús F. de la Teja and John Wheat, "Béxar: Profile of a Tejano Community," *Southwestern Historical Quarterly* 89, 1 (1985): 7–34.

Theodore Gentilz, *Aguador: Water Seller*. Mules and donkeys constituted the backbone of commercial transportation on the Texas frontier. Although carts operated locally, for long-distance hauling over rough trails and low-water crossings mules were preferred because of their strength and endurance. Like their bigger relatives, donkeys had stamina and were easy to care for, but unlike their larger equine cousins, they were not attractive to the independent Indian raiders who often target military and civilian herds. Courtesy of Daughters of the Republic of Texas Library.

The Saltillo Fair and Its
San Antonio Connections*

On March 1, 1790, a self-appointed San Antonio citizens' committee presented Texas governor Rafael Martínez Pacheco with a petition. On their return from a campaign against the Lipan Apaches in which they had participated as citizen militia, they had discovered that the previous year's town council had in their absence taken the liberty to reappoint itself—illegally—for the current year. The petitioners requested justice from the governor, noting that he had "helped the town councils in office since [his] arrival by taking on their duties so the members could take care of their needs, such as planting, going to their ranches, and in August to Saltillo for the fair at the end of September, where they trade what they have produced the whole year for the necessary goods for the coming one."[1] The petition, on the surface little more than a petty grievance, is in reality a window on the world of eighteenth-century San Antonio, the life of which revolved around farming, ranching, Indian fighting, and dependence on economic ties with the interior of Mexico as represented in the Saltillo Fair.[2]

Documentation regarding business and military activity in San Antonio during the colonial period is replete with references to Saltillo and its annual fair. Men responsible for underwriting San Antonio's annual religious celebrations note their need to do business at the fair in order to acquire the means to meet their obligations. Creditors owed money by Bexareños (citizens of San Antonio de Béxar, Spanish Texas' major settlement and capital after 1771) explain that their deadbeat business associates had promised to pay at the fair. Governors' correspondence regularly refers to sending an armed escort to await the return of residents and the garrison's quartermaster, who have gone to Saltillo for the fair. Saltillo, in other words, was the major economic (and social) destination for the people of

---

*First published in Arnoldo De León, ed., *Tejano Epic: Essays in Honor of Félix D. Almaráz, Jr.* (Austin: Texas State Historical Association, 2005), 15–27.

San Antonio in the colonial period, and by the late eighteenth century the fair had become the best time of year to make the trip.

Despite its apparent importance to Bexareños and to the population of northeastern colonial Mexico generally, the fair remains underappreciated by both Texas and Mexican historians. Among those who have mentioned the fair, Vito Alessio Robles provides the most details in two of his major works, *Coahuila y Texas en la época colonial* and *Saltillo en la historia y la leyenda*. His approach is anecdotal and general, relying on a handful of readily available documents. Nevertheless, he provides a clear indication of the socio-economic importance of the annual gathering:

> Saltillo was the commercial emporium of northeastern New Spain. At its famous fairs, held every year in the months of September and October, there gathered all the stockmen, agriculturalists, and merchants of the four eastern interior provinces[3] to sell their products, and a great number of merchants from central Mexico attended to acquire said goods and sell foreign merchandise and those produced in the heart of the viceroyalty.[4]

Clearly, then, Bexareños were part of an economic region that stretched from the Gulf of Mexico to the Bolsón de Mapimí, from the pine forests of East Texas to the mountain valleys of the Sierra Madre Oriental and was linked, through Saltillo, to the world beyond. But, what was their role in this system? What does their participation say about their economic behaviors and interests? Specifically, how can the study of their participation at the fair illustrate the nature of northern New Spain's socio-economic system? These are some of the questions this essay seeks to answer.

Before addressing these topics, let us briefly discuss what fairs are, what role they play in a country's social and economic development, and how the Saltillo Fair developed. First, fairs are worldwide and ancient in origin. Many had their start as religious events that soon acquired a commercial importance. Unlike markets, which occur on a regular basis, oftentimes weekly or daily, fairs normally occur only annually or semi-annually. Markets usually bring together area agricultural producers, artisans, and petty merchants with local consumers. Fairs are gatherings of large merchant houses with local producers, manufacturers, and consumers. Writing on the purpose of fairs, the French social historian Fernand Braudel states:

> Their function was to interrupt the tight circle of everyday exchanges.... They could mobilize the economy of a huge region: sometimes the entire business community of western Europe would meet at them, to take advan-

tage of the liberties and franchises they offered which wiped out for a brief moment the obstacles caused by the numerous taxes and tolls."[5]

One additional point to be made about the economic character of officially sanctioned fairs was their special tax status. Unlike markets, chartered fairs were tax-free events. Often, such as in the Saltillo case, it was many years before the crown granted approval for the fair; nevertheless these gatherings were known as fairs because of their annual occurrence, the participation of import-export merchants, and the great festivals that accompanied them.

Because they were large and elaborate events held over an extended period of time, fairs were seen as special social occasions offering greater opportunities for entertainment and religious celebration. In fact some fairs, such as the one at Saltillo, owed their existence to pre-existing religious feast days. Braudel stresses that "fairs meant noise, tumult, music, popular rejoicing, the world turned upside down, disorder and sometimes disturbances."[6] Later he makes an assertion that applied as much to Saltillo as it did to the European fairs, of which he writes: "in this essentially agricultural world, all fairs, even the very grand ones, were open to the overwhelming presence of country people. Alongside the main Leipzig fairs, large horse- and livestock fairs were also held."[7]

In fact, commercial fairs were often the outgrowth of religious celebrations. Historian William Christian, writing on sixteenth-century Spain, cites how the annual feast at a Benedictine shrine had grown into an important commercial gathering:

> All of these villages come in procession the Wednesday of Litanies, the day before Ascension, and a great fair is held in this place attended by merchants of silk and woolen cloth, goldsmiths and silversmiths, vendors of dry goods and numerous artisans of all kinds because of the multitude of people who come from so many places.[8]

Mexican historian María Villanueva Saldivar, writing about the influence that medieval Spanish fairs had on those of New Spain, comments that the earliest fairs were usually associated with religious events and their settings were considered sacred places.[9] With its origins in early seventeenth-century pilgrimages to a shrine to the Virgin Mary, the fair at San Juan de los Lagos, on the road between Guadalajara and Aguascalientes, is a good example of this interplay between religion and commerce in colonial Mexico. As the number of pilgrims increased in the eighteenth century, merchants from throughout colonial Mexico made it a favorite destination.[10]

All this is not to say that fairs were a uniquely Hispanic phenomenon. In colonial times they were employed not only in Spanish America, but in British America as well. Throughout New England, fairs appeared in the initial decades of colonization, although they seem to have quickly fallen into disuse. The close proximity and abundance of urban centers soon lessened the need for periodic commercial gatherings. The more rural colonial South retained its fairs much longer. One scholar judges that "the various fairs . . . marked an important stage in the early growth and development of Virginia's towns."[11]

Consequently, modern county and state fairs only partially resemble earlier forms. Like them, the modern fair provides opportunities for entertainment, competition, and the exhibition of products. Unlike them, the fair system that came into existence in the late nineteenth century is not an avenue for regular commerce.

The Saltillo Fair was part of a hierarchy of fairs that began to emerge in Mexico in the seventeenth century, although it took more than a century for any of them to obtain royal approval. At the top of the hierarchy were two fairs of international importance: Jalapa, which dealt with trans-Atlantic trade, and Acapulco, which was supposed to have a monopoly on trans-Pacific commerce because it depended on the annual arrival of the Manila Galleon. Below these were regional fairs, such as the previously mentioned one at San Juan de los Lagos and our own Saltillo Fair, where representatives of the major merchant houses of Mexico City and Spain did wholesale business with local merchants and stockmen, and retail trade with consumers. Finally, under the right conditions, regular trade relations were established with independent Indian groups on an annual or semi-annual basis. For instance, at Taos and Santa Fe, New Mexico, these events, which were also called fairs, included the exchange of European and Mexican goods for hides, pelts, livestock, and even human captives.[12]

To the degree that "fairs" in New Spain's Far North have been examined, their true scope and character are difficult to surmise. Spanish borderlands historian Max Moorhead, in his study of trade between New Mexico and Chihuahua, comments that by the late eighteenth century the annual trade caravan to Chihuahua was timed for late autumn to avoid conflicts with the Taos fair, at which Nuevomexicano traders did business with Comanches and other Plains peoples in July or August. The schedule had to be altered again early in the nineteenth century when, beginning in 1806, the mining supply center of Valle de San Bartolomé was granted the right to hold an annual trade fair of its own.[13] Another historian writes that local traders took the items they bartered from the Plains Indians "directly to the great Chihuahua fairs,"[14] despite the absence of clear evidence that there was a "fair" at Chihuahua. It may be that the annual feast of San Francisco held at Chihuahua was acquiring the type of commercial importance for northwestern Mexico that Saltillo's feast of Santiago had acquired for the northeastern part of the colony, hence reference to it as a fair.[15]

Saltillo's importance as a colonial economic and social center grew in the course of its first two centuries of existence. Founded by former slavers, it was strategically located in a fertile valley from which its agricultural production could easily be transported to mining centers to the south and west. As the settlement grew, especially with the addition of the neighboring Tlaxcalan Indian town of San Esteban, Saltillo was able to provide the seed populations of new settlements in Nuevo León, Coahuila, and eventually as far as Texas and Nuevo Santander. As Indian role models, royal officials employed many of San Esteban's Tlaxcalans to found communities near missions for the aboriginal peoples of northeastern Mexico. Occupying a well-watered and protected valley, the people of the Saltillo area developed a prosperous agricultural economy that rested on wheat and livestock. Permanence, economic growth, and geographic centrality endowed Saltillo with a regional leadership role that was in large measure expressed, as was natural in the Spanish-Catholic world, through religious celebration.

Settled at the end of New Spain's first great period of frontier expansion in the 1570s, the town had been named Villa de Santiago del Saltillo, honoring the patron saint of the *conquistadores*, Santiago Matamoros (St. James, Moorslayer), whose association with victory over the infidels during the *Reconquista* (the Christian reconquest of Spain from the Muslims) had made him a natural spiritual force in the conquest of the heathen Indians. St. James is said to have appeared to Hernan Cortés and other conquistadores in the 1520s and 1530s and even to Juan de Oñate's forces during the subjugation of Acoma Pueblo in New Mexico in 1598. Consequently, numerous towns throughout the Americas established during the sixteenth century employed Santiago as patron saint. For some reason, most likely because of the adverse traveling conditions of mid-summer and early harvest times in the region, by the early eighteenth century the celebrations had been moved from the official feast day, July 25, to anywhere from mid-September to early October, depending on conditions. As attendance and business opportunities increased at the week-long celebration, city fathers paid increasing attention to the secular aspects of the event. Mandatory attendance by the town's *vecinos* (citizens) at the procession of the royal standard, enclosure of the main plaza for bullfights, and the building of temporary vendors' booths were all elements of the city fathers' efforts to foster Saltillo's importance as a regional economic and religious center. The feast was good for business.[16]

Aside from celebrating the feast of the town's patron saint, an event that would have been solemnized from the earliest times with a High Mass, the early seventeenth century produced another important religious devotion that attracted outsiders to the frontier town. The Santo Cristo de la Capilla (Holy Christ of the Chapel), a statue of the crucified Savior, became a pilgrim's shrine soon after its arrival. Legend had it that a mule appeared in town on August 6, 1608, carrying a large box containing the statue, and once unloaded, the animal disappeared. Alessio Robles asserts, however, that one of Saltillo's early residents, Santos Rojo, was responsible for bringing the image back from a business trip to Veracruz. The miraculous attributes of the crucified Christ were enough to foster annual pilgrimages to its chapel from ever greater distances.[17]

Just how and when the traditions associated with the feast of St. James formed is impossible to pinpoint. Fire destroyed the town's archives in 1669, leaving the early history of Saltillo largely in the realm of myth and legend.[18] Fortunately, early eighteenth century efforts on the part of town elites to recommit the community to celebrating the feast give us a good idea of what the celebrations entailed. Each year, sometime between late August and early October, two "captains" who had spent almost a year in preparations organized a variety of functions: processions of the royal flag; masses and other religious ceremonies in the parish church; performances of Moros y Cristianos (a reenactment of the struggle between Christians and Muslims of medieval origins); and bullfights in the town plaza.[19] As early as 1682 a lieutenant governor's order refers to the obligation of residents to hold the feast and of area farmers and ranchers to enclose the plaza, "as is the custom," for bullfights.[20] With modifications, these basic elements remained in place until the middle of the nineteenth century.

Saltillo, then, was the economic, social, and religious hub of an expanding frontier region that stretched for hundreds of miles to the north and east. Among the places within its sphere of influence was San Antonio de Béxar, the most import settlement in colonial Texas, and its capital after 1771. Spanish occupation of Texas in the early eighteenth century came in response to French activities in the Mississippi Valley and Gulf of Mexico. Spanish imperial officials, concerned about the possibility of their chief imperial rival setting up shop so close to the rich silver mines of New Spain, established a presidio-mission complex in East Texas among the area's Hasinai Indians. Fearful of exposing coastal traffic to privateers and enemy navies, royal officials insisted on making Texas an inland province—all authorized communication between Texas and the rest of Mexico would take place over the Camino Real. With the four-hundred-mile distance between the East Texas missions and presidios too great to be traveled without a layover, the upper course of the San Antonio River became the logical location for a waystation. San Antonio de Béxar was founded for that purpose in 1718.

As an economic venture Texas proved a great disappointment to the Spanish crown. With no precious metals or other easily exploitable resources found in the region, there was little to attract settlers to the Texas frontier. Throughout the eighteenth century, then, Texas was essentially a military-religious enterprise. Beyond these two spheres, the lion's share of historical attention has focused on a small group of Canary Islander (Isleños) immigrants who arrived in Béxar in 1731. Despite being a small minority of the overall population of the province, the Isleños reaped the benefits of being "Spanish" and received royal honors such as the right to establish the first chartered town in the province and carrying the title of "hidalgo." In reality, however, the population of Spanish Texas consisted of a mixed bag of mestizos, mulattoes, creoles, and mission Indians who lived a meager existence well beyond the real line of settlement hundreds of miles to the south.

By 1731, the parameters of Spanish Texas were set. The Franciscans and the military led the vanguard of Spanish activity in the province, while the Canary Islanders constituted the most "visible" element of the civilian population. Initiatives to protect the province from the French threat eventually produced two small areas of Spanish control—one along the San Antonio River valley and the other in what is now deep East Texas and western Louisiana—and then periodic abortive efforts to occupy other strategic locations as circumstances required. All these elements taken together have produced a skewed perception of early Texas history, obscuring the socio-economic roots of Tejanos in New Spain's northern frontier civilian settlement experience. Historians have perpetuated the notion that a combination of administrative indifference on the part of royal officials and slothful dissoluteness on the part of the province's inhabitants contributed to the backwardness of Texas. As we shall see, even under chronically adverse conditions, Tejanos, in particular those of San Antonio, set about organizing economic activities that would bring them wealth and status. Bexareño participation at the Saltillo Fair, and in their trade relations with Saltillo generally, provide us with a good case study of Tejano entrepreneurship.

While the record for Béxar's participation at the Saltillo Fair dates to the last quarter of the eighteenth century, a commercial relationship between San Antonio and Saltillo dates to the earliest days of Spanish Texas. So far, the evidence for this trade is skimpy. We know, for instance, that Francisco Duval, the Frenchman who escorted the first and only group of Isleño colonists from Mexico City to San Antonio in 1731, purchased goods at Saltillo for sale in Texas. Not long afterwards, one of the quickly disheartened Isleño immigrants, Felipe Pérez, used the excuse of taking a shipment of hides and suede for sale at Saltillo in an attempt to escape Texas and return to the Canary Islands. Also doing business in Saltillo during this early period were Texas governor Manuel Sandoval and José de Urrutia, commander of Béxar's presidio. Although the exact nature of the commodities remains for the most part unknown, Urrutia did list ninety-five rams as part of what he had bought there. In the 1760s another presidio commander, Capt. Luis Antonio Menchaca, was even more closely associated with Saltillo, making use of one of that city's merchants as the principal supplier for the garrison.[21] By the 1790s, after a series of military and fiscal reforms had been put into place, Saltillo became the regular destination of Texas garrisons' quartermasters, who not only purchased supplies at Saltillo, but who also picked up payrolls from the newly established subtreasury there.

For civilian Tejanos, business opportunities at Saltillo were varied, although the list of Texas exports was always headed by cattle and cattle byproducts. While the driving of cattle into New Spain, including to Saltillo was a fairly late development, cattle products made the trip south much earlier. Through the middle of the eighteenth century, the practice was to conduct cattle slaughters in the countryside, render the grease, fat, and tallow, and dry the meat. The resulting products could fulfill both local needs and find a market in the interior. Texas cowhides, deerskins, and buffalo hides—the latter often acquired through trade with Indians—typically made up the mule trains that plied the often dangerous trails linking Texas to the rest of the Spanish empire. At least one San Antonio entrepreneur regularly took mule-loads of pecans into Coahuila late in the eighteenth century.[22]

Not surprisingly, as the Saltillo Fair grew in importance in the last decades of the eighteenth century it became a regular destination for Béxar merchants. It was, however, only part of an extensive commercial network encompassing Louisiana, Coahuila, Nuevo León, and Nuevo Santander, as well as Saltillo. Business trips out of Texas were timed to coincide with the agricultural-climatic cycle and to allow the person making the trip the opportunity to conduct transactions at more than one place. Manuel González, a native of the Canary Islands looking for a way to return to his homeland, managed to raise a small herd, the proceeds from which were to pay for his travel. According to him, his goal was "to have gone with some beeves with the intention of selling them at the presidio of Santa Rosa and with the proceeds go on to the fair in Saltillo to employ said money and see if I could alleviate my situation and transport myself to my homeland." Unfortunately for him, he got involved with Manuel Monjaras, one of Béxar's many petty merchant-cattlemen, who almost succeeded in defrauding González of the proceeds from the sale of his stock.[23]

In the money-tight world of colonial Mexico most commercial transactions were conducted on credit, and Béxar's merchants were in perpetual debt to those of Saltillo and to each other. Going to the fair was both an opportunity and a risk, since merchants were liable to run into creditors eager for their loans to be repaid. The case of petty-merchant Francisco Javier Rodríguez illustrates this dilemma for San Antonio entrepreneurs. Having contracted a debt of 380 pesos in the Saltillo store of Francisco Meléndez Valdez in 1780, Rodríguez was not eager to return to the fair in following years. Unfortunately for Mariano Menchaca (Rodríguez's surety), when he showed up at the fair in 1782, he "was accosted by [Rodríguez's] creditors who demanded payment from me of the principal and penalty." Menchaca promised that Rodríguez's debt would be paid at the 1783 fair, and to make sure, he asked the alcalde to prevent Rodríguez from leaving on a business trip to Louisiana without giving Menchaca the required sum. Rodríguez insisted that while he recognized the debt, he did not have the means to pay it off and was going to Louisiana precisely to raise the necessary funds. To this Menchaca answered that if Rodríguez had the means to go to Louisiana, he had enough funds to take care of his old business in Saltillo. Rodríguez insisted on going to Louisiana, however, promising to pay the debt during the coming September, that is during the fair, and both pledged his property against the debt and named Mariana Curbelo and Miguel Gortari of San Antonio as guarantors. The governor, who had now intervened in the case, accepted the change in sureties and relieved Menchaca of all responsibility. In the end, Rodríguez came through on the new deal, paying off what he owed as he said he would.[24]

Creditors were not the only unpleasantry awaiting Béxar businessmen journeying to the fair; there was always the taxman. Because it remained unchartered, that is lacking in royal sanction, the annual gathering at Saltillo was not a tax-exempt function. Consequently, all merchandise coming into Saltillo, even for the fair, was subject to the colonial excise tax known as *alcabalas*. Until 1767, the tax was set at 2 percent owing to Saltillo's frontier location. It rose over the next dozen years to 8 percent during the financial reform efforts of the 1770s, before again dropping to 2 percent following the protests of city fathers and merchants.[25]

In Texas, which was not just on the frontier but beyond it, there was no collection of *alcabalas*, but any Texas resident taking goods into the interior became subject to all the royal taxes along the way. Added to the sheer cost of transport, particularly in the form of labor, and the tithe and *mesteña* (livestock tax) taxes that had to be paid in Texas, *alcabalas* could and did represent a potentially ruinous burden. When the tax collector at Saltillo complained to Governor Rafael Martínez Pacheco that three Bexareños had brought herds into the city at fair time, but left without paying the *alcabalas*, the governor launched an investigation. The three men, Felipe García, Vicente Flores, and Juan Romero, complained that having lost many animals on the road and not having gotten a good price because of the survivors' condition, they did not have the means to pay the tax at the appraised rate.[26]

Although much research remains to be done, particularly on the volume, value, and scope of the goods bought and sold at the fair, from the above discussion we can generalize as to the meaning of the fair and as to what role it played in the formation of a regional society. As an outgrowth of seventeenth-century celebrations of St. James the Great, the feast survived well into the nineteenth century. It served the needs of regional ranching and farming for access to manufactured goods and markets for their livestock commodities and crops. It provided economic and recreational opportunities for commoners and elites alike. Until the end of the colonial period it served to reinforce a sense of Spanish life on the frontier by publicly highlighting ties to the Catholic Church, the Crown, and Spanish culture.

The fair demonstrates that colonial frontier society was socially and economically dynamic, adaptive, and capable of successfully defending local interests against government officials. In their efforts to avoid paying what they considered excessive taxes, for instance, the merchants of Saltillo appealed the decisions of powerful government officials until they won not only a tax reduction but a rebate of taxes already paid. Maintaining low taxes was only one way that Saltillo merchants drew trade to the town, for they also extended credit to the petty merchants and rancheros who did business at Saltillo, both at fair time and throughout the rest of the year. Saltillo's business elites also understood the powerful attraction of religious spectacle and deliberately tailored the feast day of the town's patron saint to best suit their business ends.

With regard to Texas, to the degree that it reflects the emergence of increased economic activity throughout northeastern New Spain, the Saltillo Fair served as an essential stimulant to frontier commerce, as Bexareños saw it as a desirable business destination. The record makes clear that although the Camino Real posed its share of threats, the weather often took the role of malevolent foe, and distances involved required extraordinary feats of planning, Texas—at least San Antonio de Béxar—was not as isolated from the rest of New Spain as it is so often portrayed. In Saltillo, and especially during the fair, which brought together merchants, mule-skinners, and artisans from throughout the viceroyalty, Tejanos could learn of the latest fashions, fads, and cultural trends. Texas communities gained much more than knowledge of the prevailing customs or current events from these annual fairs, however. The return journey brought manufactured merchandise unavailable in the hinterland. The fair supplied Texas settlements with essentials like flour and salt, soaps and notions, as well as kitchen utensils and footwear, to say little of intoxicating spirits and much more.

Enticing as the opportunities at the fair were, making a peso was an iffy proposition in light of the expenses attached to getting Texas goods to Saltillo. The evidence makes clear, however, that Tejanos were not the complete economic disasters so often portrayed in histories of Texas. Some Bexareños, such as Tomás Travieso and Mariano Menchaca, became successful businessmen who overcame considerable obstacles of the types discussed earlier. As conditions permitted, Tejanos organized business activities that allowed them to produce commodities for market; often these were commodities which they produced by their own hand or with the assistance of paid workers. Bexareño farmers, ranchers, and merchants, while not capitalists, can certainly not be considered feudal, economically static, or un-enterprising.[27] In the specie-scarce environment that was the Spanish colonial world, they had to rely on credit and barter to transact business, which prevented them from accumulating capital and, often, from paying cash wages. The limited market opportunities within Texas itself meant that the country below the Rio Grande, particularly Saltillo at fair time, presented Bexareños with the best opportunity to participate in an exchange economy. Such an entrepreneurial spirit could only give a desired edge to San Antonio's men (and a few women) of substance. The Saltillo Fair's impact extended onto the northern regions, therefore, contributing to existing social distinctions and helping to fortify the influence the elites had on local politics.

In sum, the record makes plain that Bexareños were neither victims of an uncaring and incompetent monolithic government, nor lazy, insubordinate riffraff. They in fact had considerable freedom of movement, enjoyed substantial economic mobility, and eagerly sought ways to engage in the market economy. At the Saltillo Fair they found an important opportunity to participate in the economic and social world of northeastern colonial Mexico, and they took advantage of it to the best of their abilities.

NOTES

1. Representation of republicanos and vecinos of Bexar, March 1, 1790, Bexar Archives (hereafter BA).

2. This essay is part of an ongoing research project that employs the Saltillo Fair as the mechanism through which to study the development of a northeastern Mexican socio-economic region. For a more detailed overview of the fair and its significance see Jesús F. de la Teja, "St. James at the Fair: Religious Ceremony, Civic Boosterism, and Commercial Development on the Colonial Mexican Frontier," *The Americas: A Quarterly Review of Inter-American Cultural History* 57, 3 (2001), 395–416.

3. Texas, Nuevo Santander, Nuevo León, and Coahuila.

4. Vito Alessio Robles, *Acapulco, Saltillo y Monterrey en la historia y en la leyenda*, combined ed. (Mexico: Editorial Porrúa, 1978), 116.

5. Fernand Braudel, *Civilization and Capitalism, 15th–18th Century*, Volume II: *The Wheels of Commerce*, trans. Siân Reynolds (New York: Harper & Row, 1982), 82.

6. Ibid., 85.

7. Ibid., 90.

8. William Christian, *Local Religion in Sixteenth-Century Spain* (Princeton: Princeton University Press, 1981), 118.

9. Quoted in María Villanueva Saldivar, *Las ferias medievales y su influencia en las ferias mexicanas* (Thesis, Universidad Nacional Autónoma de México, 1963), 14.

10. Manuel Carrera Stampa, "Las ferias novohispanas," *Historia Mexicana*, 2 (1952–53): pp. 334–35; Luis Weckmann, *La herencia medieval de México*, 2nd ed. (Mexico: Fondo de Cultura Económica, 1994), 393.

11. Quote: Joseph A. Ernst and H. Roy Merrens, "'Camden's Turrets pierce the skies!': The Urban Process in the Southern Colonies during the Eighteenth Century," *William and Mary Quarterly*, 3rd Ser., 30, 4 (1973), 573. Also see Richard R. Beeman, "Social Change and Cultural Conflict in Virginia: Lunenberg County, 1746 to 1774," *William and Mary Quarterly* 3rd Ser., 35, 3 (1978), 458; Winifred B. Rothenberg, "The Market and Massachusetts Farmers, 1750–1855," *Journal of Economic History* 41, 2 (1981), 312–13; Darret B. Rutman, "Governor Winthrop's Garden Crop: The Significance of Agriculture in the Early Commerce of Massachusetts Bay," *William and Mary Quarterly* 3rd Ser., 20, 3 (1963), 408.

12. Manuel Carrera Stampa, "Las ferias novohispanas"; María Angeles Gálvez and Antonio Ibarra, "Comercio local y circulación regional de importaciones: la feria de San Juan de los Lagos en la Nueva España," *Historia Mexicana* 46, 3 (1997), 581–616; Max Moorhead, *New Mexico's Royal Road: Trade and Travel on the Chihuahua Trail* (1958, reprint, Norman: University of Oklahoma Press, 1994), 42–43; Charles L. Kenner, *The Comanchero Frontier: A History of New Mexico–Plains Indian Relations* (1969, reprint, Norman: University of Oklahoma Press, 1994), 40.

13. Moorhead, *New Mexico's Royal Road*, 42–43.

14. Kenner, *The Comanchero Frontier*, 40.

15. Cheryl English Martin, *Governance and Society in Colonial Mexico: Chihuahua in the Eighteenth Century* (Stanford: Stanford University Press, 1996), 116, 120–21.

16. "Quejas, reclamos, peticiones y otros negocios de ningún valor, 1683," Archivo Municipal de Saltillo, Presidencia Municipal, caja 3/1, exp. 60, doc. 17 (hereafter AMS PM); Cabildo minutes, Sept. 23, 1696, Archivo Municipal de Saltillo, Actas de Cabildo, libro 1-III, acta 15 (hereafter cited as AMS AC, L=libro, A=acta); AMS AC Aug. 29, 1700, AMS AC L2 A1; "Cuadernos de nombramientos de regidores del cabildo," July 28, 1738, AMS PM, caja 14, exp. 32 [this document is mistitled, as it refers to the town's obligation to the feast and the naming of captains].

17. Alessio Robles, *Acapulco, Saltillo y Monterrey en la historia y la Leyenda*, 163–67.

18. Pablo M. Cuellar Valdés, *Historia de la ciudad de Saltillo* (Saltillo: Biblioteca de la Universidad de Coahuila, 1982), 24.

19. September 23, 1696, AMS AC L1 A15; Aug. 29, 1700, AMS AC L2 A1; Cuaderno de nombramientos, AMS PM C14, E32.

20. "Quejas, reclamos, peticiones," AMS PM C 3/1, E60, d-17.

21. Petition of Vicente Alvarez Travieso, Bexar, January 30, 1735, Archivo General de la Nación de México, ramo Provincias Internas, vol. 236 (hereafter AGN PI); Autos de pedimiento de varios soldados del presidio de S. Antonio de Béjar, provincia de Texas, contra su gobernador, D. Manuel de Sandoval sobre abusos. 1735. Bexar, May 29, 1735, AGN PI, vol. 163; Proceso de diligencias seguidas en virtud de superior mandamiento del Ilmo. y Exmo. Señor Arsobispo Virrey de esta Nueva España, por D. Manuel de Sandoval, gobernador de la Provincia de Texas contra los bienes de D. José de Urrutia Capitán del Presidio de San Antonio de Béjar, para el recobro del rédito que el expresado Capitán debía a la Real Hacienda. 1737, ibid; Copia de la carta que comprehende las resoluciones tomadas en la revista de inspección pasado por mi el mariscal de campo marqués de Rubí, en 12 de agosto de 1767, a la compañía del Presidio de San Antonio de Béxar, Gobernación de la provincia de Texas, y cargo de su capitán Dn. Luis Antonio Menchaca. Bexar, Aug. 17, 1767, Archivo General de Indias, Audiencia de Guadalajara, 104-6-13, vol. 45, 211, Center for American History, University of Texas at Austin.

22. Jesús F. de la Teja, *San Antonio de Béxar: A Community on New Spain's Northern Frontier* (Albuquerque: University of New Mexico Press, 1995), 105.

23. Escrito presentado por Manuel González, y diligencias practicadas a continuación, como se consta por el protocolo, September 19, 1780, BA.

24. Presentación hecha por Luis Mariano Menchaca, vecino de esta Villa de San Fernando contra Francisco Xavier Rodríguez, sobre haberle sido fiador en la Villa del Saltillo, March 31, 1783, BA.

25. Moderación de alcabalas en la Villa del Saltillo, 1782, Archivo General del Estado de Coahuila, Fondo Colonial, caja 10, exp. 27.

26. Collector of alcabalas of Saltillo José Pereira de Castro to Rafael Martínez Pacheco, November 13, 1788, Martínez Pacheco to Pereira de Castro, December 8, 1788, Pereira de Castro to Martínez Pacheco, December 26, 1788, BA.

27. The debate over the nature of the frontier colonial system—capitalist, pre-capitalist, non-capitalist, feudal, quasi-feudal—will probably never end. As Gilbert G. González and Raúl Fernández, "Chicano History: Transcending Cultural Models," *Pacific Historical Review* 18, 4 (1994), 469–97, make clear, historians arguing for one characterization or another base their arguments on very different criteria and definitions of terms. Particularly damaging has been the label of "feudal" or "quasi-feudal," which as Antonio José Ríos-Bustamante, "New Mexico in the Eighteenth Century: Life, Labor and Trade in la Villa de San Felipe de Albuquerque, 1706–1790," *Aztlán* 7, 3 (1976), 357–89, argues, has supported the "viewpoint that Mexican society in the far north was a static society until the incorporation of the area into the United States in 1848" (p. 359).

Theodore Gentilz, *San Juan Capistrano*. In the isolated frontier community, marriages between people of different racial groups were rather common. Nevertheless, status and personal interests could and did often interject themselves into marriage choices, particularly when they involved members of the mission communities. Strong relationships between some San Antonio families and particular missions endured until the end of the Franciscan presence in the city in the 1820s. Courtesy of Daughters of the Republic of Texas Library, San Antonio, Texas.

Why Urbano and María Trinidad Can't Get Married

Social Relations in Late Colonial San Antonio*

Our case study begins on the evening of June 3, 1781 when troopers José Miguel and Francisco Sales Games and Pedro Hernández (acting on behalf of his brother Carlos) presented themselves before Texas governor Domingo Cabello. The Sales Games brothers were the paternal uncles and the Hernándezes were the step-brothers of Ana María de la Trinidad Games, the first banns for whom had been pronounced at Sunday Mass in the parish church earlier that day. The soldiers informed the governor that the proclamation of banns for Urbano Hinojosa and their niece and step-sister was an affront to their honor, as Urbano was an Indian of unknown parentage from Mission San Antonio de Valero. They complained to the governor that the day before, they had attempted to talk María Trinidad's widowed mother, Gertrudis Pérez, out of agreeing to the marriage as it was dishonorable, and that she had agreed to bring the matter to a close. Now, discovering that she had disregarded their will, they sought relief from Cabello. They asserted that Pérez was a woman of poor judgment and a spendthrift who had been manipulated by Fray José María Salas, the missionary at Mission Valero, who made a deal with her so she would consent to her underage daughter's marriage. Citing the Pragmática Sanción of 1776 regulating the marriage of minors, they requested that the governor prevent the wedding. Governor Cabello, in view that the men were soldiers in the presidio company of Béxar, granted them relief, advised parish priest Father Pedro Fuentes of his decision, and deposited María Trinidad in the home of Don José de la Santa, a "man of known good repute," where she might be properly taught Christian doctrine.[1]

On August 27 Urbano, having waited for a proper resolution of the mat-

---

*First published in *Southwestern Historical Quarterly* 112, 2 (Oct. 2008): 121–46.

ter, presented his side of the case, not to the governor but to Father Fuentes. Urbano still wished to contract matrimony with María Trinidad, whom he described as a *mulata*. According to him, Father Fuentes had received all the necessary information in the course of the required prenuptial investigation and found nothing to prevent the marriage. Urbano claimed that the girl's uncles and stepbrothers had no standing to invoke the Pragmática Sanción of 1776 as they were not the girl's parents or legal guardians. He then went on to respond to the charges made by the girl's male relatives. The charge that María Trinidad was too young was false, as her birth certificate showed that she was thirteen years and five months old. Furthermore, she knew all the principal prayers as required. As to the charge that she was forced or deceived into the marriage, that too was false since after two months away from her home she still wanted to marry him.

Having addressed the overt questions, Urbano turned his attention to the racial subtext. To quote him directly:

> To all this said brothers and uncles of María Trinidad add the feigned dishonor (*desdoro*) that would follow, because being soldiers it would not look right for their niece and sister to marry an Indian. It is very clear that the dishonor is feigned, for they did not consider nor declare what they are and with whom they are married, it being notorious and public knowledge that they are mulattoes on all four sides. And, being mulattoes, although they are soldiers, neither are they Spaniards nor of better status, or of better or purer blood than that of an Indian; carrying within themselves the tarnished honor that their origins give them and that they shall take to the grave. Therefore, they suffer no dishonor, as they did not suffer it when Felia Games [María Trinidad's aunt] married José María Camberos, an Indian who was so new to the faith [*neófito*] that his baptism and marriage took place at the same time without it having prevented them from living as Christians and true Catholics.[2]

Urbano concluded by addressing the gender issue, stating that no greater proof existed that the marriage was not forced than that neither woman, despite threats and cajoling and their weak female nature, had backed down. Consequently—and here we see the heavy hand of Fray Salas:

> Said brothers and uncles can and should open their eyes and recognize the injury and grave sin that they have committed, because in addition to acting in a matter that does not concern them they leave María Trinidad exposed to being kidnapped by her intended and taken to the wilderness to live as

heathens or that she surrender herself to turpitude, making her a public spectacle with illegitimate births (as experience teaches) and disregard for religion, with scandal to the community and revilement and shame of those very same ones who obstructed her will to receive such a holy sacrament; thus putting in jeopardy her eternal salvation.[3]

On September 6 José Miguel Games responded to Urbano's charges. José Miguel began by stating that he was not a mulatto. Even if he were, however, he would still be more worthy than a mission Indian, and an illegitimate one at that, since he like his brother and nephews had shed blood in the service of the king. In addition, he charged Fray Salas with being behind the whole affair, for it was clear he had written Urbano's declaration in its entirety, even down to the signature. Moreover, he, his brother, and his nephews did have the right to intervene because Gertrudis Pérez was a woman of bad character who, along with María Trinidad, was supported by her son Carlos until he married, and since then by Pedro and her other son José Mariano. As for the marriage between Felipa Games and the Indian José Camberos, that only demonstrated the mixing with better quality people that had taken place among the mission Indians and the fact that the Pragmática Sanción had not yet been promulgated. It also showed the disregard with which such royal pronouncements were taken at the missions, for having a number of Indian women at the missions with whom Fray Salas might have married Urbano, the missionary chose to wed him to one of the townspeople.[4]

As to the friar's charges of injury and grave sin, José Miguel was dismissive, countercharging that they were beneath the dignity of a man of God. The soldier saved his most damning response to the threat that if the marriage did not take place Urbano might elope to the hills with María Trinidad to live like heathens: "No one would find it odd that the Indian Hinojosa would go live in the woods as one among the heathens, as the Indian Arcón from that same mission did and as many others of the same ilk have done and do every day, which is the example of the fruit produced by mission Indians." In closing, José Miguel pleaded to be relieved of having to make further declarations, both because he lacked the wherewithal and because of the threats he had received from Fray Salas. Not knowing how to write, the document was written and signed on his behalf by the schoolteacher, José Marcos Aguilar, who had previously prepared José Miguel's original petition.[5]

Finding the matter more than he could deal with, Cabello sent the proceedings to a lawyer in Saltillo for his opinion. Communications with

Saltillo were a slow thing in the eighteenth century, however, and the lawyer had not responded by November 23, 1781, when Urbano appeared before Governor Cabello yet again. Stating that he had decided to marry a woman of his own mission, he asked that his decision be communicated to María Trinidad for her approval. Cabello, probably very eager to have done with the matter, approached Trinidad, who granted Urbano "his freedom."[6]

So, what goes on here? How can racial identities jump from mulatto to Spaniard, and what made an Indian equal to or better than a mulatto and vice versa? Why would María Trinidad's relatives intervene in her betrothal to a mission Indian whose qualifications for marriage had been promoted by one man of the cloth and certified by another? What did Fray Salas (through Urbano) hope to accomplish by calling the Games and Hernándezes mulattos? Why would the brothers-in-law and sons of Gertrudis Pérez attempt to usurp her parental rights and accuse her of being motivated by self-interest in agreeing to her daughter's marriage to Urbano? What on the surface seems a trivial case of petty family squabbling does not quite reach Shakespearian proportions, but it does open a window on a variety of social and cultural issues that bear examination from the perspectives of race, gender, status, and honor.

At the center of the story are two unlikely survivors in the historical record, a mission Indian and an adolescent girl. The case is in certain respects unique, and it is only one of two extant records of marriage opposition in Spanish colonial Texas. The involvement of the governor, the parish priest, and a missionary, among others, helps us better understand the dynamics of social roles and relations across the entire spectrum of colonial San Antonio society. Whether or not Urbano and María Trinidad loved each other, whether or not her uncles and stepbrothers were motivated by concern for their honor, and whether or not the missionary at Mission Valero was manipulating María Trinidad's mother, the arguments made by the various parties and the procedures and decisions executed by the governor and the parish priest all have much to tell us about how the participants saw themselves as part of the Spanish colonial order.[7]

Things appeared to have ended well for everyone concerned. Urbano did not flee to the hills to live as a heathen, and in fact proved to be a very different fruit of the mission system. His story makes clear that he was an unlikely candidate for "heathenism." As a Payaya Indian, the son of Francisco and Ana María, he was only illegitimate in the technical sense that his parents appear to have themselves been unbaptized and therefore unmarried in the eyes of the Church. The Payayas, a Coahuiltecan group that included at least three bands, were one of the original groups at Valero in 1718, but some of the bands continued to reside beyond the mission for decades. Urbano, born in December 1746, may have been the son of late arrivals to the mission who either passed away before receiving the sacrament of baptism or who themselves fled to the hills leaving their son behind.[8]

Either circumstance would not have been an extraordinary event, as mid-eighteenth century Valero, like the other San Antonio missions, was the scene of racial and ethnic mixing not only between distinct Coahuiltecan groups but also with Apaches and Comanches. Eighteen months before our Urbano was born, a two-year-old Apache Indian by the same name had come to Valero with two brothers, Benito and Masimo, where they were immediately baptized. In September 1743 Fray Diego García baptized María Gertrudis, the child of Luisa, "a Comanche Indian." Another Comanche woman, Lucia, was baptized on her deathbed at about this time, as was Juan Ignacio, an adult Indian whom visiting Apaches had brought to Governor Manuel Sandoval, who in turn traded him to Joseph Leal for a younger native. These individuals are representative of a population of victims of the endemic warfare that marked Spanish-Indian and inter-Indian relations throughout the northern frontier of New Spain. At least through the end of the 1740s, the missionaries in San Antonio railed against Indian hunting expeditions by the settlers thinly disguised as retaliatory raids. As for the Apache Urbano, in 1768 he married Thecla Salazar, an Ypandi Indian maiden who died childless sometime around 1780, remaining a good son of Mission Valero to his death.[9]

While his marriage to María Trinidad would have cemented his place in the broader San Antonio community and completed his transformation into a Tejano, if only at the lower rungs of society, he and Fray Salas had to content themselves with a more humble union. Urbano married the widow Luisa de los Santos, a fellow Mission Valero Indian. In 1793 the couple participated in the distribution of land and property when the mission was finally secularized. Along with a plot of land for farming and a house lot, Urbano, Luisa, and their two daughters received a little over ten bushels of corn, one yoke of oxen, one plow, one hoe, and one cow. Urbano continued to live and farm at Valero, appearing in the records with the status of *labrador*, or landholding farmer, until passing away sometime around the turn of the century. To the degree that he was a successful farmer and family man, Urbano proved José Miguel's opinion of mission Indians wrong. If the friars measured success by the outward signs of good Christian living among their charges, then Urbano's success would have made Fray Salas and his fellow Franciscans content that in him they had accomplished their mission.[10]

María Trinidad fared less well than Urbano. Soon after the breakup with him she wed Francisco de los Santos, a man about whose economic, social, and racial status we know nothing, but the marriage did not last as he died in June 1782. The following January she married Félix Castañeda, a Pajalate Indian of Mission Concepción and himself a widower, and between 1784 and 1785 they started a family. María Trinidad, then, married by age fifteen, a common first marriage age for women in New Spain and other parts of the Spanish colonial world, and the most common age in San Antonio. In fact, her marriage to Urbano at age thirteen would not have been unique, there being evidence for at least one other female marriage age of thirteen during the same period—three others married at age fourteen. Of ninety-eight surviving marriage petitions for the period 1762–1800, sixty-eight indicate a female marriage age of twenty or younger. Widows begin to appear in the petitions by age twenty-four, and of the eleven petitions for women ages thirty-two to forty-nine, all were widows.[11]

Félix Castañeda, of whom we know little other than what appears in the census reports, was also not an unusual husband in terms of marriage age. Like Urbano, he was a widower. He would have been in his early thirties when he married María Trinidad in January 1783. How long his first marriage to Feliciana Villegas lasted is unknown, but assuming a trajectory similar to Urbano's, he probably married between ages twenty-one and twenty-eight, the typical age for men. Unlike for females, teenage marriage for boys was unusual, the two youngest males being sixteen at time of marriage, with three marrying at age eighteen and one at age nineteen. This difference should not surprise, as many of the activities involved in the domestic role of women were routinely accomplished by adolescent girls, whereas the income earning roles of men required more maturity. Moreover, operating within a patriarchal society, the typical older male–younger female marriage pattern allowed husbands to more easily exercise their dominant role.[12]

If María Trinidad's and Félix's marriage ages were not at all unusual, their family's racial designations in the records certainly merit analysis. The couple appears in the town censuses of 1793, by which time another son had been added to the family, and 1796, when they are listed as having three boys and three girls. What makes these entries interesting is that while in the 1792 Concepción census María Trinidad is listed as an *española*, she is listed as a mestiza in the town's census of the following year, and worst of all, as an Indian in the list of 1796. Félix, however, was consistently identified as an Indian. Baptismal records for their children bear out the decline in caste: a girl born in 1795 is listed as a mestiza, while a boy born in

1797 is entered as a *lobo*, the designation for an Indian-African mix. In the latter baptismal entry María Trinidad is listed as a *mulata*, the designation she also carries in a subsequent town census in which she also is recorded as a widow.[13]

María Trinidad's shifting racial status, a theme to which I shall return below in the context of her male relatives' concerns over social status, needs to be understood in terms of the elaborate system that Spaniards created in an attempt to bridge the distinct socio-economic and racial hierarchies required to control their empire. Already racially conscious from their encounters with African peoples, Spaniards brought to America a racialized view of society. One's place in society was not only determined by one's estate—noble, clergy, commoner—but also by one's race. Racial mixing produced results that upset the natural order, especially as relatively few Spaniards migrated to the Americas. The result was that "racialized identities (coded by skin color and defined by collective stereotypes) played a major role in organizing human relations at all levels." In this "caste system" (*sociedad* or *sistema de castas*) Spaniards from Europe saw themselves at the top of the ladder, followed by American-born Spaniards; below them ranged the mestizos (Spanish-Indian mixed-bloods), other Spanish-Indian-African mixes (*castas*), mulattoes (Spanish-African mixed-bloods), free Africans, Indians, and slaves. Of course, as the centuries progressed it became more and more difficult to maintain a simple hierarchy, so that by the eighteenth century the terms *castas* or *color quebrado* (broken color) were commonly used to refer to mixed-bloods in general. Historians continuously grapple with making use of the various factors involved in *calidad* to properly understand the social system. Some have turned to analyzing the non-narrative representations of the system for clues. Colonial artists, particularly in New Spain, attempted to capture this increasingly fanciful mélange through painting collective family scenes consisting of sixteen frames, each depicting parents of different racial groups and an offspring representative of one of the *castas*. Thus, the frame for a mestizo would depict Spaniard and Indian parents with a mestizo child.[14]

If María Trinidad's peregrination through the various racial labels assigned to her in the course of her life provides clear evidence of the artificiality and arbitrariness of the system, it also reveals the nebulousness of her socio-economic status. Her low status is confirmed by her husband's designation. In both the mission and town lists Félix Castañeda is entered as an Indian native of Mission Concepción. Moreover, his status of *jornalero*, or agricultural laborer, is lower than her old suitor Urbano's status, which means he did not participate in the 1794 distribution of property when Mission Concepción was secularized. In fact, the absence of Castañeda from any record other than the census reports confirms his low socioeconomic status. Despite her humble social position, María Trinidad did manage to acquire some property. She was among a substantial number of widows who headed households and conducted their own business affairs. As in the case of her husband, clear evidence is lacking of where and when María Trinidad passed away, but as late as May 1812 she was active giving permission for her daughter María Castañéda, herself a widow and a self-declared mestiza, to wed Tomás Cantu, a local mestizo.[15]

We now turn to the other figures involved in the case, particularly José Miguel de Sales Games and María Trinidad's other male relatives. After all, it was they who protested her marriage to Urbano on the basis that they were both Spaniards and soldiers, and he an Indian. Both the Games and Hernández brothers were from Los Adaes, with José Miguel, his brother, and Carlos Hernández having transferred to the Bexar command in 1773 when the first capital of Texas was decommissioned as a result of the presidio reforms recommended by the Marqués de Rubí. José Miguel, the oldest of the four men, is sparingly listed in the records, appearing mostly as an invalid on the presidio rosters. Like most of his fellow Adaesaños who chose to stay in San Antonio instead of following Antonio Gil Ybarbo back to East Texas, José Miguel lived a humble, marginal existence.[16]

His brother Francisco, who like José Miguel had entered the service at Los Adaes, attempted to retire from the military in 1783, after about eighteen years of service. Apparently he found employment opportunities limited, and he re-enlisted within a few months. Baptismal register entries for the years 1772, 1776, 1777, and 1779 note Francisco and María Ojeda as the parents of a boy listed as a Spaniard and three girls entered as mestizas. His daughters' caste status makes clear that even if Francisco continued to be identified as *español*, either his wife was herself an Indian or the priest making the annotations considered one or both to be of mixed-blood. The absence of property records or his appearance in any census after 1790 suggests that he too died in rather humble circumstances about this time.[17]

Carlos and Pedro Hernández, María Trinidad's step-brothers, both continued in the service and started families. Carlos too had joined the military at Los Adaes. A competent young soldier, he was assigned to the heavy cavalry company as a *soldado de cuera* when the garrison was divided into heavy and light cavalry as a result of the same reforms that had brought about his transfer to San Antonio. In 1786 he received one further promotion, to the rank of *carabinero*, but by 1788 a prolonged illness required him to retire. Carlos was obviously proud of his record, commenting that he lamented requesting his discharge from the service, "because I have embraced it with such love—as is well known and as my noteworthy conduct makes clear—for more than fifteen years, during which I have served without interruption." Indeed, if the Carlos Hernández listed in the burial register for January 29, 1789, as married to María Luisa Hidalgo, is our man, then he died as an *español*.[18]

The younger Hernández brother, Pedro, was not nearly as accomplished or of as sterling a character as Carlos, although he had assumed primary responsibility for maintaining his mother and step-sister after Carlos's marriage. Pedro, who joined the garrison just before the flap over Urbano and Trinidad, had already had at least one run-in with the law, having participated as a cowboy on an illegal cattle roundup. Although he apparently received a medical discharge from Governor Cabello in 1786, the new governor, Rafael Martínez Pacheco, re-enlisted Pedro the following year. The re-enlistment was later criticized by yet another governor, Manuel Muñoz, who wrote in 1791 that the "Soldier Hernández should be discharged because of his many faults, as was done at the time of Don Domingo Cabello, though Pacheco re-enlisted him." That discharge finally took place sometime between 1792 and 1796. The single record indicating caste, his daughter's 1782 baptismal entry, lists both him and his wife as *españoles*. Although the evidence is sparse, it is likely that Carlos and Pedro were both firmly established in their *español* status, unlike the Games family, whose status was still in flux.[19]

Nevertheless, as men born and raised at Los Adaes, Carlos and Pedro, like their step-uncles, were tainted by their status as Adaesaños. Except for José Miguel and his fellow soldiers, between their arrival in 1773 and January 1778 the Adaesaños had drifted into a hand-to-mouth existence that had them sharing in all the duties and obligations of Indian defense and local public works without any prospects of gaining property of their own. When the Caballero de Croix, commandant general of the Interior Provinces, a new administrative unit carved out of northern frontier provinces, arrived for an inspection and war council in San Antonio in January 1778, he was deluged with petitions and complaints from the locals, among them that of the Adaesaños. Sixty-three former Adaes householders signed a petition that bemoaned their second-class citizenship in Béxar and asked for prompt redress. In the more than four years since they had been forced to abandon Los Adaes, where they had property and means of subsistence, they had been treated as if they were foreigners rather than men who had been willing to spill their blood for their king. "At present we are living here, but without land on which to place our dwellings, much less land to sow, nor to maintain ourselves; and the only thing we are good for is to provide the same service as those who enjoy the privileges we do not enjoy, although on all occasions we provide assistance and lend a strong hand." Conditions had not improved by 1781, when Bernardo Cervantes showed up at Croix's headquarters in Chihuahua to complain that nothing had yet been done to alleviate the condition of his fellow Adaesaños. For the most part they remained unwelcome outsiders with no social standing. Consequently, it should not surprise that despite having obtained an affidavit from family acquaintances asserting his parents' caste as *españoles*, José Miguel's October 1796 burial record lists him as a mulatto.[20]

There is one more male member of the Games-Hernández family for whom we must account. In his argument against María Trinidad's marriage to Urbano, José Miguel Games mentioned his nephew José Mariano, who along with Pedro was responsible for maintaining his mother and sister. Like his uncles and step-brothers, José Mariano too entered military service, enlisting sometime before the end of 1783. Over the course of the next few years he married Rita Vargas before receiving a discharge sometime in 1790. Not surprisingly, the baptismal record for his first child, a boy born in 1784, lists his son as *español*, as is the case with a second son born in 1787. A shift occurs at the time of José Mariano's discharge, however, for a son born in 1791 is entered as a mulatto, while a daughter born in 1793 and a son born in 1795 are recorded as mestizos. The 1793 entry makes clear that it was not just Rita Vargas, the mother, who carried the lower caste status, for the notation refers to both parents as mestizos. The record is further complicated by the fact that at the marriage of one of their sons in 1818, the marriage record refers to the son as *español*, and to them as "the late Don Mariano Games and the late Doña Rita Vargas."[21]

This curious elevation in José Mariano's and Rita's social status is unprecedented for any of the principal parties to the case. Elevated social status is indicated by use of the terms *don* and *doña*. Traditionally, historians have accepted the explanation that the honorific stemmed from the association of all Spaniards in the New World with the conquistadores, since by royal decree first settlers of a new district were granted noble status as "*hidalgos*", along with land and other privileges. By the late eighteenth century, both in Spain and in the Americas, the term had broadened to include anyone meriting public respect. The 1791 edition of the dictionary of the Real Academia (and subsequent editions through the mid-nineteenth century) defined *don* as "a title of honor and dignity that formerly was given to very few, even among the highest nobility, but which has now become distinctive of all nobles, although it is commonly granted to those who are not [noble] merely out of tolerance or abuse." The definition goes on to explain that it can also mean sir or mister (*señor*).²²

In San Antonio in the late eighteenth and early nineteenth centuries, the documentary evidence makes clear that use of *don* remained reserved for higher status members of the community. The Cabello census of 1779, which included 293 civilian households noted that thirty-one were headed by men addressed as *don* and five headed by women, all widows, addressed as *doña*. Of the thirty-one men, twenty-one were listed with the occupation of *labrador*, although there were a number of other men categorized as *labradores* who were not addressed as *don*. On the other hand, all seven men reported as being merchants were also labeled *don*. Two other men addressed as *don* had no occupation, and one was a carpenter. By 1793, when the population had grown substantially, *labradores* still made up the single largest group of men addressed as *don* in the census—thirty-six. Again, all seven men described as merchants were also addressed as *don*. The most significant difference between the 1779 and 1793 censuses is that in the latter one a number of other men addressed as *don* had lower status occupations, for instance the town notary, four *jornaleros*, one carpenter, and a field hand. In the case of the latter individual, Francisco Travieso, it helped that he belonged to one of the most important of the original Canary Islander families and that his brother Tomás was the only individual listed as an *hacendero*, that is, hacienda owner. One last observation worth noting is that not a single individual in either census holding the honorific of *don* or *doña* was from Los Adaes, although a number of other towns, both in New Spain and Europe, were mentioned, and in one case a former resident of Natchitoches. In sum, as an agricultural community, being a landowning farmer and having commercial ties to the outside world provided significant status benefits in the community. Further research will be needed to reveal what circumstances might have led Mariano and Rita to climb above the humble station to which they were born.²³

The other family members mentioned in the proceedings are the least represented in the records. Trinidad's father, Ildefonso Games, is listed in the rosters of the presidio, and he has a rather substantial entry in the account book for those soldiers from Los Adaes stationed at San Antonio in 1770–71. According to the May 1777 roster and a September 1777 entry in the parish burial register, he passed away while in the service. His wife and María Trinidad's mother, Gertrudis Pérez, is completely absent from the censuses and sacramental registers this author has consulted. She apparently never established a household on her own or she would have been accorded some recognition as a head of household. The same is true for the maligned Felipa Games, whom Urbano and Fray Salas accused of being a *mulata* and who married the Indian José María Camberos—unless she is one of two widows surnamed Games, both from Los Adaes, and both appearing in the records as *mulatas*, who maintained independent households in the 1790s.[24]

To complete the cast we must not overlook the non-family members embroiled—willingly or not—in this melodrama. At the top of Spanish Texas' socio-political hierarchy was Don Domingo Cabello y Robles, "Colonel in the Royal Armies, Governor and Military Commandant of the Province of the Texas, its missions, conquests, and frontiers, Captain of the cavalry company of the Royal Presidio of San Antonio de Béxar, Inspector General of militia units and presidio troops of said province by commission conferred by the Lord Commandant General of the Interior Provinces of this Kingdom of New Spain." A native of León, Spain, the fifty-six-year-old career military man was one of only a few true Spaniards in the province. A veteran of war with England, having seen action during the siege of Havana of 1762, the crown rewarded him with the governorship of Nicaragua. From his correspondence with friends and superiors it is obvious that he must have often wondered what sin he might have committed to deserve posting to such a godforsaken place as Texas, or as he once declared, "because this place is worse than Siberia or Lapland." And he did not hold Bexareños in high regard, particularly the Adaesaños, at one point requesting of the governor of Louisiana that he acquire for him a male slave cook or a female slave who could also "sew, wash, and iron" because all those things were entirely lacking in San Antonio. He had to take José Miguel and his relatives seriously as soldiers under his command, but it is not hard to imagine that he might have seen very little real difference, either culturally or physiologically, between them and the Indian Urbano who was the butt of their insults.[25]

The second most important person in the capital of Spanish Texas was the parish priest, Father Pedro Fuentes. Born in Saltillo and well educated, Fuentes went on to write a history of his home town that is now lost, an indication that he was a man of some polish and accomplishment. During his twenty years of ministry in San Antonio he built the first two-story house in the town proper, he put parish affairs in order, and he attempted as best he could to make Bexareños behave properly. He attempted to wield the kind of old-fashioned clerical authority that was increasingly at odds with the regalist tenor of the times. Even in frontier Texas, clergy in the second half of the eighteenth century could no longer hope to go unchallenged by their flock, which found government officials more than willing to take their side in disputes with the Church. Not surprisingly, Fuentes was the target of numerous complaints during a visit by the commandant general at the beginning of 1778. People lined up outside the quarters of the most senior royal official ever to set foot in Béxar for a chance to complain about how the priest had acted in some high-handed and unfair manner against him or her.[26]

For Fuentes the complaint by the Games and Hernández men must have come as something of a surprise, for although the record does not survive, our case file makes clear that the required investigation for impediments to the marriage had taken place, during which no obstacles to the nuptials had been raised. In fact, this was not Father Fuentes's first marriage opposition case. Eight years earlier, near the beginning of his tenure as parish priest, he had passed judgment on Basilio de Armas's request to prevent the marriage of Marcos Montes de Oca and María Margarita Ximenes. In that case, Father Fuentes had carefully weighed the evidence and "after reading some passages from the Bible," had decided in favor of the couple. Given his penchant for doing things by the book, it is highly unlikely that he either botched the investigation or intentionally overlooked some impediment. Father Fuentes' role in the case assures us that Urbano would have been fully capable of living out his obligations as a Christian husband.[27]

Fray José María Salas, the alleged instigator of Urbano's efforts to wed María Trinidad, was one of eight Franciscans serving in the five San Antonio missions in the early 1780s. His position in Béxar society, and that of his fellow friars, was even more ambivalent than that of Father Fuentes. As José Miguel's comments make clear, the missionaries were not beyond the criticisms of the Tejano population, which often saw them as economic rivals and social meddlers. Former Texas governor Hugo Oconor's comment to Governor Juan María Barón de Ripperdá that in the past royal policy had favored the interests of "infidels and neophytes over those of the other vassals of these kingdoms," was no exaggeration. In large part, the tensions between the Franciscans and the settler population in Texas and elsewhere resulted from the prerogatives that the missionaries had long enjoyed in managing the affairs of their neophyte charges. At San Antonio, for instance, disputes between missionaries and townspeople had begun soon after the 1731 arrival of the Canary Islanders, who had immediately challenged the missions' monopoly over the supply of foodstuffs to the presidio. And, just as in the case of the secular church, the regalist efforts of Spanish officials beginning in the mid-eighteenth century, Fray Salas and his co-religious found themselves increasingly constrained in how they could manage the affairs of their missions and defend the rights of the Indians.[28]

Like many of his brethren, Fray Salas is an enigmatic figure. Nothing is known of his personal background. A member of the Apostolic College of Nuestra Señora de Guadalupe de Zacatecas, he served as missionary of San Antonio de Valero from 1777 to 1783, then served at San José until his death in 1790. One thing about Fray Salas is clear—he had a deep love for his charges, for whom he was willing to be rather duplicitous. There is no doubt that José Miguel Games's accusation that Fray Salas wrote Urbano's petition and signed it for him is correct, for when one of the governor's witnesses went to notify Urbano that María Trinidad had released him from his vow, Urbano had not been able to sign the required acknowledgment. How the collapse of Fray Salas's small social engineering experiment affected him may be unknown to us, but María Trinidad's relatives' complaint makes clear that it was not a unique occurrence.[29]

Already in 1779 the first secularization order for Mission Valero had arrived in Béxar. The plan, developed out of a San Antonio town council memorial in which the city fathers pointed out that Valero had the best developed irrigation works of any mission, or even the town, recommended that the mission be suppressed and the land, not allotted to the existing neophyte population, be distributed among the Adaesaños and landless townspeople. Although Governor Cabello did not comply with the order, Fray Salas may well have felt that the interests of his native charges would best be protected by firmly integrating them into the Tejano population that the order seemed to favor—low status Bexareños. There is evidence, therefore, that contrary to the longstanding view that the mixing between townspeople and mission Indians took place contrary to the wishes of the friars, Fray Salas and some of his brethren were actively engaged in the incorporation of sufficiently acculturated neophytes into the general Tejano population.[30]

That population, despite its frontier character, was based on cultural norms consistent throughout the empire, chief among them perceived piety and commercial success. María Trinidad was deposited into the care of Don José de la Santa, an approximately sixty-one-year-old petty merchant who had previous experience serving as depository for women at a time when jail was strictly for men. A native of Tenerife, he was among a handful of merchants, including Ángel Navarro and Fernando Veramendi, who by about 1770 had made their way to San Antonio from various parts of the empire. The same reform efforts that were responsible for the political, religious, and military reorganization of the frontier were depriving presidio commanders of a monopoly over retail trade, and petty merchants such as Santa, who were at a competitive disadvantage in the more established parts of New Spain, found opportunity on the frontier. Like the other merchant newcomers he quickly established himself as a leading member of the community, a distinction recognized by the appellation *don* before his name. While Veramendi and Navarro, both younger men, married their way into insider status by wedding the daughters of old San Antonio families, Santa, as a widower, did so by maintaining a substantial and apparently devout household of older daughters and servants. Apparently he also benefitted from having been a cousin of Fray Pedro Ramírez, former president of the Zacatecas missionaries in Texas. In these respects he was an apt choice for supervising María Trinidad.[31]

However, chronically in debt—like almost anyone doing business in late eighteenth-century San Antonio—Santa's luck ran out in the mid-1780s, when various financial obligations led him to take an extended trip to Mexico City from which he never returned. His son, who also went into commerce, remained behind, however. Juan José de la Santa established himself as one of the leading Bexareños of the late eighteenth century, serving numerous times as *alcalde*, as an alderman, and even as an officer for the town's religious feasts. As their involvement in the town's public life and the deferential attitudes toward them makes clear, in places such as San Antonio men of commerce such as Santa enjoyed a prestige second only to government service and the religious life.[32]

One last figure participating in the events under study deserves mention, the schoolteacher Marcos de Aguilar. His presence in the proceedings dispels the common notion that San Antonio lacked for educational efforts until the early nineteenth century. Almost nothing is known about Aguilar. He was part of the committee that selected the officers for the annual religious feasts in the early 1780s, but does not otherwise appear in the records. The honor of serving on such a committee, however, indicates that even though an outsider he occupied a position of respect and some prestige in town.[33]

Illiteracy and ignorance may have run rampant among the town's general population, but that does not mean that men of learning—even limited learning—were not held in high regard. In fact, Aguilar was not the first schoolteacher in Béxar. As early as the 1740s Cristóbal de los Santos Coy petitioned the town council for a town lot because he did not have a proper school in which to conduct classes. In 1759, when Bishop Martínez y Tejada visited San Antonio he instructed the parish priest that

> with all effort and care he make sure that the town continues to have a schoolteacher . . . and that all the residents send their sons to learn to read

and write, and that they learn their prayers and Christian doctrine; teaching them at a tender age good customs and a holy fear of God for their better education and spiritual welfare; forcing their parents to contribute what is just for his weekly or monthly maintenance.[34]

Still, in 1778 a lot set aside for a school, as requested five years earlier by the then schoolmaster, Pedro José Agapito Tejada, still was vacant. Perhaps the lack of support drove Aguilar away, for he was gone by 1786, his place eventually taken by José Francisco de la Mata, who having noticed that children were without proper training, "running around, wasting their time on idle games," set up a school for the boys. Besides asking that the boys pay tuition, he requested that parents be restrained from complaining and even yelling at him when he punished a child. Collectively, Aguilar and the other men who attempted to provide San Antonio educational services had some success, for by the late eighteenth century a handful of the town's boys against great odds had gone off to Mexico City and Monterrey to study for the priesthood.[35]

What, then, does the case of Urbano and María Trinidad have to tell us about social relations in late colonial Texas? First, San Antonio society should not be seen—as it continues to be seen—simply in the dichotomous terms of Canary Islanders and everyone else. Royal law for the Indies established that the designated first settlers of a place were entitled to deferential treatment—membership in the municipal council, grants of public lands, and, very importantly, *hidalguía*, that is, nobility—but that did not mean that other factors did not contribute to social status. Race, gender, occupation, and origins all contributed to one's place in society. San Antonio was undergoing rapid social change in the last third of the eighteenth century and community members attempted to take advantage of the transformation.

Until relatively recently historians thought of issues of honor and status as matters of concern only to Spaniards of higher status. The Spanish minor nobility, the *hidalguía*, was particularly noted for its culture of honor, with its strict requirements for the defense of personal and family honor, and for the severe generational penalties for the dishonor brought about by illegitimacy and lack of *limpieza de sangre*, or purity of blood. From Spain, where proof of Old Christian blood and legitimacy had become a progressively important element in determining whether an individual could aspire to public office, university training, or the clergy, this royally sanctioned mechanism for determining a person's standing in society had traveled to the New World. In the Americas the concept of *limpieza de sangre* had been expanded to include *calidad*, which was affected by contamination of African blood and, unofficially, Indian blood.[36]

How was the whole *calidad* concept applicable in a place like San Antonio, Texas, where Indians, Spaniards, Afro-Mexicans, Frenchmen, and others mingled on the outer fringes of empire? One could ask Simón Francisco de Arocha and María Ignacia de Urrutia, parents of José Clemente, whom they wished to see study for the priesthood in Mexico City. Before he could be ordained, Father Fuentes, the parish priest, would be required to carry out an investigation of José Clemente's worthiness. Among the thirteen questions to be asked of the witnesses were:

- If he is the legitimate son of a legitimate marriage and who are his parents;
- Are the parents *españoles* and clean of "all bad race of Moors, Jews, and heretics";
- If they knew the paternal and maternal grandparents of said Clemente, their names, their residence, and if they were Christians;
- If they know said Clemente to have some physical deformity, sickness, epilepsy, mental illness, or possession by evil spirits or other grave defect;
- If there are any Jews, Moors, heretics or penitents of the Holy Office among the ancestors or collateral relatives of said Clemente;
- If they know him to be free of all slavery, or servitude by way of debts, or of him having practiced any unworthy occupations such as comedian or shoemaker, or vile ones such as gamecock breeder, innkeeper, gambler, etc.[37]

In other words, social worth was not simply the product of one's accomplishments; it was the result of circumstances and actions of one's ancestors and relatives. The Games family had invested quite a bit in gaining status as Spanish military men. For their niece to marry an Indian, and an illegitimate one at that, would bring dishonor and loss of status to the Games and Hernández brothers, and to their children and grandchildren besides.

On the frontier, where Spanish colonials were few and isolated and often in confrontation with hostile Indians, the issue of race, or *calidad*, was particularly complex. Limits on potential marriage partners, reduced population sizes generally, and individual achievement all worked against the proper functioning of the *sistema de castas*. Another important contributing factor on the frontier was the Spanish military code, which itself ran on the basis of the *sistema*. Soldiers were expected to be *españoles* unless they were members of separate units composed of black-mulatto enlisted men, or Indian auxiliaries. Consequently, no matter the physical characteristics of the enlistee, presidio rosters typically labeled all members of a unit as *españoles*, regardless of their lineage. This practice was not confined to the northern edges of Spain's American empire; it extended into the Portuguese world as well, as the response to the query of an early nineteenth-century English visitor to Brazil regarding the race of a military officer makes clear. Questioning why an obviously mulatto officer was referred to as "white," the reply was simply that "he was a mulatto, but he is now a white, for how can a mulatto be a *capit o mor*?" Thus, the convenient fiction for officers who had to keep garrisons fully staffed in the face of a shortage of pure-blooded Spaniards, worked to the benefit of *casta* men who saw their racial and therefore their social status elevated through military service.[38] Hinojosa, when he challenged the Games-Hernández men's racial background, was putting the lie to the system. They might be *españoles* on paper, but everyone in the community knew—for they could see it physically—that they were something else.

But what was that something else? The fact that census, parish, and other public records could record the same individual under different racial categories attests not so much to "passing," the conscious effort on the part of an individual to gain higher status through claims of being something other than what he or she truly was, but of the subjective and arbitrary nature of a system that ran counter to the everyday circumstances of the population. Mulattos might claim to be mestizos because an Indian-Spanish mix was of higher status than an African-Spanish one, but a mestizo and a mulatto might actually look very similar, and a public official having to record the race of such individuals might easily confuse one for the other. Marriage might similarly work to change the status of a spouse in the eyes of a public official who might find it unseemly that an *indio* was married to an *española*. Thus, while Trinidad Hernández might have been considered an *española* at Mission Concepción, once her Indian husband brought her to town her status was open to reinterpretation. Consequently, in the town censuses she devolves even beyond her original background, from mestiza to *india*. Race, then, became a value rather than an objective characteristic. Being Spanish was valued higher than being mestizo, being mestizo was valued more than being mulatto, and being black or Indian was least valued of all.

All of this happened because a system of social control was in place that relied on honor, status, and race as tools of public policy. From Spain came the estate system, imperfect and ill-fitting as it was to the American context. Where nobility did not exist, Spanish colonials created it because it was comfortable. Hence, María Trinidad was placed in the home of Don José de la Santa, a leading member of the community. How do we know his status? Because the honorific "don" precedes his name and tells us that although he would not be considered a noble back in Spain he had earned the deference of his social lowers and the esteem of his social equals. María Trinidad's uncles and stepbrothers attempted to prevent her marriage because they believed it would negatively impact the honor and status of the family. Because they were in a higher status position—soldiers—and because the position entitled them, even if temporarily, to the status of *españoles*, they claimed that the Pragmática allowed them to defend their honor against their female relative's bad marriage.

As the questionnaire in regard to Clemente Arocha's studies for the priesthood make clear, not only the Crown subscribed to a racial-status construct for society, so did the Church. As an instrument of government, but also as an institution in its own right, the Church walked a fine line between the ideals of the Bible and the realities of hierarchical society. Marrying an Indian to a Spaniard, as ostensibly was the case with Urbano and Trinidad, was one thing; who performed the marriage was another. Public and Church officials had to have the right stuff—*calidad*. Consequently, the background check for admittance to the seminary included some questions regarding the ethnic and racial heritage of the applicant.

The case of Urbano and María Trinidad challenges us to look at San Antonio as a complex set of social relations in which the values of the overarching Spanish culture were accepted as the norm, even as they were modified or undermined by behaviors shaped by local circumstances. Bexareños may have been largely illiterate but they were not ignorant. Even seemingly esoteric royal decrees such as the Pragmática Sanción were published in this frontier outpost and resorted to by individuals who could make a rather sophisticated case for themselves. They could certainly attempt to play the system, as the Games and Hernández brothers did when claiming *in loco parentis* rights to defend their *español* status despite their obvious physical appearance. Women, too, understood their rights, particularly to act as independent agents and to seek marriage partners for themselves and their children according to their own desires. Gertrudis Pérez may not have presented herself formally in the course of the proceedings under review, but her wishes were well known. In fact, it appears that Pérez's first marriage was to an *español*—Carlos' and Pedro's father—while her second marriage was to someone who outside the military environment would not be considered an *español*.

By the late eighteenth century, the Spanish values of honor, status, and race were well understood by a very broad cross-section of colonial Mexico's population. How do we know? Because, as our case demonstrates, even in isolated and backwards San Antonio, Texas, people were attempting to establish or defend their place in society based on these values. Honor, status, and race mattered to everyone from a mission Indian looking to promote himself into the general town population, to recently arrived mixed-blood soldiers attempting to recast themselves as honorable, Spanish servants of the king. In late eighteenth-century Texas Spain's imperial mechanisms of social control were alive and well. That everybody "gamed" the system was to be expected, and therein rest future stories to be told.

NOTES

1. The case of Urbano and María Trinidad is contained in "Año de 1781. Diligencias practicadas sobre la oposición hecha por José Miguel y Francisco de Sales Games, Carlos y Pedro Hernández, tíos y hermanos de María de la Trinidad Hernández para que no efectue matrimonio con Urbano Ynojosa indio de la misión de San Antonio consecuente a lo resuelto por Su Majestad en la Pragmática Sanción expedida en 23 de marzo de 1776 y 7 de abril de el de 1778. Número 51," Bexar Archives (Center for American History, University of Texas at Austin; hereafter cited as CAH).

Banns are the formal announcement of a proposed marriage required by the Catholic Church as one of the reforms of the Council of Trent. Technically, the marriage was to be announced on three successive feast days (a requirement subject to considerable latitude in interpretation) to allow anyone knowing of a reason why the couple should not wed to come forward. The Council of Trent gave bishops considerable discretion in dispensing with the requirement. See Patricia Seed, *To Love, Honor, and Obey in Colonial Mexico: Conflicts over Marriage Choice, 1574–1821* (Stanford: Stanford University Press, 1988), 75–76.

The Pragmática Sanción of 1776 was a royal decree issued in Spain by Charles III requiring parental approval for a marriage of all individuals under the age of twenty-five and notification of parents for individuals over the age of twenty-five. The Pragmática was extended to Spanish America in 1778. See Seed, *To Love, Honor, and Obey*, 200.

2. "Año de 1781," (quotation), Bexar Archives (CAH).

3. Ibid.

4. In fact, Fray José Francisco López, president of the San Antonio missions, had commented on how the Indians of Mission Valero and the others increasingly spoke Spanish on account of having "married mulattoes and mestizos, who are called coyotes here." Quoted in Jesús F. de la Teja, *San Antonio de Béxar: A Community on New Spain's Northern Frontier* (Albuquerque: University of New Mexico Press, 1995), 26.

5. "Año de 1781," (quotation), Bexar Archives (CAH).

6. Ibid.

7. The other case is that of Marcos Montes de Oca and María Margarita Ximenes, Apr. 28, 1773, Marriage Petitions and Permissions of San Fernando Church, John Ogden Leal translations (Daughters of the Republic of Texas Library, San Antonio) (cited hereafter as Leal transcripts).

8. Entry 726, [Baptisms] Mission San Francisco de Solano (Mexico) and Mission San Antonio

de Valero (Alamo), San Antonio, 1703–83, Leal transcripts; entry 342, Marriage Records of Mission San Antonio de Valero (Alamo), 1709–88, Leal transcripts; "Payaya Indians," *Handbook of Texas Online*, www.tshaonline.org/handbook/online/articles/PP/bmp53.html (accessed May 21, 2008); David La Vere, *The Texas Indians* (College Station: Texas A&M University Press, 2004), 65.

9. *Race* is here used in reference to the broad categories of purely phonologically distinct groups in Spanish colonial society, the three basic ones being European, Indian, and African. *Ethnic* refers to the groups having distinct social, cultural, and linguistic characteristics and who may be part of a specific racial group. Consequently, "Apache," "Comanche," and "Coahuiltecan" are ethnic groups within the "Indian" racial category.

Entries 629, 632, 637 (quotation), 694–96, [Baptisms] Mission San Francisco de Solano (Mexico) and Mission San Antonio de Valero (Alamo), San Antonio, Texas, 1703–83, Leal transcripts; Juan Agustín Morfi, *History of Texas, 1673–1779*, trans. and annot. Carlos Eduardo Castañeda (Albuquerque: Quivira Society, 1935), 94. The Ypandi were one of the Apache bands of Central Texas; see Elizabeth Howard West (trans. and annot.), "Bonilla's Brief Compendium of the History of Texas, 1772," *Quarterly of the Texas State Historical Association Online* 8 (July 1904), 52, www.tshaonline.org/shqonline/apager.php?vol=008&pag=052 (accessed May 21, 2008). For a discussion of the role of captive-taking in the introduction of young Indian children into the San Antonio community, see De la Teja, *San Antonio de Béxar*, 122–23, and Gilberto M. Hinojosa and Anne A. Fox, "Indians and Their Culture in San Fernando de Béxar," in *Tejano Origins in Eighteenth-Century San Antonio*, ed. Gerald E. Poyo and Gilberto M. Hinojosa (Austin: University of Texas Press for the University of Texas Institute of Texan Cultures at San Antonio, 1991), 110. In New Mexico, with its much denser population, the large number of non-Pueblo Indian captives who were incorporated into local society were referred to as *genízaros*. By the turn of the nineteenth century, at least some Comanche men were marrying into Nuevomexicano families to incorporate themselves into local society. See James F. Brooks, *Captives and Cousins: Slavery, Kinship, and Community in the Southwest Borderlands* (Chapel Hill: University of North Carolina Press for Omonhundro Institute of Early American History and Culture, 2002), 121–48, 195–96. See also David J. Weber, *Bárbaros: Spaniards and Their Savages in the Age of Enlightenment* (New Haven: Yale University Press, 2005), 234–41.

10. *Tejano* refers to any Spanish-speaking resident of Texas sharing in the culture of New Spain; entry 372, Marriage Records of Mission San Antonio de Valero (Alamo), 1709–88, Leal transcripts; "Padrón de las almas," Dec. 31, 1792, and "Padrón de las almas," Dec. 31, 1796, Bexar Archives (CAH); Distribution of effects to Indians of San Antonio Mission as per instructions, Apr. 11, 1793, List of fields left uncultivated in 1809, Aug. 18, 1809, Nacogdoches Archives, transcripts, Texas State Archives, Austin (cited hereafter as Nacogdoches Archives); Carlos E. Castañeda, *The Mission Era: The End of the Spanish Regime, 1780–1810*, vol. 5 of *Our Catholic Heritage in Texas, 1519–1936* (7 vols. 1942; repr., New York: Arno Press, 1976), 41–42. Marion A. Habig, in *The Alamo Chain of Missions: A History of San Antonio's Five Old Missions* (1968; rev. ed., Chicago: Franciscan Herald Press, 1976), 19, comments of the Franciscans that "they were as much interested in improving the Indians' temporal status as they were in promoting their eternal salvation."

11. Entry 883, San Fernando Church Burials, vol. 2, Leal transcripts, entry 235, Mission Concepción Marriages, Leal transcripts; "Misión de la Purísima Concepción ... Padrón de las almas," Dec. 31, 1792, Bexar Archives (CAH); Claude Morin, "Age at Marriage and Female Employment in Colonial Mexico," paper read at the International Conference "Women's Employment, Marriage-Age and Population Change," University of Delhi, Developing Countries Research Center, March 3–5, 1997, www.hst.umontreal.ca/U/morin/pub/CIDHInd97.htm [accessed May 15, 2008]; Julia Tuñón Pablos, *Women in Mexico: A Past Unveiled* (Austin: University of Texas Press, 1999), 31; Susan M. Socolow, "Acceptable Partners: Marriage Choice in Colonial Argentina, 1778–1810," in *Sexuality and Marriage in Colonial Latin America*, ed. Asunción Lavrin (Lincoln: University of Nebraska Press, 1989), 212. Analysis of marriage ages is based on Marriage Petitions and Permissions of San Fernando Church, Leal transcripts.

12. Tuñón Pablos, *Women in Mexico*, 31; Ramón Gutiérrez, *When Jesus Came, the Corn Mothers Went Away: Marriage, Sexuality, and Power in New Mexico, 1500–1846* (Stanford: Stanford University Press, 1991), 271–81.

13. "Padrón de las almas," Dec. 31, 1793, "Padrón de las familias," Dec. 31, 1796, and "Relación de las familias," 1803, Bexar Archives (CAH); entries 155 and 312, [Baptisms] Mission San Francisco de Solano (Mexico) and Mission San Antonio de Valero (Alamo), 1793–1812, Leal transcripts; De la Teja, *San Antonio de Béxar*, 24–28; José Cuello, "Racialized Hierarchies of Power in Colonial Mexican Society: The Sistema de Castas as a Form of Social Control in Saltillo," in *Choice, Persuasion, and Coercion: Social Control on Spain's North American Frontiers*, ed. Jesús F. de la Teja and Ross Frank (Albuquerque: University of New Mexico Press, 2005), 212–13.

14. Cuello, "Racialized Hierarchies of Power in Colonial Mexican Society," 24–28; Ilona Katzew, *Casta Painting: Images of Race in Eighteenth-Century Mexico* (New Haven: Yale University Press, 2004), 5. Douglas Cope, in his seminal study of race relations in Mexico City, *The Limits of Racial Domination: Plebian Society in Colonial Mexico City, 1660–1720* (Madison: University of Wisconsin Press, 1994), argues that not too much should be made of changing racial identities, since they tended to be much more important for Spanish elites than for the lower classes. See pp. 161–65 for a summary of his arguments. Richard Boyer, in an interesting working paper, "Caste and Identity in Colonial Mexico: A Proposal and an Example," Latin American Studies Consortium of New England Occasional Papers, n.d., http://clacs.uconn.edu/pdf/RBoyer.pdf [accessed May 27, 2008], uses a case study based on the *mulatto* named Gabriel Pérez from the Atrisco Valley of Puebla in the early eighteenth century to ponder the fluidity of race and status within the concept of *calidad*; or, as he writes, "to view status and identity as a construct that might shift with audience and situation" (p. 4).

15. "Venta de una casa por Margarita Falcón a Gavino Váldes, año de 1795, y traspaso de las misma a favor de María Trinidad Gámez, año de 1804," June 6, 1795, and Ana María de la Trinidad Games to María Clemencia Hernández, deed of sale, Aug. 18, 1808, Land Grants, Bexar County Spanish Archives, microfilm transcripts (Tarlton Law Library, University of Texas at Austin); Cantu-Castañeda, May 30, 1812, Marriage Petitions and Permissions of San Fernando Church, Leal transcripts; Castañeda, *The Mission Era*, 57; De la Teja, *San Antonio de Béxar*, 40, 41, 115, 123.

16. For an overview of the decommissioning of Los Adaes and transfer of the population to San Antonio, see Donald E. Chipman, *Spanish Texas, 1519–1821* (Austin: University of Texas Press, 1992), 184–87. The best detailed narrative remains Herbert E. Bolton, *Texas in the Middle Eighteenth Century: Studies in Spanish Colonial History and Administration* (1915; reprint, Austin: University of Texas Press, Texas History Paperbacks, 1970), 375–93. The story of the Adaeseños in San Antonio is summarized in Gerald E. Poyo, "Immigrants and Integration in Late Eighteenth-Century Béxar," in *Tejano Origins in Eighteenth-Century San Antonio*, ed. Gerald E. Poyo and Gilberto M. Hinojosa (Austin: University of Texas Press for the University of Texas Institute of Texan Cultures at San Antonio, 1991), 96–102.

"Libro de cuentas de los soldados del Real Presidio de Nuestra Señora del Pilar de los Adaes destacados en este de San Antonio de Béxar," Jan. 1, 1771, "Pie de lista de la expresada Compa," Feb. 3, 1774, "Autos practicados por el Coronel D. Domingo Cabello Gobernador y comte. de las Armas de la Pra. de los Texas, contra la persona de Felipe Flores," Apr. 5, 1783, Petition of Francisco Xavier Rodríguez, Mar. 29, 1784, "Diligencias practicadas por el coronel D. Domingo Cabello ... para el número de ganado vacuno orejano que el capitán reformado D. Luis Antonio Menchaca ha señalado y herrado en su rancho de San Francisco," Aug. 8, 1786, Extracto de la revista, Jan. 1, 1797, Bexar Archives (CAH); "Provincia de Texas: Estado general de la tropa de el presidio y vecindario de la Villa de San Fernando," July 30, 1779, legajo 283, Ramo Audiencia de Guadalajara, Archivo General de Indias, microfilm (University of Texas at San Antonio Institute of Texan Cultures) (cited hereafter as "Provincia de Texas"); Extracto de la revista, July 1, 1796, Nacogdoches Archives; entry 1689, San Fernando Church Burials, vol. 2, Leal transcripts.

17. "Libro de cuentas de los soldados del Real Presidio de Nuestra Señora del Pilar de los Adaes

destacados en este de San Antonio de Béxar," Jan., 1, 1771, "Pie de lista de la expresada Compañía," Feb. 3, 1774, "Testimonio de la sumaria información recibida por el coronel D. Domingo Cabello," July 15, 1779, "Extracto de la revista," Dec. 2, 1783, "Extracto de la revista," Feb. 3, 1784, "Provincia de Texas, Jurisdicción de San Antonio de Béxar," n.d. [1790], Bexar Archives (CAH); "Provincia de Texas"; entries 489, 728, 810, 930, vol. 2, San Fernando Church Baptismals, Leal transcripts.

18. "Pie de lista de la expresada Compañía," Feb. 3, 1774, "Extracto de la revista," Jan. 3, 1782 and July 1, 1786, Rafael Martínez Pacheco to Ugalde, Aug. 2, 1788, Bexar Archives (CAH); "Provincia de Texas"; entry 1297, San Fernando Church Burials, Leal transcripts.

19. "Autos formados contra Juan José Flores de Abrego y otros Rancheros por varios robos de ganado orejano en los agostaderos de la Misión de Espíritu Santo," Sept. 23, 1778, "Extracto de la revista," Aug. 1, 1782, June 1, 1786, Mar. 1, 1787, and Feb. 1, 1792, Manuel Muñoz to D. Ramón Castro, Apr. 8 and Apr. 19, 1791, in "Correspondencia con los Sres. Comandantes Generales, Brigadier D. Pedro de Nava y Coronel D. Ramón de Castro, Nov. 2, 1790, Bexar Archives (CAH); "Extracto de la revista," July 1, 1796, Nacogdoches Archives; entry 1113, vol. 2, San Fernando Church Baptismals, Leal transcripts.

20. "Expediente promovido por los vecinos del extinguido Presidio de Los Adaes para que se les conceda algún establecimiento donde puedan subsistir con sus familias," Jan. 4, 1778, Spanish Materials from Various Sources, vol. 48 (quotation) (CAH); Castañeda, *The Mission Era: The Passing of the Missions, 1762–1782*, vol. 4 of *Our Catholic Heritage in Texas, 1519–1936* (1942; reprint, New York: Arno Press, 1976), 354–56; Certifications of race, Sept. 2, 1781, Bexar Archives (CAH).

21. "Extracto de la revista," Nov. 3, 1783, Sept. 1, 1786, Sept. 1, 1790, "Provincia de Texas, Jurisdicción de San Antonio de Béxar," n.d. [1790], Bexar Archives (CAH); entries 1251, 1395, 1676, vol. 2, San Fernando Church Baptismals, Leal transcripts; entries 15, 150, vol. 3, San Fernando Church Baptismals, Leal transcripts; entry 209, San Fernando Marriages, 1798–1856, Leal transcripts.

22. Stuart Schwartz, "The Landed Elite," in *The Countryside in Colonial Latin America*, ed. by Louisa Schell Hoberman and Susan Migden Socolow (Albuquerque: University of New Mexico Press, 1996), 98; Oakah L. Jones, Jr., *Los Paisanos: Spanish Settlers on the Northern Frontier of New Spain* (Norman: University of Oklahoma Press, 1979), 9–10. A good summary of the complexities of Spanish nobility is found in I. A. A. Thompson, "Hidalgo and Pechero in Castile," *History Today* 37(Jan. 1987): 23–29, web.ebscohost.com/ehost/pdf?vid=5&hid=103&sid= 72f6b6a1-78c5-4ffd-8f97-64276445e030%40sessionmgr108 [accessed May 28, 2008].

23. "Provincia de Texas"; Padrón de las almas, Dec. 31, 1793, Bexar Archives (CAH).

24. "Libro de cuentas de los soldados del Real Presidio de Nuestra Señora del Pilar de los Adaes destacados en este de San Antonio de Béxar," Jan. 1, 1771, "Pie de lista de la expresada Compañía . . . ," Feb. 3, 1774, Bexar Archives (CAH); "Extracto de la revista," May 6, 1777, Nacogdoches Archives; entry 620, San Fernando Church Burials, Leal transcripts; "Provincia de Texas"; "Padrón de las familias," Dec. 31, 1796, Bexar Archives (CAH).

25. "Año de 1781" (1st quotation), Bexar Archives (CAH); Domingo Cabello to Bernardo de Gálvez, July 25, 1779, Archivo General de Indias Papeles de Cuba, Leg. 70, transcript (2nd and 3rd quotation), Texas State Archives, Austin. Carlos Castañeda comes to the same conclusion regarding Cabello's attitude toward the Adaeseños in *Our Catholic Heritage*, IV, 356. For a biographical sketch of Governor Cabello focusing on his administration of Texas, see Donald E. Chipman and Denise Joseph, *Notable Men and Women of Spanish Texas* (Austin: University of Texas Press, 1995), 202–25.

26. Croix to Pedro de Fuentes, Jan. 6, 1778, Bexar Archives (CAH); "El Ayuntamiento de la villa de San Fernando queja contra el Cura y a consecuencia se previene el modo en que se han de hacer las elecciones anuales de oficios concegiles. Año de 1778," Archivo de Gobierno, Saltillo Leg. 5 exp. 270a, Spanish Material from Various Sources, vol. 840, no. 4 (CAH); "Quejas de María Rosa Pérez, mujer de Miguel de Bergara, vecino de San Antonio de Béxar, contra su cura pár-

roco, el Bachiller Don Pedro Fuentes, que la puso en prisión por sospechas de incontinencia con José Marcelino Martínez," Archivo de Gobierno, Saltillo Leg. 5, exp. 270b, ibid.; "Instancia de Mateo Rodríguez Maderos, vecino de San Antonio de Béxar sobre que se le devuelva una hija suya depositada por el cura párroco. Año de 1778," Archivo de Gobierno, Saltillo Leg. 5 exp. 313, ibid.; "Juan Agustín Bueno, queja contra el cura de la villa de San Fernando sobre haberle castigado a su mujer y depositado a sus hijos," Archivo de Gobierno, Saltillo Leg. 5 exp. 314, ibid.; "Expediente sobre permitir a Juana Francisca Rodríguez su residencia en esta provincia," Archivo de Gobierno, Saltillo, Leg. 5 exp. 315, ibid.; "Quejas de Cristóbal Casio vecino de la villa de San Fernando, contra el Sr. Gobernador de la Provincia y su cura párroco por haberle castigado el primero y quitado dos hijos el segundo. Año de 1778," Archivo de Gobierno, Saltillo Leg. 5 exp. 338, ibid.; De la Teja, *San Antonio de Béxar*, 25, 47. On the impact of regalist reforms on the status of priests elsewhere in New Spain, see William B. Taylor, *Magistrates of the Sacred: Priests and Parishioners in Eighteenth-Century Mexico* (Stanford: Stanford University Press, 1996), especially 420–23.

27. Of the surviving prenuptial investigations, this is the only one documenting an opposition. Its occurrence some years just before the proclamation of the Pragmática Sanción is indicative of the power the Church had in such matters. Father Fuentes overruled the wishes of Margarita's father in deciding in favor of the marriage. After 1776, he would not have had the authority to perform the marriage over the objections of a parent. Marcos Montes de Oca and María Margarita Ximenes, Apr. 28, 1773, Marriage Petitions and Permissions of San Fernando Church, Leal transcripts.

28. Gilberto M. Hinojosa, "The Religious-Indian Communities: The Goals of the Friars," in *Tejano Origins in Eighteenth-Century San Antonio* ed. by Gerald E. Poyo and Gilberto M. Hinojosa (Austin: University of Texas Press for the Institute of Texan Cultures, 1991), 61–83; De la Teja, *San Antonio de Béxar*, 89–90, 120. A good article summarizing these issues in neighboring New Mexico is Rick Hendricks, "Church-State Relations in Anza's New Mexico, 1777–1787," *Catholic Southwest: A Journal of History and Culture* 9 (1998), 25–42. For a broader discussion of the changing status of the missionaries in the Spanish world, see Weber, *Bárbaros*, 102 (quotation), 103–109.

29. On the Franciscans serving the San Antonio missions, see Habig, *Alamo Chain of Missions*, particularly the biographical entry on Fray Salas on page 252.

30. De la Teja, *San Antonio de Béxar*, 84–85; Hinojosa, "The Religious-Indian Communities," 82.

31. Order of Governor Ripperdá, Mar. 27, 1775, Bexar Archives (CAH); "Quejas de María Rosa Pérez, mujer de Miguel de Bergara, vecino de San Antonio de Béxar, contra su cura párroco, el bachiller don Pedro Fuentes, que la puso en prisión por sospechas de incontinencia con José Marcelino Martínez, Archivo de Gobierno, Saltillo Leg. 5, exp. 270b, Spanish Material from Various Sources, vol. 840 no. 4 (CAH); "Autos y diligencias practicadas por el coronel don Domingo Cabello, gobernador y comandante de las armas de esta provincia de los Texas sobre haberse opuesto los vecinos pobladores de las orillas del arroyo del Cíbolo," Dec. 14, 1778, Bexar Archives (CAH); Cabello to Neve, Sept. 18, 1784, ibid.; De la Teja, *San Antonio de Béxar*, 133–34.

32. "Posesiones de oficios de alcaldes y regidores de esta villa de San Fernando," Dec. 20, 1779, Neve to Cabello, July 10, 1784, Cabello to Neve, Sept. 18, 1784, Cabello to Rengel, April 9, 1786, Bexar Archives (CAH); "Provincia de Texas."

33. Appointment of officers for feasts of Guadalupe and Purísima Concepción, Jan. 10, 1782, in Papers Relative to Religious Feasts, Feb. 12, 1772, Nacogdoches Archives.

34. Auto de visita del Ilmo. Sr. Dn. Fr. Francisco de San Buenaventura Martínez de Tejada y Diez de Velasco, dignísimo Obispo de Guadalajara, etc., a la villa de S. Fernando y Presidio de San Antonio de Béjar el año de 1759, vol. 81 (quotation), Spanish Material from Various Sources (CAH).

35. Donación de tierra a Cristóbal de los Santos Coy, Jan. 7, 1746, roll 65, Donación de un solar a Pedro José Agapito Tejada, Sept. 15, 1773, roll 67, Donación de un solar a favor de Gertru-

dis Sánchez, Apr. 6, 1778, roll 67, Testamento de Teresa Saenz de Zevallos, Bexar June 11, 1802, roll 61, Bexar County Spanish Archives, microfilm transcripts, Tarlton Law Library University of Texas at Austin; Auto de visita del Ilmo. Sr. Dn. Fr. Francisco de San Buenaventura Martínez de Tejada y Diez de Velasco, dignísimo Obispo de Guadalajara, etc., a la villa de S. Fernando y Presidio de San Antonio de Béjar el año de 1759, vol. 81, Spanish Material from Various Sources (CAH); Petition of José Francisco de la Mata, May 1, 1789, (quotation) Bexar Archives (CAH).

36. Richard Boyer, "Honor Among Plebians: *Mala Sangre* and Social Reputation," in *The Faces of Honor: Sex, Shame, and Violence in Colonial Latin America*, ed. by Lyman Johnson and Sonya Lipsett-Rivera (Albuquerque: University of New Mexico Press, 1998), 153–55; Magali M. Carrera, *Imagining Identity in New Spain: Race, Lineage, and the Colonial Body in Portraiture and Casta Paintings* (Austin: University of Texas Press, 2003), 12–14. A good overview of the general characteristics of the intertwined concepts of nobility, honor, *limpieza de sangre*, and education can be found in Mark A. Burkholder, "Honor and Honors in Colonial Spanish America," in *The Faces of Honor*, 18–44.

37. Questionnaire on eligibility to study for the priesthood, May 17, 1786, Nacogdoches Archives.

38. Ben Vinson III, *Bearing Arms for His Majesty* (Stanford: Stanford University Press, 2001), 11; Donald Pierson, "The Educational Process and the Brazilian Negro," *American Journal of Sociology* 48 (May, 1943), 693 (1st and 2nd quotations). Unfortunately, there is as yet no comprehensive study of the social history of the presidio system. In fact, Max L. Moorhead's *The Presidio: Bastion of the Spanish Borderlands* (Norman: University of Oklahoma Press, 1975), an institutional history, is the only comprehensive look at New Spain's northern frontier defensive system. Vinson provides a general discussion on the role of race in the evolution of New Spain's military system in pp. 7–45. A useful survey of the role of race in the Spanish colonial military, although limited in its coverage of the presidio system, is Ben Vinson III and Matthew Restall, "Black Soldiers, Native Soldiers: Meanings of Military Service in the Spanish American Colonies," in *Beyond Black and Red: African-Native Relations in Colonial Latin America*, ed. by Matthew Restall (Albuquerque: University of New Mexico Press, 2005), 15–52.

Theodore Gentilz, *Corrida de la sandía*. San Antonio's holiday schedule included a number of opportunities for celebrating in ways appropriate to the horse culture that came to Texas with the north Mexican frontiersmen that made up most of the town's population. Although not to the liking of the more refined governors and clergy, equestrian events allowed Bexareños to show off talents honed in the process of working cattle and pursuing Indians. Even women participated in the fun, a particularly scandalous aspect of local culture to outsiders. Courtesy of Daughters of the Republic of Texas Library, San Antonio, Texas.

7

"Buena gana tenía de ir a jugar"

THE RECREATIONAL WORLD OF EARLY SAN ANTONIO, TEXAS, 1718–1845*

San Antonio de Béxar, today's San Antonio, Texas, came into existence in spring 1718 as a way station between New Spain's frontier settlement line hundreds of miles to the south on the Rio Grande and the border with French Louisiana hundreds of miles to the northeast.[1] As the largest and most robust of the settlements occupying the northeastern end of the viceroyalty of New Spain (colonial Mexico), the city's history illustrates many of the characteristics common to Spanish settlements throughout the region. Isolated and lightly populated, San Antonio had few amenities to offer either its own residents or visitors. Nevertheless, Bexareños, as scholars commonly refer to the people of the area, managed to find ways of amusing and entertaining themselves.

Although the record is sparse, enough documentation survives to give some idea of how the people of San Antonio celebrated life even under the most difficult of circumstances from the first arrival of Mexican frontiersmen in the early eighteenth century until the arrival of Anglo-American and European immigrants over a century later. Sports as we have come to understand the term in the course of the twentieth century—regularly practiced and organized competitions of physical skill and endurance, including both amateur and professional practitioners—were unknown in eighteenth and early nineteenth-century Texas. Nevertheless, Bexareños did participate in recreational activities calling for physical prowess, some of which, as the reader will see, have contemporary analogues in the sports world—horse racing, bocce, rodeo. Other activities, also very much

---

*First published in *The International Journal of the History of Sport* 26, no. 7 (June 2009): 889–905, and as revised in *More Than Just Peloteros: Sports and U.S. Latino Communities* (Lubbock: Texas Tech University Press, 2014), 15–38. The phrase in the title means "I had a strong urge to go play."

familiar to us today, such as dancing and gambling, played import roles in filling the leisure time of all classes of people. Bexareños, then, were not just reduced to fighting Indians, surviving natural disasters, and eking out a hand-to-mouth existence on a remote frontier.

To understand what was possible by way of recreation and leisure to Spanish colonial frontiersmen (and not just in Texas but throughout much of the Spanish world), one should understand the role that Bexareños filled within that empire. At the turn of the eighteenth century Spain, France, and England had become involved in a series of dynastic/colonial wars that led each nation to seek strategic advantage in the interior of North America. Spain, fearful for its silver-producing colony of New Spain, met French penetration into the Gulf of Mexico region by exploring and eventually settling Texas as a buffer to encroachments of its valuable Mexican possessions. In the process, the native peoples of the region became the objects of attention of Spanish missionaries and French traders. In establishing its forward line of defense in the Texas-Louisiana border area, Spaniards had to overcome a five-hundred-mile-wide gap in settlement. Military officials chose the vicinity of present-day San Antonio as the most suitable location for an entrepôt between the Spanish outpost of San Juan Bautista del Río Grande (present-day Guerrero, in the Mexican state of Coahuila) and the Spanish Texas capital at Los Adaes (present-day Robeline, Louisiana).

San Antonio started as a mission-presidio complex—that is, a collaborative project between religious and military agents of the Spanish crown. Aside from the regional Indian groups gathered into Mission San Antonio de Valero (the facility better known as the Alamo), the first settlers were a motley collection of mixed-blooded frontier men and women. Within two years of its founding the Franciscans had established a second mission, and a decade later three more dotted the banks of the San Antonio River as it flowed in a southeasterly direction toward the Gulf of Mexico. Also, in 1731 a group of Canary Islander families, totaling fifty-six individuals, received a royal charter to found a town and acquire land in the area. In the century that followed, the descendants of these original Mexican, Canary Islander, and Indian inhabitants were joined by other subjects of His Catholic Majesty, and later by Mexican citizens, Anglo-American frontiersmen, and European immigrants. From an original population of about one hundred, San Antonio grew into a city of about four thousand souls by the time Texas joined the United States in 1845.

From its founding and through the changes in sovereignty until Texas annexation, San Antonio was a military town (in fact, it still is). The presidio, or garrison, was the single largest employer. The vast majority of recruits were locals or men from the two other Texas settlements of La Bahía (today Goliad) and Los Adaes/Nacogdoches, and the neighboring provinces of Nuevo León and Coahuila. The size of the garrison fluctuated, but by the late decades of the eighteenth century it included well over one hundred men. Hundreds more troops came to San Antonio in the early years of the nineteenth century as the Louisiana Purchase gave Spain a dangerous new neighbor, the land-hungry Americans, on Texas' eastern border. At this time the settlement's oldest mission, San Antonio de Valero, found a new role as the headquarters for a cavalry company transferred from San Carlos del Alamo de Parras, a name often shortened to Alamo.

Just about everyone in San Antonio was connected to the presidio in some way. The missionaries relied on soldiers to provide guard and escort duty for them as they went about their tasks of collecting, converting, and "civilizing" the Indians. The missionaries, as well as area civilian farmers and ranchers, also looked to the presidio as a market for some of the surplus agricultural products that the mission Indians grew. Craftsmen and merchants relied on the presidio for work as tailors, cobblers, and carpenters and as a market for goods imported from the interior of Mexico or smuggled in from Louisiana. And, of course, many families were composed of soldiers' kinfolk.

To make the settlement work, Bexareños relied on the river that coursed through or by each community and on the fertile lands the river watered. The site had originally been chosen for its abundant and accessible water supply, its fertile soil, and its plentiful timber resources. In the course of the eighteenth century an intricate water-delivery system of *acequias* (ditches), dams, and aqueducts provided drinking water and irrigation for the agricultural fields of townspeople and mission Indians, and for the orchards and gardens of the town's residents. Farther away from the San Antonio River, other area streams allowed for the watering of the large herds of cattle that made the region the birthplace of the Texas cattle industry.

The agricultural infrastructure that Bexareños put in place supplied the population of the San Antonio River valley to meet its subsistence needs and produced a small surplus for sale in neighboring provinces. By the 1770s, a full century before the great cattle drives of the post-Civil War era (1865–90), Texas cattlemen drove large herds south into the interior of Mexico and eastward to Louisiana. When crops were abundant enough, mule trains delivered Texas corn and other crop products, sometimes even pecans, to markets in Mexico. This traffic took place over *caminos* (byways) that were little more than deer tracks and Indian trails.

San Antonio was not a wealthy community. Surrounded by vast

expanses of Indian-controlled lands, suffering from inadequate communications with other parts of New Spain, and lacking in precious metals or other resources capable of attracting a large population, the settlement remained a simple frontier outpost. The most imposing structures in the area were the missions and the town's church. By the 1770s all five missions were enclosed by stone stockades that also served as the outer walls to Indian apartments, workshops, offices, and storage rooms. The chapels, two of which are handsome structures even in the early twenty-first century, were the product of Indian laborers working under the supervision of stonemasons and other artisans imported from the interior of New Spain. In the town itself, a few stone houses belonging to the most affluent Bexareños neighbored the two plazas, one of which was dominated by the parish church of San Fernando and the other by the buildings that made up the presidio. Most dwellings in the settlement were made of adobe or were *jacales*, a form of thatch-roofed hut of upright poles and mud.

Under such circumstances, opportunities for education or substantial social mobility were limited. Although there is patchy evidence for the presence of teachers throughout the eighteenth and early nineteenth centuries, there is little reason to think that most boys—girls were not thought of as needing formal education—received little more than the basics. A handful did make it out, however, to study for the priesthood or to gain practical experience in the bigger towns and cities of the interior. The presence of books in town is known from a few wills and legal cases for which inventories were made of personal possessions. Nothing suggests, however, that there was much sense of "refined" culture until after Mexican independence, although along with other activities commemorating public holidays, performances of one sort or another and meant to serve the cause of religious edification or respectable entertainment did take place. In the 1820s a group of leading men made an effort to establish a cultural association to stage plays, but the success of that endeavor is unknown. The first documentation of regular "professional" entertainment dates to the Republic of Texas period (1836–45), when the presence of comedy troupes and mountebanks is mentioned in travelers' journals.[2]

Similarly, there is no evidence for any kind of organized sporting activity in early Texas. That is not to say that organized sports were lacking in New Spain generally, however. By the eighteenth century Mexico City boasted a number of *pelota* courts, the precursor to modern jai-alai. Immigrants from northern Spain, particularly the Basque country, were very fond of the sport and the merchants among them who could afford to sponsor professional *pelota* players, on whose performances—as in jai-alai—there was always considerable wagering. Likewise, Mexico City and the other major urban centers of the viceroyalty each had bull rings where young men tested their horsemanship and other athletic skills for the pleasure of large audiences, if not always to the liking of "enlightened" churchmen and nobles. The native Mesoamericans had their own games, particularly variations on ancient ball games that often served religious purposes as well as entertainment. However, nothing in the historical record indicates that any of these competitive activities made it to the northern frontier regions.[3]

To be sure, there were ball games and bullfights in San Antonio, but they played different roles than they did in the metropolises of the interior. Bullfights were held in conjunction with the annual town feasts surrounding the Christmas season, and on other very special occasions, from the mid-eighteenth century until well after Mexican independence in 1821. From early December until the Feast of the Epiphany (January 6), Bexareños held religious and secular feasts that included enclosing one of the town plazas as a makeshift bullring and setting up booths and stalls on the periphery for games and food sales. Although we lack clear descriptions of the bullfights and bullfighters, we can assume that they were much anticipated opportunities for some of the locals to show off their equestrian skills and personal courage in the manner of the professional events held in Mexico City. There, bulls were fought both from horseback and on foot, in a style that was the direct antecedent to today's elaborate ritual. Aside from providing a special form of entertainment, the bullfights also reaffirmed the population's status as members of the Spanish cultural and religious world—despite official displeasure, both secular and religious—a not unimportant function on a remote and often hostile Indian frontier.[4]

Boys played ball games that could turn quite as dangerous as any encounter with a bull. In summer 1769 Ignacio Flores and Francisco Salinas were playing "a little game of *bolas*" in "the field the children and adolescents play in"[5] when an argument broke out between the two fifteen-year-olds. Flores struck Salinas with the ball, killing him instantly. Although the boys were related and the families argued that the incident was an accident owing to the boys' hotheadedness, the governor sentenced Flores to a year's exile, with the admonition that should he run away the crime would be raised to the level of a capital offense. Given the damage that Flores did, and the description of the accident scene, the game the boys were involved in was probably some variant of bocce, a game widespread throughout Spain's American empire by the mid-eighteenth century. Although subject to wagering, *bolas* appears to have been recognized as a legitimate form of recreation even among adults, and by 1782 the governor had granted a concession for that game and also for bowling to local merchant Juan Manuel Ruiz.[6]

Unfortunately, no identification or descriptions of children's games such as marbles or hide and seek have surfaced in the available records. Neither are attitudes toward such games clear from archival documents. When José Francisco de la Mata petitioned for a contract to serve as the town's schoolteacher, he prefaced his request by stating that he had observed the town's children "running around, wasting their time on idle games."[7] Of course he meant boys, since girls were not permitted access to public education. A later set of school regulations makes clear that when schools did operate there was little leisure time and that sports was not part of the curriculum.[8] Given the amount of physical exertion that frontier life demanded of average males, including work on horseback and agricultural chores, the omission of physical education from the school day is not at all surprising.

There is some evidence, however, that horseback riding was not just a utilitarian skill but an accepted recreational activity. In 1781 Governor Domingo Cabello banned the custom of men, women, and youths racing horseback "through the streets of the presidio and villa on the feast days of S. Juan, S. Pedro, Santiago, and Sta. Ana causing much harm." The activity must certainly have been disruptive, for the penalty for youths convicted of this offense was forfeiture of the horse and twenty-five lashes and for adults forfeiture of the animal and one month's labor on reconstruction of the town hall.[9] Cabello's ban proved as ineffective as other efforts to curtail such uses of town streets, for the equestrian custom remained popular in San Antonio well into the nineteenth century. Governor Manuel Salcedo opted for a more measured response to this continued unsavory practice, especially as it was one way in which the sexes might interact in an inappropriate manner. In 1809 and 1810 he issued orders to prevent men and women from riding together on the same horse, galloping through the streets, and most ominously, riding after curfew.[10] As late as 1849 a German visitor to San Antonio noted that on St. Peter's Day, "Young people of both sexes dashed through the streets on horseback and yelled. Mud splashed up to their ears, and the muddier they became the better."[11]

Horseback riding and sporting contests remained popular well into the Anglo-American era. In fact, from that period we have our first depictions of what such events entailed. French immigrant artist Theodore Gentilz painted a "watermelon race" through town streets in the 1840s. The object of the contest was to cross the finish line with an intact watermelon as competing riders tried to take it away by pursuing and jostling the one carrying the fruit. Another similar competition involved snatching a live rooster from the ground or a pole and trying to make it across the finish line as competitors reached for the hapless fowl. John Duvall, a veteran of the Texas War of Independence, recorded a riding match between Tejanos, rangers,[12] and Comanches at about the same time the whole town turned out to witness it.[13]

Equestrian displays were not the only physical exertions through which Bexareños enjoyed their leisure time. Although names and descriptions are lacking for San Antonio itself, mention of games among the Mexican population of the area is available in various records. German immigrant Eduard Ludecus described two games in one of his 1834 letters to his relatives from the Rio Grande country to the southwest of San Antonio. The first consisted of two opponents being bound by the wrists and placed in a crouching position with a stick locking their elbows and knees together. Facing each other toe-to-toe, each opponent was given another stick that was to be used in an attempt to knock each other over. The winner of the game, crouching over his helpless opponent, would then poke him in the groin. "The constrained position of the two players produces an extremely comical spectacle, and the laughter does not stop until one of the spectators takes pity on the loser and helps him up again." In the second game a group of people sat in a circle with their feet together, their legs covered by a blanket. Into the center of the circle stepped another person, who was pushed over and twirled around the circle by the prone players. The person who pushed over the standing person would then take his place in the center.[14] Unfortunately, similar descriptions of other physical games have yet to come to light.

In contrast, officials' efforts to regulate one form of recreational exercise—dancing—provide an abundance of documentation on a ubiquitous activity. Dancing was considered morally suspect, particularly as practiced among the popular classes. Men and women in too close proximity, authorities believed, led to no good.[15] Friar Ilarione da Bergamo, an Italian Capuchin who traveled in New Spain collecting alms for his order's missions in Tibet, commented on this popular entertainment that "ordinarily their songs are quite shameless, but still worse are their dances, which include rather indecent gestures." After noting that there existed three social levels of *fiestas*, he noted that "the third ... is the so-called *fandango*, which is the most universal one among the common people and where, for the most part, they perform the dances they call the *chuchumbé, bamba*, and *guesito*, which are all quite indecent."[16] The opening stanza of *Chuchumbé* makes clear what Friar Ilarione and Father Fuentes found so objectionable in what went on at fandangos:

> *En la esquina está parado*
> *un fraile de la Merced,*
> *con los ábitos alzados*
> *enceñando el chuchumbé*[17]

> Standing at the corner
> Is a friar of the Merced,
> With his habit lifted up
> Showing off his *chuchumbé*

In San Antonio about a decade later, songs being sung at dances included *fandangos*, *la chinita*, and *seguidillas*, which the singer, who was in trouble with Father Fuentes for singing what the priest considered lascivious lyrics, maintained were "harmless *juguetes*," that is, happy and festive tunes.[18]

To men such as Governor Salcedo, who had been educated in the best tradition of the Catholic Enlightenment and whose entire family was composed of government officials, good governance entailed the moral uplifting of the population. His ordinance for good government included the following view of nocturnal entertainments:

> Having come to my attention the disorders committed in the streets at night by men and women who in scandalous terms wander the streets, as well as in the fandangos which are held with too much frequency, and under which pretense people stay out and commit themselves to all sort of vice....
>
> [However,] because I do not seek to take away diversions, but rather to promote wholesome ones, I decree the following:
>
> There will be no fandangos or dances held except in the homes of trusted owners who will not permit the sale of liquors, *aguardiente*, or wine, will permit no disorders, and will keep the room well lit.
>
> The dance should not go beyond midnight, unless there is a particular license for it, and there should be no one standing outside the dance or around the building, since the judges or patrols will arrest such individuals no matter their class.[19]

Salcedo was sensible to the fact that such fandangos were among the few recreational activities available to the population in general, and his action merely restated longstanding governmental practice. As early as 1760 the town council attempted to regulate fandangos and the practice of nighttime strolls, by prohibiting both activities after 8 p.m., penalizing lawbreakers with an eight-peso fine and two days in jail. The measure seems to have done little to curtail such activities, however, for in the following year *Alcalde*[20] Alberto López issued an ordinance prohibiting fandangos and music after curfew and imposing stiff penalties for both the hosts and the attendees. At a time when the daily wage of a common laborer was a quarter peso, fines were set at a steep twelve pesos for the host and six pesos for those in attendance. The restriction, with a curfew set at 9 p.m., was repeated in 1776 by *Alcalde* José Salvador Díaz.[21] In 1783 the town council at something of wits' end complained to the governor because much of the crowd attending or congregating outside fandangos was composed of "unbridled youths and marked women." They asked that fandangos should be restricted to certain hours and confined to the inside of houses, "making the homeowners responsible for the offenses to God committed through the bad things that are sung, the fights, and disorders that occur."[22]

Fandangos remained popular and rather rowdy affairs, so the authorities eventually came to terms with them through another means of regulation. By the 1820s regulation took the form of exacting fees, which helped to fill government coffers and give us some idea of the frequency of the events. During the mid-1820s, for instance, it cost an individual one-half peso to hold a dance in a private residence, so the fees collected tell us that Bexareños could attend more than one fandango per week, although only on weekends or on holiday eves. In the period immediately after Mexican independence, the regulations were relaxed somewhat, as travelers reported multiple fandangos available on any given evening.[23] The best description of a San Antonio dance comes down to us from this period. Auguste Frételière, an early Alsatian immigrant to Texas, provides a word portrait of a fandango in 1837 that closely matches Theodore Gentilz's painting *Fandango*,[24] created a few years later:

> The sound of the violin drew us to the spot where the *fête* was in full swing. It was in a rather large room of an adobe house, earthen floored, lighted by six tallow candles placed at equal distances from each other. At the back a great chimney in which a fire of dry wood served to reheat the *café*, the *tamales*, and the *enchiladas*: opposite, some planks resting on frames and covered with a cloth, formed a table on which cups and saucers were set out.... At the upper end of the room, seated on a chair which had been placed on an empty box, was the musician, which was a violin.... The airs, for the most part Mexican, were new to me. The women were seated on benches placed on each side of the room.... The dance which I liked best was called the quadrille. It is a waltz in four-time with a step crossed on [e]very slow measure.... When the quadrille is finished, the cavalier accompanies his partner to the buffet, where they are served a cup of coffee and cakes. Then he conducts the young lady to her mother or to her chaperon to whom the girl delivers the cakes that she has taken care to reap at the buffet. The mother puts them in her handkerchief, and if the girl is pretty and has not missed a quadrille, the mama carries away an assortment of cakes to last the family more than a week.[25]

An even more common diversion, and an even more problematic one for the authorities, was gambling. The Spanish Bourbon monarchs, concerned as they were with reform of society, looked upon games of chance and wagering in general as contributing to laziness and immorality. Efforts to prohibit gaming were a staple of royal policy throughout the later colonial period, and San Antonio authorities wrestled with prohibition from an early date.[26] As early as 1724 a dispute between the presidio commander and missionaries led to the latter's accusations of Capt. Nicolás Flores allowing soldiers to gamble, which the captain strenuously denied. A senior official reviewing the case ridiculed the missionaries' recommendation that soldiers be paid in coin rather than in goods by commenting that "were they to be paid in coin they would soon gamble and whore it away."[27] Even more serious charges were made in 1749 by *Regidor*[28] Antonio Rodríguez Mederos against Governor Pedro del Barrio in a case involving Rodríguez Mederos's rivals on the town council. According to Rodríguez Mederos, since Barrio had arrived in town there had been "perpetual gambling at his house in spite of the royal decree forbidding it."[29]

To the public corruption to which gambling contributed, games of chance, like dancing, also resulted in another moral lapse—the improper mixing of the sexes. In fact, authorities believed that gambling and prostitution were closely related. In 1745 a new arrival in town was considered suspicious not only because he was of mixed blood but also because he had no apparent livelihood, and there were rumors about the woman he lived with not being his wife. Confronted by the authorities, he admitted that he did in fact live from his gambling, although the record did not clarify the state of his "wife."[30] In 1783 the town council sought clarification of civilian officials' authority over the homes of soldiers where "townspeople gather, both men and women, to play prohibited games, commit offenses against God [euphemism for sex], and other things worthy of reform."[31]

Although royal laws against games of chance were well known, if not well respected, by the middle of the century local officials found it necessary to take more direct action. In 1754 *Alcalde* José Curbelo issued an ordinance that made the association between gambling and other social ills explicitly clear. The rule attempted to prohibit loitering, the carrying of concealed weapons, and—because it was the "cause of laziness and disregard for work among many"—gambling.[32] When in 1778 Toribio Farías petitioned for a license to hold cockfights, Governor Barón de Ripperdá recommended to his superior that the request be denied because "the establishment of a cockfight in San Antonio would lead to more gambling than already takes place illegally, since the population is given to drinking and gambling." Subsequent prohibitions of gambling were issued by governors and local officials alike in 1783, 1786, and 1809. In 1825 Governor Rafael González notified the local authorities that he could not approve their request to allow public games of chance, since they were prohibited by state law.[33]

Governor Ripperdá knew of what he spoke. Many Bexareños found themselves drawn too heavily into the addictive qualities of gambling. Francisco de Estrada faced foreclosure on his home, which he had put up as collateral, for what was in part a gambling debt incurred without his wife's knowledge. When parish priest Father Pedro Fuentes placed Juan Agustín Bueno's wife in shackles, had him physically punished, and removed their daughters from their home because of the couple's gambling, Mrs. Bueno exclaimed, according to Fuentes, that "even if the devils took her body and soul, she would not do as he said." What Father Fuentes sought was that the couple stop gambling, which provided their daughters with a very poor example. In the proceedings regarding a murder case, the victim's wife declared that he had been a drunkard, a gambler, and had even attempted to sell her body.[34] In his first full inspection of the garrison, Governor Cabello reported on Lt. José Menchaca that although capable as an Indian fighter, he "could not be trusted with financial affairs as he is very fond of gaming and a spendthrift."[35]

The theft of seven hundred pesos from the home of merchant Santiago Villaseñor in 1774 provides evidence of the widespread nature of gambling in the San Antonio community. According to the documents in the extensive case file, gambling took place in various homes, in nearby woods, and behind corrals, both day and night. One gambler, a tailor, lost five military uniforms worth of work to another player. In fact, the break-in at Villaseñor's house took place while he was gambling. At one of the games was a man whose wife gave birth to their child while he was playing. Pedro Leal, who was arrested but never stood trial, came under suspicion when he left one of the games for two hours then returned to pay off his IOUs. Suspicion mounted when he and his wife began buying bread in larger amounts than normal on succeeding days. Eventually, all but 137 pesos were recovered, and Leal was released from jail having been admonished regarding the perils of gambling.[36]

As the cases above demonstrate, gambling was a recreational activity that brought together people of different socio-economic status. Cockfights, which eventually became legal once the government decided to turn the activity into a revenue-generating opportunity (and which remained popular until the late nineteenth century), required financial resources on the part of the individual or group responsible for building and running the cockpit, modest resources on the part of breeders and trainers of roosters, and just enough money on the part of anyone else interested in placing a bet.[37] Similarly, other than pick-up games, cards required that a few individuals serve as hosts and banks, but the majority of participants only had to show up with betting money or a line of credit. Because San Antonio was a small community, not enough men of substance could keep games socially stratified, so class mixing was inevitable.

Unlike dice, which appear in the records only on the rarest occasion, because of the frequency of official proceedings involving card games, we have the names of some of the games played by Bexareños. One was called *treinta* or *treinta y una*, and like blackjack (twenty-one) consisted of players drawing cards in an effort to get to thirty (or thirty-one) points. In the game *albures*, a game in Spain called *parar*, cards were dealt out to all the players who made bets against the dealer. Subsequently cards were dealt out until there was a match, with the bank losing to the player making the match or winning all the bets if it received the matching card. *Monte* made its appearance in the nineteenth century and should not be confused with three-card monte. The Spanish game involved dealing four cards, two for the dealer and two for the player, and then drawing more cards until a pair was made with one of the four dealt cards. The dealer either lost the amount bet by the other player or won it depending who made the winning pair. At least one parlor card game (although also subject to wagering) also was popular in the late eighteenth century and remains popular in Mexico today—*malilla*. Played by four persons in two teams, it involved dealing all the cards from the deck, with the lead player turning over a trump card. Players won tricks by having a trump or high card in each round. When all the cards had been played the two teams counted the points (cards have different values). The team with the most points won.

One other Spanish parlor game played in San Antonio, which could be played with cards or with other objects, was called *pares y nones* and involved guessing odd or even on whatever object was being hidden. In 1737 Governor Carlos de Franquis Benítez de Lugo ran into accusations that he brought "suspicious women" to his home to play the game at late hours of the night. Because of the possibility of legitimate "recreational" card games, the authorities could not ban the sale and use of playing cards. Indeed, so profitable did the authorities consider the playing card market that by the 1760s the crown decreed a royal monopoly on the sale of playing cards, along with tobacco, gunpowder, and other lucrative products.[38]

Although public gambling remained illegal during the Mexican period, restrictions on this activity were lifted in the post-Texas independence period. Travelers to San Antonio during the 1830s and 1840s commented on the universal popularity of games of chance, but focused on the Bexareño population's particular zeal for the sport. One observed that on the Sabbath, "Many Mexicans leave chapel even before mass was concluded, and repair to the gaming table; where they spent the remainder of the day, and perhaps the whole night." Another visitor to San Antonio commented that "so strong is this passion that even the priests sometimes forget their sacred office and are seen dealing monte, the favorite game of the Mexicans."[39] How disappointed Father Fuentes would have been to learn of some of his successors' weakness for gambling.

Our inventory of recreational activities in early San Antonio would not be complete without a brief comment on alcohol. Already in the 1740s, there is evidence of efforts on the part of town officials to enforce the royal prohibition on contraband liquor, and as early as 1761 *Alcalde* Alberto López's police ordinance reiterated the royal ban on home distillation of sugarcane alcohol, commonly referred to as *aguardiente de caña* or *chinguirito* to distinguish it from regular *aguardiente* (brandy). He then elusively decreed that "because of the grave consequences to this town, no one is allowed to bring *aguardiente* into town except that which is from Castile and brought in for necessary reasons," an amount he estimated at one to two barrels.[40] A few years later Governor Ripperdá carried out the penalty for the production and sale of *aguardiente de caña* and adulterated *aguardiente*—dumping in the plaza tainted liquor belonging to a handful of sellers.[41]

As noted above, drinking accompanied dancing and gambling, which is why it concerned public officials. For instance, during the investigation on the murder of José Antonio Ballejo his wife testified that he was "a drunkard and a gambler." When Governor Ripperdá recommended against permitting Toribio Farías from establishing a cockpit in San Antonio, he specifically mentioned that Bexareños were already too addicted to "drinking and gambling." Governor Salcedo's ordinance regulating fandangos specifically prohibited "the sale of liquors, *aguardiente,* or wine" at the dances.[42]

Among the cases for drunkenness, that of Sub-Lieutenant Manuel de Urrutia stands out for illustrating the range of social ills clergy and officials attempted to fight by regulating the sale and consumption of alcohol. On the night of September 7, 1791, Urrutia attended a fandango held at the home of Corporal José Granados, despite the fact that he was officer of the guard that day. He was drunk on *aguardiente,* "a defect of his that has been his custom for many years." Nothing that Governor Manuel Muñoz did remedied Urrutia, who was in the habit of being drunk on and off duty, and who had developed a severe hatred for the governor. According to *Alcalde* Juan José de la Santa, who made the statement, not only had Urrutia once told him of a plot to kill the governor, it was also notorious that he had an illicit affair with an Indian woman.[43] Hence, alcohol contributed to dereliction of duty, contempt for senior officers, violence, and dissolute behavior.

Our perspective on diversions in early San Antonio is unfortunately skewed by the records upon which we must rely to document recreational and entertainment activities. Except by way of serendipity, missing are the innocent games of children and social leisure activities of adults. The harmless strolls and picnics in neighboring fields during lulls in Indian warfare that allowed for family interaction did not make it into the written record. Storytelling and the arts of painting and sculpture have not been treated in this article, although circumstantial evidence supports the presence of both.[44]

Also, as mentioned earlier, public celebrations sometimes created opportunities for special entertainments. Game booths and food stalls encircled the plaza during the festive season at the end of each year. The bullfights, horse races, and other competitions that took place broke the monotony of everyday existence. Even more special, because of the added entertainments, were extraordinary celebrations like a royal wedding or the birth of an heir to the throne. Fortunately, a report on the celebrations surrounding the ascension of a new king give us a glimpse of just how elaborate such events could become, even in backwaters such as San Antonio de Béxar.[45] After six months of mourning for the departed Philip V, the authorities advised the townspeople to prepare for a celebration and oath to Fernando VI on January 27, 1748. Governor Francisco García Larios requested that residents and soldiers display lights in front of their homes for the three evenings preceding the celebration. On the day of the ceremony, a military escort carried the royal standard to the governor's residence, whence he read the royal decree, which concluded with cries of "Long Live the King" from the citizenry, along with musketry and artillery fire and a speech by García Larios. At three in the afternoon the royal standard-bearer placed the flag to the right of the governor, who—accompanied by the town council and the presidio commander—marched to the parish church. They were preceded in the march by a company of "Moors" with its Grand Turk and officers and a company of "Christians" with its field marshal and officers.[46] After the church blessing, the whole assembly marched to the town plaza where a four-sided castle had been built for the occasion. With the town assembled there, the standard-bearer knocked at the castle door and the "castellan" responded by letting him in so that the royal standard could be hoisted at the topmost part of the structure and the guards set. The governor and town council then retired while the "Moors" made their passes around the castle.

So began the celebrations, which went on for another eight days. On the second day of the festivities, the procession to the church with the royal standard was repeated, and a mass of thanksgiving was sung, after which the "Moors" and "Christians" made processions. The following four days witnessed bullfights, followed by a day of skirmishes between the "Christians" and "Moors" and another day of bullfights. Finally,

> On the morning of February 4 the Moors and Christians held their battle, with all possible luster and with the Moorish prisoners carrying the [image] of the town's patron saint in procession to the church, where mass was sung and St. Ferdinand was left in his church. The promenade then resumed, making a turn about the plaza with the Moorish prisoners. At three in the afternoon a comedy was presented, which everyone attended, and after which the artillery fired three volleys and the [celebration] concluded with the oath to Our King and Lord, whom God protect.

The festivities surrounding the oath to the new king were neither unique to San Antonio nor exotic.[47] They were, however, the clearest indication of how closely Bexareños culturally identified with the Spanish world. Bullfights, *moros y cristianos*, and processions with Christian religious icons were all parts of a pageant meant to remind the population of its Spanish heritage even as it provided relief from the daily routine. Despite their own chronic warfare with the autonomous tribes that surrounded them, Bexareños never attempted to stage a mock battle between Christians and Indians. And the other forms of entertainment we have reviewed here, while limited to those for which documentation exists, point equally strongly to a Spanish culture that served as a source for popular culture in the Mestizo world of northern New Spain. European-origin ball and card games, music, and liquor, were accompanied by equestrian and religious displays that also drew from Iberian practices.

As Anglo Americans and European immigrants, particularly Germans, overwhelmed the Tejano population of San Antonio in the mid-nineteenth century, the local Bexareño culture began to adopt and adapt cultural practices from those sources, including American baseball and German polkas. Eventually, as Bexareños blended the customs of Mexico with those of the

United States, they enriched both their own Hispanic culture and American culture at large. At least one modern organized sport can trace its heritage back to Spanish colonial times. The sport of rodeo owes more than just its name to the early Mexican pioneers who brought the associated ranching skills to the American Southwest. To the degree that the modern "cowboy sport" reflects skills, equipment, and dress that had their origin in Spanish colonial Texas and other parts of what is now the American Southwest, it unwittingly celebrates the way that Tejanos, Nuevomexicanos, and Californianos lived, worked, and entertained themselves.

NOTES

1. The following description of San Antonio and its environs is based on Jesús F. de la Teja, *San Antonio de Béxar: A Community on New Spain's Northern Frontier* (Albuquerque: University of New Mexico Press, 1995). For a historical survey of colonial Texas see Donald E. Chipman, *Spanish Texas, 1519–1821* (Austin: University of Texas Press, 1992).

2. Jesús F. de la Teja, ed., *A Revolution Remembered: The Memoirs and Selected Correspondence of Juan N. Seguín*, 2nd ed. (Austin: Texas State Historical Association, 2002), 16; Jesús F. de la Teja, "Discovering the Tejano Community in 'Early' Texas," *Journal of the Early Republic* vol. 18, no. 1 (Spring 1998): 92–93.

3. Robert Ryal Miller and William J. Orr, eds., *Daily Life in Colonial Mexico: The Journey of Friar Ilariano da Bergamo, 1761–1768*, trans. William J. Orr (Norman: University of Oklahoma Press, 2000), 118–21; Juan Pedro Viqueira Albán, *Propriety and Permissiveness in Bourbon Mexico*, trans. Sonya Lipsett-Rivera and Sergio Rivera Ayala (Wilmington, DE: Scholarly Resources, 1999), 185–87, 200–201.

4. Activities surrounding the succession of Fernando VI, May 25, 1747, Bexar Archives, Center for American History, University of Texas at Austin (hereafter cited as BA); Petition to be exempted from hauling stone for the erection of public buildings, Feb. 7, 1771, Nacogdoches Archives Transcripts, Texas State Library, Austin (hereafter cited as NAT); Representation of republicanos and vecinos of Béxar, March 1, 1790, BA; Bandos of Governor Manuel Salcedo continued, January 16, 1809, BA; Cabildo minutes book, January 17, 1821, p. 125, BA. A good contemporary description of a Mexico City bullfight, complete with moralistic commentary, can be found in Miller and Orr, *Daily Life in Colonial Mexico*, 119–20. A good survey of the evolution of bullfighting in eighteenth-century New Spain is Benjamín Flores Hernández, "Organización de corridas de toros en la Nueva España del siglo xviii y primeros años del xix," *Anuario de Estudios Americanos* vol. 61, no. 2 (2004): 491–515.

5. Sentence against Ignacio Flores, September 15, 1769, BA.

6. Auto of Governor Barón de Ripperdá, August 13, 1770, BA; Petition of Juan Manuel Ruiz, July 14, 1782, BA.

7. Petition of José Francisco de la Mata, May 1, 1789, BA.

8. School code, March 13, 1828, BA.

9. Bando of Governor Domingo Cabello, June 24, 1781, BA.

10. Bandos of Governor Salcedo continued.

11. W. Steinert, quoted in De la Teja, "Discovering the Tejano Community in 'Early' Texas," 96.

12. Until the term became synonymous with the post-Civil War law enforcement organization known as the Texas Rangers, rangers were horsemen who acted as a frontier defense force. Composed mostly of Anglo Americans, these early ranger forces also contained Tejanos.

13. Dorothy Steinbomer Kendall, *Gentilz, Artist of the Old Southwest* (Austin: University of

Texas Press, 1974), 27, 84–85; De la Teja, "Discovering the Tejano Community in 'Early' Texas," 95–96; Joel Huerta, "Red, Brown, and Blue: A History and Cultural Poetics of High School Football in Mexican America" (Ph.D. diss., University of Texas at Austin, 2005), 35–45.

14. Louis E. Brister, trans. and ed., *John Charles Beales's Rio Grande Colony: Letters by Eduard Ludecus, a German Colonist, to Friends in Germany in 1833–1834, Recounting His Journey, Trials, and Observations in Early Texas* (Austin: Texas State Historical Association, 2008), 146.

15. Viqueira Albán, *Propriety and Permissiveness*, 123–24. An analysis of these dances and songs, based on documentation from the records of the Holy Inquisition, is found in Sergio Rivera Ayala, "Lewd Songs and Dances from the Streets of Eighteenth-Century New Spain," in *Rituals of Rule, Rituals of Resistance: Public Celebrations and Popular Culture in Mexico*, ed. William H. Beezley, Cheryl English Martin, and William E. French (Wilmington, DE: Scholarly Resources, 1994), 27–46.

16. Miller and Orr, *Daily Life in Colonial Mexico*, 116.

17. Rivera Ayala, "Lewd Songs and Dances," 31. I have replaced the original English translation in the article with my own.

18. Francisco García vecino de la villa de S. Antonio de Béxar, contra el Sr. Gobernador de la provincia por haberlo castigado por delitos que se expresan. Año de 1778, Archivo de Gobierno, Saltillo Leg. 5 exp. 314, Spanish Materials from Various Sources, vol. 840, no. 4 (transcript), Center for American History, University of Texas at Austin.

19. Bandos of Governor Salcedo continued.

20. The Spanish office of *alcalde* combined administrative and judicial duties, and can be roughly translated as "magistrate." In modern times, the office has become akin to that of mayor in many parts of the Hispanic world.

21. Bando of Cabildo, October 26, 1760, BA; Bando of Alberto López, January 10, 1761, BA; Bando of José Salvador Díaz, January 21, 1776, BA.

22. Cabildo to Cabello, February 28, 1783, BA.

23. Arnoldo De León, *The Tejano Community, 1836–1900* (Albuquerque: University of New Mexico Press, 1982), 172–73; Jesús F. de la Teja and John Wheat, "Bexar: Profile of a Tejano Community," *Southwestern Historical Quarterly* vol. 89, no. 1 (July 1985): 23; De la Teja, "Discovering the Tejano Community," 90.

24. Kendall, *Gentilz*, 10, 25, 59.

25. Quoted in De la Teja, "Discovering the Tejano Community," 90.

26. A summary of government efforts to prohibit and control games of chance can be found in Teresa Lozano, "Los juegos de azar. ¿Una pasión novohispana? Legislación sobre juegos de azar en Nueva España. Siglo xviii," *Estudios de Histora Novohispana* vol. 11 (1991): 155–81. See also, Teresa Lozano Armendares, "Tablajeros coimes y tahures en la Nueva España ilustrada," *Estudios de Historia Novohispana* vol. 15 (1995): 67–86.

27. Autos sobre diferentes puntos consultados por el gobernador de la Provincia de los Texas muerte de un correo y otras materias. Año de 1724, Archivo General de la Nación de México, ramo Provincias Internas vol. 183 (microfilm), Benson Latin American Collection, University of Texas at Austin.

28. The office of *regidor* is akin to that of alderman, although there were specific administrative tasks assigned to each *regidor*. By royal charter, San Antonio was entitled to six *regidores* on its town council.

29. Autos fhos. a representación de D. Antonio Rodríguez Mederos, regidor decano de la Villa de San Fernando en la Provincia de Texas, sobre que salgan de dha. Villa D. Vicente Travieso, alguacil mayor, y D. Francisco de Arocha escribano de cabildo, por falsos, reboltosos, y pertubadores de la paz pública, July 19, 1749, BA.

30. Proceedings on legitimacy of a marriage, October 4, 1745, BA.

31. Cabildo to Cabello, January 24, 1783, BA.

32. Bando of José Curbelo, January 12, 1754, BA.

33. Petition of Toribio Farías, January 12, 1778, BA; Order of Gov. Cabello, October 7, 1786,

BA; Bandos of Governor Salcedo continued; Governor Rafael González to Jefe Político of Béxar, November 18, 1825, BA.

34. Petition of Juan José Flores, January 26, 1754, BA; Criminal investigation on the death of José Antonio Ballejo, June 4, 1776, BA; Juan Agustín Bueno, queja contra el cura de la villa de Sn. Fernando sobre haberle castigado a su mujer y depositado a sus hijos. Archivo de Gobierno, Saltillo Leg. 5, exp. 314 (transcript), Spanish Material from Various Sources, vol. 840, no. 4, Center for American History, University of Texas at Austin; Extracto de la revista de inspección ejecutada por mí el Coronel de Infantería Don Domingo Cabello, July 1, 1779, Archivo General de Indias, Audiencia de Guadalajara 104-6-20 (transcript), Texas State Archives, Austin.

35. Extracto de la revista.

36. Sumaria del robo hecho a D. Santiago Villaseñor, entrando por una ventana de su casa la noche del 24 al 25 de Octre. de 1774, de la cantidad de 700p, en Sn. Antonio de Bexar, October 28, 1774, BA.

37. Petition of Toribio Farias; Vicente Bernabeu to Gov. Manuel Muñoz, December 27, 1790, BA; Intendente Bruno Díaz de Salcedo to Gov. Muñoz, January 4, 1796, BA; De León, *The Tejano Community*, 184–85. The history of this activity in colonial Mexico can be found in María Justina Sarabia Viejo, *El juego de los gallos en la Nueva España* (Seville: Escuela de Estudios Hispanoamericanos, 1972).

38. Testimonio de las diligencias ejecutadas en la Provincia de Texas en virtud de superior despacho del Exmo. Sor. Virrey de este Reino, por el gobernador del Nuevo Reino. de León contra el coronel don Carlos de Franquis Benítez de Lugo actual gobernador. de la Provincia de los Texas y electo de la de Tlaxcala, April 17, 1737, Archivo General de Indias, Audiencia de Guadalajara 67-2-27, Spanish Materials from Various Sources vol. 29, Center for American History, University of Texas at Austin; Order of Gov. Cabello, October 7, 1786, BA; Causa criminal formada de oficio por el Governador contra Prudencio Barrón, Vecino del Preso. de Sn. Anto. de Béxar, y Villa de Sn. Ferndo. sobre la muerte ridenta de Clemente Xavier Méndez, March 12, 1775, BA; Order of Gov. Cabello, October 7, 1786, BA; De la Teja, "Discovering the Tejano Community," 92; Susan Deans-Smith, *Bureaucrats, Planters, and Workers: The Making of the Tobacco Monopoly in Bourbon Mexico* (Austin: University of Texas Press, 1992), 7. The names and descriptions of the card games mentioned come from various editions of the *Diccionario de la lengua española*, dating between 1726 and 1899—see "Nuevo Tesoro Lexográfico de la Lengua Española," http://buscon.rae.es/ntlle/SrvltGUILoginNtlle (accessed July 18, 2008). Additional information on *malilla* was taken from "Malilla," http://www.pagat.com/manille/malilla.html (accessed July 18, 2008).

39. Quoted in De la Teja, "Discovering the Tejano Community," 92.

40. Quote, Bando of Alberto López, January 10, 1761, BA; Case of Isleños v. Mederos, June 17, 1750, BA.

41. Order of Gov. Ripperdá, March 27, 1775, BA.

42. Criminal investigation on the death of Jose Antonio Ballejo; Petition of Toribio Farias; Bandos of Gov. Salcedo continued.

43. Certification of Alférez Manuel de Urrutia's conduct by D. Juan José de la Santa, *regidor* and acting *alcalde* in absence of Francisco Arocha, September 9, 1791, BA.

44. See, for instance, Adina De Zavala, *History and Legends of the Alamo and Other Missions in and Around San Antonio*, reprint ed. (Houston: Arte Público Press, 1996); and Gilberto M. Hinojosa and Anne A. Fox, "Indians and Their Culture in San Fernando de Béxar," in *Tejano Origins in Eighteenth-Century San Antonio*, ed. Gerald E. Poyo and Gilberto M. Hinojosa (Austin: University of Texas Press for the Institute of Texan Cultures, 1991), 113–18.

45. Activities surrounding the succession of Fernando VI.

46. On the Reconquista reenactment spectacle known as "Moros y Cristianos" see Mas Harris, *Aztecs, Moors, and Christians: Festivals of Reconquista in Mexico and Spain* (Austin: University of Texas Press, 2000).

47. See, for example, Cheryl English Martin, *Governance and Society in Colonial Mexico: Chihuahua in the Eighteenth Century* (Stanford, CA: Stanford University Press, 1996), 100–105.

Theodore Gentilz, *La cocina*. Processing maize into corn meal and then into tortillas and tamales was long and laborious work for women, who had to be up long before everyone else to prepare the hardy breakfast that would keep men in the fields and in the saddle for the day. All the hard work produced food items the savory nature of which could not help but impress Anglo Americans who otherwise found little of worth in Mexican culture. Courtesy of Daughters of the Republic of Texas Library, San Antonio, Texas.

8

Discovering the Tejano Community in "Early" Texas*

Most Anglo-American writers refer to the Texas of the 1820s, 1830s, and 1840s as early Texas, and in one sense they are right. The transformation of Texas into a member state of the American Union began in those years. Most of the country that the Anglo-American colonies and later the Republic occupied was wilderness, as that term was defined by Euro-American concepts of wilderness and civilization. Unquestionably, however, there was an even earlier Texas; a Texas that existed within a Hispanic historical context and responded to Spanish-Mexican social, economic, political, and religious norms. Before that, there had been no Texas. To the Indian peoples who inhabited the coastal prairies, the piney woods, the high plains, and the mountains and basins of the extreme southern Rockies, there were very different economic and political geographies, most of which remain a mystery to us today.[1] Nevertheless, in this essay "Early Texas" denotes the span between the 1820s and 1850s, during which Texas in its modern form came into being.

The foundations of this work are based on what other scholars have had to say about everyday life in nineteenth-century Texas. Fifty years ago William Ransom Hogan published *The Texas Republic: A Social and Economic History*, a path-breaking work that remains unsurpassed in breadth of scope and depth of understanding. Not surprisingly for his time, Hogan was primarily interested in the immigrant white population, not the pre-existing Hispanic one. His references to the Tejanos (Texans of Spanish-Mexican heritage) are few and most often incidental. For instance, in six pages devoted to Republic-period housing, there is only one paragraph on Tejano architecture. In the six pages devoted to clothing there is one paragraph on how slaves were dressed, but not one line on Tejano fashions.

---

*First published in *Journal of the Early Republic* 18, no. 1 (Spring 1998): 73–98.

This coverage is generous by comparison with Joseph Schmitz's earlier social history of the Republic of Texas, *Thus They Lived*. Schmitz explicitly limited attention to the Anglo Americans "since they constituted the overwhelming majority of the inhabitants." For him the black population was beneath attention and the Mexicans could be dismissed in the following terms: "These people were not assimilated, but neither did they in the least retard the progressive Americans."[2]

About a dozen years ago another important work in Texas social history appeared, Arnoldo De León's *The Tejano Community, 1836–1900*. Although encompassing a much broader time span than *The Texas Republic*, De León's work dealt with many of the same issues. He looked at how Mexican Texans, the Tejanos, went about constructing and reconstructing their communities to meet the exigencies of the environment, both physical and social. De León's most important contribution was his description of a complex economic, political, and social life among people usually dismissed simply as Mexicans.[3] Curiously, many of Hogan's descriptions of Republic-era customs, practices, and material culture among Anglo-American settlers bear considerable resemblance to ones described by De León for the Tejano community.

The purpose of this essay is to make some of these connections. Focusing primarily on Tejanos, it points out how the two "early Texases," one largely descended from southern United States colonial and early national experiences, the other from Mexican colonial culture, compared. The evidence demonstrates that despite suspicions, and sometimes overt racism and antipathy, there existed between early Texans and Tejanos much common ground. In what they ate, how they lived, what they enjoyed, and what they suffered, Tejanos and Texians had more in common than they realized. How the two groups drifted increasingly apart is another story, however, and comment on the political and legal status of Tejanos is beyond the scope of the present work.[4]

Corn—*maiz* to the Spanish world—was easy to grow under a variety of conditions; could be consumed before ripening; and was the most important gift of the New World to the Old. It was already being grown in Texas when the first Hispanic settlers arrived in the early eighteenth century to establish permanent residence. For hundreds of years the Caddoan people of East Texas, part of the Mississippian culture group, had raised corn, as had the Jumanos of the trans-Pecos and, perhaps, even the ancestors of the Lipan Apaches. What the Spanish colonial settlers and missionaries introduced was the application of Spanish technologies—plowing, *acequia* irrigation, and new varieties of the staple. Even in the advanced state of decay in which Hispanic agriculture found itself following the hostilities of the 1830s, Thomas W. Bell, a Texas army recruit could recognize that "the country around this place or rather immediately in the valley of the San Antonio river has been in a high state of cultivation . . . . By ditches from the river the whole valley has been irrigated and thus entirely obviate the necessity of rain in the cultivation of the soil."[5]

The importance of corn to both the Anglo-American population and the Tejanos cannot be overstated. Boiled ears of corn and mush kept many a family from starving on both the Anglo-American and Mexican frontiers. In the *Texas Republic* William Hogan writes that "newly arrived pioneers always hastened to plant patches of corn, a grain distinctly adapted to its role as a fundamental factor in the conquest of the wilderness." Yet Hogan does not draw the connection between Tejanos and Anglos with regard to this fundamental aspect of frontier life. For both Mexican and Anglo-American frontier farmers, corn was the first crop in the ground, and its hardiness, versatility, and quick consumability made it much more popular than wheat. An 1840 immigrants' guide to Texas reported that

> At present but little else than corn and rye, and very little of the latter grain, are cultivated in any part of the country. This crop gives bread to the family, fattens their pork, feeds their working horses and oxen, and furnishes corn blades, usually called fodder, which serve here all the purposes of hay in the northern states. Thus this one single article, comprises nearly all the products of field husbandry throughout the republic.

As a matter of fact, from Spanish-colonial times until the last days of the Republic wheat remained an imported luxury.[6]

If the Republic-era Tejana used a *metate* and *mano* while the Anglo-American frontierswoman used an Armstrong mill, the result was the same, a coarse meal that could be used in numerous ways. In the absence of American grinding tools, some Anglo women adopted Mexican methods, as Mrs. Dilue Harris reminisced: "Mrs. Roark had a Mexican utensil for grinding corn, called a *metate*. It was a large rock which had a place scooped out of the center that would hold a peck of corn. It had a stone roller. It was hard work to grind corn on it, but the meal made good bread." The *tortilla* may have had its counterpart in cornbread, but the *tamale* stood alone as the one Mexican item that appears to have won universal approval (other than silver) from Anglo Americans otherwise quick to disparage everything Hispanic. J. C. Duval gave an unqualified endorsement: "I have often 'worried them down' . . . without being fatigued, and I can recommend them as an excellent dish." So did Capt. W. S. Henry, US Army, who had the opportunity to try tamales while in Corpus Christi in August 1845. "This afternoon, at Mrs. B.'s, I ate a Mexican preparation called *themales*. It is made of corn-meal, chopped meat, and Cayenne pepper, nicely wrapped in a piece of corn-husk, and boiled. I know of nothing more palatable."[7]

Livestock provided food, clothing, transportation, and entertainment not only for Tejanos, but Indians and Anglos as well. From an early date Texas acquired a reputation as prime ranching country, and Tejanos as natural pastoralists. Hogan, however, finds almost nothing to say about Tejanos and ranching. Yet with only minimal editing William Bollaert's description of Tejano *vaqueros* in 1843 could easily be applied to later cowboys: "*Rancheros*, . . . [are] a rude uncultivated race of beings, who pass the greater part of their lives in the saddle, . . . Unused to comfort, and regardless alike of ease and danger, they have a hardy, brigand sun-burnt appearance, especially when seen with a slouched hat, leather hunting shirt, leggings and Indian moccasins, armed with a large knife, musket, or rifle, and sometimes pistols." Somewhat later, Frederick Law Olmstead, who was quite condescending in his remarks about Tejanos, described them as "excellent drovers and shepherds." The anonymous informant of *Texas in 1837* asserted that the landscape drew people and livestock together. "Almost all of them have given their attention to the growth of stock and have bestowed no more labor upon agriculture than was necessary to supply their own limited wants." A decade later an old Texas settler put it more bluntly, commenting, "The most profitable business which a person can follow in this country is stock-raising; especially if he has but a small force."[8] No wonder that the oft-described "indolent" Tejanos had been practicing stock raising as their principal profit-making business for generations.

Tejanos, moreover, had learned to make as much use of cattle as Comanches did of buffalo. One Anglo American observer was struck by the variety of uses to which Tejanos subjected rawhide.

> Some say Texas is made of rawhides & Spanish horses. Bless me, they apply rawhides to more uses than we can conceive of. Rawhides constitute the carpets, chairbottoms, cots, beds, shelves, partitions, wagon beds, packs, withers, ropes, saddle-trumpery in part, and numberless other contrivances of

the Mexicans. The lariat for noosing wilde horses, or stacking [sic] horses out to grass, is braided rope of rawhide strands.

He might well have added that Tejanos made soap and candles from the tallow and jerky from the dried beef, just as did Anglo-American frontier folk. Yet, Tejanos did draw the line at certain uses, as the French visitor Auguste Frétellière remarked in 1843: "sweetbreads, calves' flesh and head not being appreciated by the Mexicans, they gave them to us for nothing."[9]

The first commercial cattle drives from Texas took place by the early 1770s. From that time forward, what little export earnings, legal and illegal, Tejanos experienced came from the livestock trade. Cattle drives to Coahuila, while legal, were not as lucrative as drives to Louisiana, where the booming frontier market created a steady demand. Picking up on Tejano tradition, Texan stockmen continued to take their herds into Louisiana, more often than not breaking the same kinds of laws which had been passed in colonial Texas for similar reasons. "Before the Revolution," one contemporary observed, "the Texian found a market for his cattle at New Orleans, where they were driven in large droves, and at the island of. . . . Cuba. . . . Cattle are still driven across the Sabine, notwithstanding the great exertions of the authorities to prevent it."[10]

One of the more careful and observant visitors to the western frontier, a German by the name of W. Steinert, distinguished among various classes of horse and mule stock. American and "Spanish" horses were the best and most valuable, costing $100 or more. More common was the "Mexican" horse, "which is very hardy and makes out on ordinary feed," and which could be had for between $10 and $30. Below this was the mustang, to which the author of *Texas in 1840* referred. "The mustangs cannot be used much because they rarely become entirely tame. You can buy them for five to ten dollars, but as a rule they run off if they have not been thoroughly tamed. Catching and taming them is breakneck work, and it is performed mostly by Mexicans."

As for mules, the American variety cost between $70 and $100, while Mexican mules went for no more than $60, and could "also be bought very cheaply from the Indians." Thomas Bell lamented that the Indians made the horse–mule trade unacceptably risky, for "it would be a fine business to bring fine horses here and sell them and then take a drove of mules back to the states of Miss. & La. Mules can be bought low from the Mexicans about San Antonio and the rivers west of this."[11]

Not surprisingly, Tejanos and Texans shared the concept of utility in their fashions. Once again, the frontier environment intruded into the choices people made. That the results could be strikingly dissimilar in outward appearance has obscured the underlying similarity of function. In the absence of an efficient commercial network and a stable and sufficient money supply, people made do with few garments and created their own fashion trends. Hogan makes clear that homespuns, home-tanned, and home-sewn were the order of the day for most people in the Republic era. Furthermore, a considerable number of people went barefoot or made use of home constructed shoes.[12]

Aside from the "style," there was little to distinguish the Anglo Texan from the Tejano. As a matter of fact, from the Mexican perspective, Tejanos had already abandoned their cultural heritage in this regard. Two members of the Gen. Manuel de Mier y Terán's boundary commission to Texas in 1828 found Tejanos to have come under foreign influence in their customs. Jean Louis Berlandier, the expedition botanist, noted that "In their gatherings, the women prefer to dress in the fashion of Louisiana, and by so doing they participate both in the customs of the neighboring nation and of their own." The commission's artist, Lieutenant José María Sánchez, was even more critical of Nacogdoches Tejanos: "Accustomed to continuous commerce with the North Americans, they have imitated their customs, and so it may truthfully be said that they are Mexican only by birth, for even the Castilian language they speak with considerable ignorance." In 1846, William McClintock also noted that among Béxar women fashion seemed to favor that of the States: "the dress is purely American in style and material, some times rich and costly, but always plain and simple, white being the color most worn by both sexes."[13]

Women's dress got no simpler than when they went about their daily chores. Climate and custom conspired to create situations of which some observers could not fail but take inspirational note. The hot work of preparing tortillas, from the grinding of corn on metates to cooking the flat cakes on the round clay or iron griddles known as *comales*, often made comfort and modesty incompatible. So did doing the wash. Robert Brahan, who arrived in the San Antonio area in the 1850s, was pleasantly confronted by the way Tejanas went about that particular chore. "Our washing days fri. & saturday," he commented, "hundreds of Mexican females (styled Greasers) can be seen in the stream up to their knees scrubbing away with only one light garment on, without sleeves, low on the breast & very short."[14]

Certainly men's apparel was more typically Mexican, at least in the vicinity of San Antonio. As Bollaert's description of ranchero attire makes clear, however, field work demanded a style almost indistinguishable from Anglo-American frontier fashion. Typical evening wear included the short jacket, wide-brimmed hat, and colorful sash. Daily dress, at least for the laboring general population, was simple and functional. "The men mostly at this season dress in white, a crimson silk sash about the waist superseded the use of suspenders." William McClintock noted. "A linnen [sic] roundabout and sugar lofe hat complete their entire dress. When the weather is cool which is the case every few days, they throw a Mexican blanket of rich and varigated colors over the shoulders. These blankets are worth from fifty to seventy five dollars."[15]

Aside from tamales, the Mexican, or Saltillo, blanket seems to have left the most unequivocally positive impression on observers. Lt. George Mead of the United States Army, camped at Corpus Christi, noted the quality and colorfulness of the blankets. In her memoirs, Annie Harris recounted the impression left by a band of Karankawas returning the horses and goods taken from a group of Mexican traders they had assaulted near Matagorda: "the Indians presented a formidable array, riding into town on the gayly caparisoned horses of the Mexicans, made still more showy by the brilliantly colored Mexican blankets." Steinert complements the imagery, noting that the Mexicans "are excellent horsemen, and their saddles are often highly ornamented. While riding their horses they throw artistically woven blankets around their bodies in a becoming manner."[16]

Whether picket hut or *jacal*, the form and function of housing were similar—simple, labor saving, inexpensive, easy to abandon and rebuild. In the absence of sawmills, or money with which to purchase dressed lumber, early Tejanos continued to employ the building techniques of their Mesoamerican forebears. The *jacal* may have been crude, but it served its purpose well from the time of the earliest Spanish colonial settlement in the region until the end of the nineteenth century. John Leonard Riddell, passing through San Antonio in September 1839, found the population at work throwing up a new subdivision, most probably what became known as La Villita, and described the *jacal* quite elegantly.

> Four-fifths of the houses are thatched with a kind of reed, the cat tail flag (*Typha angustifolia*) it may be, but I think it is some kind of sedge or grass. Some are in progress of erection on the Alamo side of the river, and from them I gathered some idea of the Mexican mode of building. A trench is dug around in a square for about 1 foot deep for the foundation of the

walls. Timbers unhewn 4 to 6 inches in diameter, and as high as the house is designed to be, are set in this trench, side by side and on end, and bound together some 5 or 8 feet above the ground with thongs of raw hide. A few poles are attached by rawhide horizontally for supporting the roof, which is thatched with reeds. The inside is plastered with mortar, except over head and under foot. The naked ground serves universally for floor.

This common structure in which the poor lived could be found masquerading behind a clapboard façade in Houston about the same time. And, according to Hogan, the "picket huts" abounded among the Anglo-American settlers of central Texas during the first decades of settlement.[17]

Only when one went up the social ladder to the few prominent families that made up a threadbare elite in every frontier town could notice be taken of the divergence between Spanish-Mexican and Anglo-American forms. Construction in stone held the same symbolism for Tejanos as dressed-lumber construction held for Anglo Americans. Mary Maverick seems to have had no problem with the "Barrera place," a stone house at the northeast corner of Commerce and Soledad streets, which her husband bought in 1839 and which remained the family residence for a decade. Her description of the place is matter-of-fact and devoid of negative language. "The main house was of stone, she remembered, "and had three rooms . . . [and] a shed in the yard along the east wall of the house towards the north end."[18] Other Anglo families also moved into the better homes surrounding the plazas, for some time sharing the space with the descendants of the people who had built them.

While some of the Tejanos' architecture performed its function suitably for Anglo immigrants, it nevertheless remained distinct. The exotic nature of this more durable architecture was noted by many a traveler through San Antonio. According to J. C. Duval, "at that time there were but few Americans in the place, and as all the houses were built in the Spanish or Morisco style, it presented a novel appearance to us." A different Old World comparison was made by J. W. Benedict, who also visited Béxar in the late 1830s: "San Antonio de Bexar is a somber looking town," he observed. "The original town is built from hewn stone and from its antiquity presents a very Gothic appearance being built about a century since."[19]

Everyday life Republic-era San Antonio was also marked by the visible reminders of warfare. Travelers commented on the evidence that San Antonio continued to be a hostile frontier, a boundary between contending forces—Indian, Mexican, and Anglo-American. Edward Stiff, author of an immigrant's guide, summed up the appearance of the town center thus: "every thing denotes a system of defence; the houses are built of stone, nearly all of only one story, with flat roofs, and a parapet or strong wall above the covering, which is pierced for fire arms as well as the walls below." Writing in a bit more detail, William Bollaert observed, "San Antonio has been the theatre of so many revolutionary scenes and skirmishes, that not a house has escaped the evidences of strife. The walls and houses on all sides are perforated by balls, and even the steeple of the church bears evidence of rough usage from cannon shot."[20]

Gonzales and Harrisburg—burned to the ground during the war for independence—experienced brief moments of tragedy compared with San Antonio. As the gateway between the interior of Texas and Mexico, it had been invaded numerous times and almost constantly harassed by Indian raiders. John Holland Jenkins, reflecting in his memoirs on an 1842 visit to Béxar, was somewhat more poetic: "What a city of devastation and bloodshed has San Antonio been! Whatever trouble ever visited Texas, this little town seemed to be heart and center of her suffering, so that she has been well-termed as a 'Slaughter Pen.'"[21]

Aside from the destruction occasioned by warfare, both to the built environment and the human population, Texans were exposed to continuous violence from other quarters. Considering the abundance of evidence, and the influence that Indian hostilities had on westward settlement, there is scant attention paid to the subject in Hogan's *The Texas Republic*. Hogan spends more time on violence within white society, having almost nothing to say about Tejanos and violence. He makes it clear that the law in Texas was often taken into private hands. "Texans commonly settled differences by personal encounters," Hogan contends. Juries, when they were employed, seemed partial to pleas of self-defense and extenuating circumstances. The German visitor Steinert sums it up well: "In your dealings with Texans of American extraction you must be very careful not to provoke them. Your reward might be a bullet in your head, and nobody would take any notice of it."[22]

Indian hostilities constituted the single most important factor in the development of Texas until the 1870s. From its permanent settlement in the early eighteenth century, Spanish Texas was a magnet for Lipan Apaches, Comanches, and other Plains peoples who, rather than breed their own horse stock, participated in elaborate round-robin forays of expropriations. One Indian group took from the Spanish, and promptly lost their equine booty to a second group, which would then ride into a Spanish settlement to barter the animals back to the frontiersmen for trade goods. One episode described by John Riddell in 1839 was an all too familiar part of everyday life to Tejanos. "The daring Comanches then were and now are known to be prowling in the neighborhood," Riddle commented. "Two nights previous . . . they murdered a man on the same road and took his wife and two horses off as booty." Matters had not improved four years later, according to John A. King, who reported that "the Indians & perhaps some white men steal horses on all occasions."[23]

Despite numerous references to the superiority of Anglos to Mexicans and Indians, the former group was not immune from the same kinds of losses experienced by the Tejanos. Mary Maverick's brief account of her family's efforts to farm in the area just north of the Alamo is instructive. "This year our negro men plowed and planted one labor above the Alamo and were attacked by Indians. Griffin and Wiley ran into the river and saved themselves. The Indians cut the traces and took off the work animals and we did not farm there again." The following passage from J. W. Benedict's journal of a campaign against the Comanches west of San Antonio makes clear that despite the vaunted Indian-fighting skills of the Anglo Americans, they were often victimized by the lords of the Plains just like Tejanos. "Our first night of encampment here we had three horses stolen by the Indians," Benedict lamented. "The horses were all tied or staked within the Guard but from the stealthiness of the Indians and the darkness of the night they succeeded in taking three horses and escaping with them about 2 hours before daybreak[.] I myself being on the guard at the time they were taken."[24]

Consistent with the marginal inclusion of Tejanos in regard to general violence in the rest of his text, Hogan presents them only in passing as victims of a gang of rustlers known as the "Band of Brothers." Yet Tejanos were affected by the lawlessness endemic to the Republic. Prince Carl of Solms-Braunfels, who was in Texas in the mid-1840s, noted that homicides were common in the Republic. He singled out the relationship of Tejanos to violence, not as perpetrators, but rather as its victims. "Burglary and violent theft are rare occurrences and happen mostly to the unfortunate Mexicans, and then they are always connected with murder."[25]

That Tejanos became subject to bullying at the hands of Texans during this period of time is clear from other sources as well. A visitor to San Antonio in 1837 described his arrival with some friends at a dance as initially tense. He remembered, "Our presence exited [sic] no agreeable sensations, as great prejudice usually prevails in the minds of the Mexicans against all Americans. It is a matter of no surprise that such is the case, as the appearance of such persons is the signal for riots and disturbances. It has happened that strangers form themselves into a company and, entering such assemblies, put the male part to flight and take possession of the house."[26] All of this is not to say that Tejanos were not violent, only that it was not as obvious as among Texians.

A rough and dangerous frontier life could hardly be expected to be the medium in which "high" culture would develop. As in other aspects of life, a great deal of similarity can be found in the pastime pursuits of Tejanos and Texians. Hogan writes that "Dancing and horse racing were among the most common amusements." And, as for games of chance: "A fever for gambling ran in the blood of the age. It was a chronic social ailment in the South and reached even higher virulence in Texas." He also mentions that theater was popular wherever the resources made it possible. Yet, as in most other areas of life during the Republic, he has little to say about Tejano pursuits in this regard. In fact, his only comment regarding Tejanos and amusements is almost an aside: "In the period of the Republic, most of the small Texas towns, including the few predominantly Spanish, had race courses."[27]

Tejanos had as rich a social life as Texans, however. Their vices were the same, and their entertainments were similar in form and often in function. Perhaps it was the town-centered living pattern of Tejanos that appeared to Anglo observers to indicate a more desultory and dissolute way of life. Anglo Americans often became converted to the new ways they discovered among the Tejanos, however, which suggests that Mexican behavior may not have been as strange as some of the writings might indicate.

The daily siesta and regular bathing were features of Tejano life that, according to some writers, symbolized the population's "unconcerned indolence and ease." William Bollaert made quick work of the Tejano's work-day, stressing the portion of leisure over strenuous activities among Béxar's town population. "Early in the morning they go to mass, work a little on the *labores*, dine, sleep the *siesta*, and in the evening amuse themselves with tinkling the guitar to their *dulcinea*, gaming, or dancing," he scorned. J. W. Benedict did not even give Tejanos the credit of working in the morning: "People here are very Indolent[,] scarcely any person stirring in fore part of the day."[28]

In the Tejano's way of life, however, "loafing," seemed to some to be a good adaptation to the environment. W. Steinert, the meticulous German observer, had the following advice for would-be settlers: "you should never ride horseback during the noon hours; from eleven to three o'clock you should look for a shady place." Mary Maverick's memoirs make equally clear that the Tejanos' behavior was rational. "During this summer [1841], the American ladies led a lazy life of ease.... We fell into the fashion of the climate, dined at twelve, then followed a siesta, until three, when we took a cup of coffee and a bath." And some Anglo observers seem to have quickly accepted this particular daily ritual: "From early evening until the soft hour of twilight the inhabitants flock to the river to bathe," William Bollaert noted, "and then the bronze-like forms of southern nymphs may be seen joyfully gamboling in the limpid stream, with their arch looks and their dark hair floating over their shoulders."[29]

After the bath, dances and gambling were the norm. Superficially, these events proved for Anglos the indolence of the Tejano population. Immediately following his description of the lazy characteristics of Tejanos, for example, the unnamed traveler who visited San Antonio in 1837 commented, "The evening is spent by a large portion of the population at the fandango, a kind of Spanish waltz. There are seldom less than three or four of this description of dances during the night in different portions of the city."[30] Frétellière has left us one of the better descriptions of such an occasion.

> The sound of the violin drew us to the spot where the *fête* was in full swing. It was in a rather large room of an adobe house, earthen floored, lighted by six-tallow candles placed at equal distances from each other. At the back a great chimney in which a fire of dry wood served to reheat the *café*, the *tamales* and *enchiladas*: opposite, some planks resting on frames and covered with a cloth, formed a table on which cups and saucers were set out. ... At the upper end of the room, seated on a chair which had been placed on an empty box, was the musician, which was a violin.... The airs, for the most part Mexican, were new to me. The women were seated on benches placed on each side of the room.... The dance which I liked best was called the quadrille. It is a waltz in four-time with a step crossed on [e]very slow measure.... When the quadrille is finished, the cavalier accompanies his partner to the buffet, where they are served a cup of coffee and cakes. Then he conducts the young lady to her mother or to her chaperon to whom the girl delivers the cakes that she has taken care to reap at the buffet. The mother puts them in her handkerchief, and if the girl is pretty and has not missed a quadrille, the mama carries away an assortment of cakes to last the family more than a week.[31]

Fandangos were typically associated with gambling, a pastime which seems to have captivated the attention of all manner of people. William Kennedy described games of chance as "one of the prominent vices of the South." He went on to add that "among all ranks and classes in Mexico, the mania for gambling ruinously prevails." A decade later William McClintock made similar observations. Gamblers had by then descended on San Antonio in order to profit off the United States Army personnel stationed there, and "day and night, with unremitting zeal and application they ply their infamous trade." Apparently, the Mexican population was also consumed in this gaming frenzy. So much so, McClintock added, that "I yesterday saw, (and the like may be seen on any Sabbath) many Mexicans leave chapel even before mass was concluded, and repair to the gaming table; where they spent the remainder of the day, and perhaps the whole night." To this sin may be added the sacrilege observed sometime earlier by another traveler. "So strong is this passion," this outsider commented, "that even the priests sometimes forget their sacred office and are seen dealing monte, the favorite game of the Mexicans."[32]

Other forms of entertainment, some familiar to the Anglo Americans, were also evident among the Tejanos. In these activities at least some Anglos perceived a kind of cultural resistance on the Tejanos' part. William Bollaert asserted that "although San Antonio is governed by Texan laws, Mexican customs prevail; rope dancing, tumbling, and plays on Sunday." He described one performance of "maromeros" he witnessed:

> The company consisted of a comical Payaso, or clown, three young men and one female. The performance was *al fresco* in the court yard of a house in a public square. At the foot of the tight rope was made two large fires, this being the only illumination for actors and audience. The rope dancing over, tumbling commenced, this being finished, upon a rude stage, a comedy and two farces followed, the three pieces occupying about twenty minutes. I cannot speak favourably of the polite composition of the dramas represented; it was indeed very *low comedy*.[33]

In the mid-1850s Anglo-American and Mexican cultures were still coexisting. Frederick Law Olmstead noted critically that a not very good theater company provided tragedies to the local American population, while Tejanos enjoyed an amusement of a different order. "There is a permanent company of Mexican mountebanks," Olmstead observed, "who give performances of agility and buffoonery two or three times a week, parading, before night, in their spangled tights with drum and trombone through the principal streets."[34]

Horse racing was one activity that Anglos, Indians, and Tejanos shared in common. Although Mexican frontier horse racing differed in form from the Anglo-American pastime, it served similar functions. Races meant opportunities for social interactions, for showing off of personal skills and mastery of good horse flesh, and for gambling. J. C. Duval's description of a meet in San Antonio around 1840 may in part be a fanciful old-age reminiscence, but it is an example of the ameliorative powers of such events.

> It was indeed a strange and novel scene that presented itself to our view. Drawn up in line on one side of the arena, and sitting like statues upon their horses, were the Comanche warriors, decked out in their savage finery of paints, feathers and beads, and looking with Indian stoicism upon all that was going on around them. Opposite to them, drawn up in single file also, were their old enemies upon many a bloody field, the Texas Rangers, and a few Mexican rancheros, dressed in their steeple crown, broad brim sombreros, showy scarfs and "slashed" trowsers, holding gracefully in check, the fiery mustangs on which they were mounted.[35]

The competition itself consisted of various skill events, including picking up objects on the ground, target practice while riding at a full gallop, and breaking in wild horses. In other words, the spectators were witnessing a kind of proto-rodeo, complete with exotic costumes, Indians, vaqueros, trick riders, and bronco busters.

Secular and religious events of various kinds are used by people, consciously and subconsciously, to celebrate their common bonds. The calendar of holidays in early Texas was somewhat fuller than Hogan described. Although he mentions the anniversaries of the battle of San Jacinto, the Texas declaration of independence, the Fourth of July, and Christmas as those holidays generally celebrated, he neglects commemorations important to Tejanos.[36] Yet, in the 1840s Mexican Texans continued to celebrate feasts, some old and some recent, analogous to Anglo-American holidays.

In the early 1840s Tejanos still commemorated Mexican independence on September 16, according to Mary Maverick. As early as the 1820s, the celebration in San Antonio contained processions, speeches, Catholic Mass, and dancing—a ball for the town's prominent families and dances for general population. At La Bahía the event's symbolism was so obvious that it could not escape comment by Mrs. Teal.

> It was Independence Day of the Indians of Mexico and was being celebrated on the 16th of September, 1832. Inside a gaily decorated carriage sat a little Indian girl, dressed in all the splendor of Indian royalty; long lines of white ribbons were fastened to the carriage and held by twelve elegantly dressed Spanish ladies who walked on either side, while the carriage was pushed forward by officers of high rank, and soldiers marched in front.[37]

Tejanos also continued to commemorate the feast of Our Lady of Guadalupe, a holiday that since colonial days had marked the beginning of the Christmas season. Mary Maverick's description of the event in the early 1840s suggests that Tejano society continued to demonstrate internal cohesion, despite the Anglicizing forces at work. After a "grand" procession through the streets on December 12, "the more prominent families taking the Patroness along with them adjourned to Mr. José Flores' house on the west side of Military Plaza, where they danced most of the night . . . . It was all quite a novel and interesting scene to me." As a matter of fact, one of the problems encountered by the new European clergy, who took over the church in 1840, probably resulted from the continued devotion to Guadalupe. According to William Bollaert, "the Sacristan or vestry clerk was polite and communicative; he told me they were in a "difficulty," not knowing exactly to whom the church was dedicated, San Fernando, or Our Lady of Guadalupe, or San Antonio." There is other evidence that San Fernando church remained Mexican in practice to the end of the Republic, for instance William McClintock's comment that "there has been a few pews erected in the chapel, I suppose for the convenience and comfort of American citizens. But the Mexicans seat themselves on the floor."[38]

The public and communal character of Catholicism was certainly lost on most writers, even those who avoided calling the Tejanos' faith superstition. J. C. Duval, who escaped the execution of Fannin's force at Goliad, claimed that it would have been "very easy" for him to have "passed" for Catholic, as "Catholicism (at least among the lower class of Mexicans) consists mainly in knowing how to make the sign of the cross, together with unbound reverence first, for the Virgin Mary, and secondly for the saints generally—and the priests." The somewhat harsher terms of an 1837 informant nonetheless convey the same sense of public religiosity: "every Mexican professes to be a Catholic and carries about his person the crucifix, the rosary, and other symbols of the mother church. But religion with him, if one is permitted to judge of the feelings of the heart by outward signs, is more a habit than a principle or feeling."³⁹

Minor religious holidays, such as St. John's and St. James's feasts, often proved perplexing to observers. Steinert could do little but describe in bewilderment one such celebration. "Yesterday [August 1, 1849] the local Mexicans celebrated Saint Peter's day, and none of them worked," he puzzled. "The ladies wore white dresses. In the afternoon the young people of both sexes dashed through the streets on horseback and yelled. Mud splashed up to their ears, and the muddier they became the better. I was not able to find out what sense there was to all these doings."⁴⁰

Not all reactions to Tejano Catholicism were negative. John Brown, on moving his family to San Antonio in the early 1830s, had his children baptized. His son reminisced that "as a child I accepted the faith most cheerfully," until his Presbyterian grandmother "took me in hand and taught me to love the scriptures." The ceremonial and celebratory character actually became an attraction for Anglo Americans. Nacogdoches businessman Adolphus Sterne, on business in Austin at the end of 1841, commented in his diary "all hands gone to San Antonio to Spend Christmas." And, for Irish immigrants, the Tejano variant on their own faith seemed not at all strange, as Mrs. Teal's reminiscence of a wedding at La Bahía shows. "After the ceremony the Mexicans fired a salute of ten guns," she recalled. "The marriage services were concluded by a Mexican priest, before daylight, at the church in La Bahia."⁴¹

Everyday life in Republic-era Texas was rough and violent. For Tejanos, it was marked by uncertainty about the future and a great deal of disconnectedness from the past. The rapid improvement of the country largely bypassed them. Still, evidence exists that Mexican Texans did not necessarily view their position in society as inferior; nor did antagonism color all relations with Anglo Texans. Among the many negative depictions of Tejanos as a group, sympathetic comments appear. Mrs. Teal reminisced that in the Refugio County area southeast of San Antonio, the settlers, "surrounded by Mexicans and Indians, . . . learned to fear neither, as they were never harmed during all the long years they lived among them." Auguste Frételière, a Frenchman and friend of the artist Gentilz, was very positive about getting to know the Tejano population of San Antonio. He noted approvingly, "My mentor spoke Spanish very well, so I made rapid progress and in a little while I understood much better the Mexican character which pleased me infinitely—they were very polite, always gay and very obliging."⁴²

At the same time, Texans, in regarding Tejanos as "Mexicans," that is foreigners, were in the process of dissolving that uneasy partnership that had been created during the Mexican era. Promises that the laws would be published in Spanish went unfulfilled. Manipulation of the legal system led to land loss. Association with the enemy—Mexico and Indians—licensed indiscriminate violence against them. Identification with Catholicism made them the enemies of progress and enlightened thinking.

The history of Texan-Tejano relations in the second half of the nineteenth century is one of increasing intolerance and segregation. Even as they accepted words into their vocabulary, livestock practices and equipment into their economy, legal principles into their system of law, and a number of dishes into their cuisines, Anglo Texans increasingly excluded the Tejanos themselves. Even so, as the work of a growing body of scholars of Mexican Texans makes clear, Tejanos managed to retain much of the culture they inherited from "early Texas," and continued to participate in Texas society, whether or not that participation was fully recognized and appreciated.

NOTES

1. In this essay, the geographic extent of Texas is defined according to colonial (1716–1821) and Mexican era (1821–36) boundaries, which coincide with that area over which the Republic exercised effective control. The historiography of Texas is extensive. The following works are listed as examples of the most recent scholarship in their particular fields, which form a good starting place for study of early Texas history. A historiographical essay covering early Texas' place in relation to United States history is Gerald E. Poyo and Gilberto M. Hinojosa, "Spanish Texas and Borderlands Historiography in Transition: Implications for United States History," *Journal of American History* 75 (Sept. 1988), 393–416. The best narrative survey of Spanish-colonial Texas history is Donald Chipman, *Spanish Texas, 1519–1821* (Austin, 1992); the best monograph on socio-economic history during that period is Jesús F. de la Teja, *San Antonio de Béxar: A Community on New Spain's Northern Frontier* (Albuquerque, 1995); a recent study of Tejanos during the Mexican period (1821–35) is Andrés Tijerina, *Tejanos and Texas Under the Mexican Flag, 1821–1836* (College Station, 1994); the best single volume on the Indian peoples of Texas remains W. W. Newcomb Jr., *The Indians of Texas: From Prehistoric to Modern Times* (Austin, 1961); a thorough study of relations among the various Indian and European groups in the region during the eighteenth century, with significant coverage of Texas, is Elizabeth A. H. John, *Storms Brewed in Other Men's Worlds: The Confrontation of Indians, Spanish, and French in the Southwest, 1540–1795* (College Station, 1975). Also very useful for background information is *The New Handbook of Texas* (6 vols., Austin, 1996).

2. Joseph W. Schmitz, *Thus They Lived: Social Life in the Republic of Texas* (San Antonio, 1935), 1; William Ransom Hogan, *The Texas Republic: A Social and Economic History* (1946; rep., Austin, 1969).

3. Arnoldo De León, *The Tejano Community, 1836–1900* (Albuquerque, 1982). In 1968 a brief note on society in Hispanic San Antonio by Caroline Remy, "Hispanic-Mexican San Antonio, 1836–1861," appeared in the *Southwestern Historical Quarterly* 71 (Apr. 1968), 564–83, including twelve pages of plates from period paintings.

4. Along with De León's work cited above, see David Montejano, *Anglos and Mexicans in the Making of Texas, 1836–1986* (Austin, 1987), for discussion of political and economic issues affecting the Tejano population. This study is grounded in an important body of sources on which Hogan also relied. Despite its remote location well into the nineteenth century, Texas got its share of travelers, immigrants, and artists who documented their adventures and observations. The men (and a few women) who wrote about Texas normally did so with their own prejudices in mind. There is in these writings, for instance, very little differentiation between "Mexicans" and Tejanos, except to point out that the latter were a particularly low subset of the former. Fortunately, many of these writers spent considerable time describing some of the basic elements of Tejano life: food, clothing, shelter, livelihood, and pastimes. On the breadth of traveler accounts see Marilyn McAdams Sibley, *Travelers in Texas, 1761–1860* (Austin, 1967). The question of Anglo-American prejudice toward Tejanos has been carefully, if controversially, studied by Arnoldo De León, *They Called Them Greasers: Anglo Attitudes toward Mexicans in Texas, 1821–1900* (Austin, 1983). An excellent brief essay covering the same issue on a borderlands-wide basis is David J. Weber, "'Scarce More than Apes': Historical Roots of Anglo-American Stereotypes of Mexicans in the Border Region," in *New Spain's Far Northern Frontier: Essays on Spain in the American West, 1540–1821*, ed. David J. Weber (Albuquerque, 1979), 293–307. A small number of artists also visited antebellum Texas and painted their impressions of the places, people, and wildlife of the region. Among these, Theodore Gentilz left the most extensive record of Tejano everyday life, and his renditions of these activities bear out the testimony of informants. The small number of his canvases included in this essay attest to this immigrant artist's sympathy for his new home on the Mexican-American frontier. The best survey of nineteenth-century Texas painting is Sam DeShong Ratcliffe, *Painting Texas History to 1900* (Austin, 1992). Also useful is Pauline A. Pinckney, *Painting in Texas: The Nineteenth Century* (Austin, 1967). On Gentilz see Dorothy Steinbomer Kendall and Carmen Perry, eds., *Gentilz: Artist of the Old Southwest* (Austin, 1974).

5. Thomas W. Bell to father, Mar. 31, 1842, quoted in "Thomas W. Bell Letters," Llerena Friend, ed., *Southwestern Historical Quarterly* 63 (Apr. 1960), 590. On Texas Indian agriculture see Newcomb, *The Indians of Texas*, 113–14, 238, 292–93; Spanish colonial agriculture is covered in De la Teja, *San Antonio de Béxar*, 75–96. A monographic study of the Texas missions as an economic system awaits publication. Two brief syntheses of missionary activities at San Antonio, including development of agricultural skills among the neophytes, are Gilberto M. Hinojosa, "The Religious-Indian Communities: The Goals of the Friars," in *Tejano Origins in Eighteenth-Century San Antonio*, ed. Gerald E. Poyo and Gilberto M. Hinojosa (Austin, 1991), 61–83, and Mardith K. Schuetz, "The Spanish Missions, Part II: The Mission Indians," in *San Antonio in the Eighteenth Century* (San Antonio, 1976), 35–46.

6. Hogan, *The Texas Republic*, 32–33, 36; A. B. Lawrence, *Texas in 1840, or the Emigrant's Guide to the New Republic*... (1840; rep., New York, 1973), 114; De la Teja, *San Antonio de Béxar*, 91, 93.

7. Dilue Harris, "Reminiscences of Mrs. Dilue Harris, I," *Southwestern Historical Quarterly* 4 (Oct. 1900), 109; J. C. Duval, *Early Times in Texas* (2 vols., Austin, 1892), II, 68; W. S. Henry, *Campaign Sketches of the War with Mexico* (New York, 1848), 27.

8. W. Eugene Hollon and Ruth Lapham Butler, eds., *William Bollaert's Texas* (Norman, 1956), quotation at 217 (this is a controversial work, the full authenticity of which has recently come into question); Frederick Law Olmstead, *A Journey Through Texas, Or, a Saddle-Trip on the Southwestern Frontier* (1857; rep., Austin, 1978), 162; Andrew Forest Muir, ed., *Texas in 1837: An Anonymous, Contemporary Narrative* (1958; rep., Austin, 1986), 120; W. B. Dewees, *Letters from an Early Settler of Texas* (1852; rep., Waco, 1968), 300; Hogan, *The Texas Republic*, 21. Unlike the subject of Tejano agriculture, which has received scant scholarly attention, early ranching continues to attract significant work. For a general explanation of ranching in the San Antonio River valley during the colonial era see De la Teja, *San Antonio de Béxar*, 97–117. Among the debates in the field is the extent and significance of Hispanic influences. See, e.g., Ray August, "Cowboys v.

Rancheros: The Origins of Western American Livestock Law," *Southwestern Historical Quarterly* 96 (Apr. 1993), 457–88; Jack Jackson, *Los Mesteños: Spanish Ranching in Texas, 1721–1821* (College Station, 1986); and Terry G. Jordan, *Trails to Texas: Southern Roots of Western Cattle Ranching* (Lincoln, 1981).

9. James O. Breeden, ed., *A Long Ride in Texas: The Explorations of John Leonard Riddell* (College Station, 1994), 55–56; Auguste Frételliére, "Adventures of a Castrovillian," in *Castro-Ville and Henry Castro, Empresario*, ed. Julia N. Waugh (San Antonio, 1934), 91.

10. Muir, ed., *Texas in 1837*, 67; Nettie Lee Benson, "Bishop Marín de Porras and Texas," *Southwestern Historical Quarterly* 51 (July 1947), 33.

11. Gilbert J. Jordan, trans. and ed., "W. Steinert's View of Texas in 1849," *Southwestern Historical Quarterly* 81 (July 1977), 46–47; Friend, ed."Thomas W. Bell Letters," 106.

12. Hogan, *The Texas Republic*, 45–47. Serious study of fashion in Spanish and Mexican Texas, as with most other aspects of material culture, has yet to be published. The one article on the subject for the republic era, Mary Reid, "Fashion of the Republic," *Southwestern Historical Quarterly* 45 (Jan. 1942), 244–54, does not contain a single reference to Mexican Texans. De León, *The Tejano Community* (133–34), devotes less than two pages on the subject.

13. Quoted in Jesús F. de la Teja and John Wheat, "Bexar: Profile of a Tejano Community, 1820–1832," *Southwestern Historical Quarterly* 89 (July 1985), 9; Mauricio Molina, ed., *Crónica de Tejas: Diario de viaje de la comisión de límites* (Mexico, 1988), 71 (author's translation); William A. McClintock, "Journal of a Trip Through Texas and Northern Mexico in 1846–1847," *Southwestern Historical Quarterly* 34 (Oct. 1930), 142.

14. Robert Weakley Brahan Jr., to John Donelson Coffee Jr., Jan. 20, 1855, in Aaron M. Boom, "Texas in the 1850's, As Viewed by a Recent Arrival." *Southwestern Historical Quarterly* 70 (Oct. 1966), 284.

15. McClintock, "Journal of a Trip," 143.

16. Ethel Mary Franklin, ed., "Memoirs of Mrs. Annie P. Harris," *Southwestern Historical Quarterly* 40 (Jan. 1937), 241; Jordan, "Steinert's View of Texas," 64. Saltillo blankets are a particular type of *serape* or *sarape*. A very brief history of the Saltillo variety, stressing technical aspects of its production, is Kathrin Colburn, "The Saltillo Serape: History and Conservation," *Hali: The International Magazine of Antique Carpet and Textile Art* 17 (Feb.–Mar. 1995), 80–87.

17. Breeden, ed., *A Long Ride in Texas*, 53–54; Hogan, *The Texas Republic*, 28, 30. Spanish colonial and Mexican architectural forms in Texas have received some attention in scholarly publications, although mostly with regard to the Rio Grande valley area of settlement, where a great deal of it survives. See Joe S. Graham, "The Jacal in South Texas: The Origins and Form of a Folk House," in *Hecho en Tejas: Texas-Mexican Folk arts and Crafts*, ed. Joe S. Graham (Denton, TX, 1991), 293–308; Joe C. Freeman, "Regional Architecture and Associated Crafts," in *A Shared Experience: The History, Architecture and Historic Designation of the Lower Rio Grande Heritage Corridor*, ed. Mario Sánchez (1992, 2d ed., Austin, 1994), 137–97; Willard B. Robinson, "Colonial Ranch Architecture in the Spanish-American Tradition," *Southwestern Historical Quarterly* 83 (Oct. 1979), 123–50. Charles Ramsdell and Carmen Perry, *San Antonio: A Historical and Pictorial Guide* (1959; 2d rev. ed., Austin, 1985), contains useful descriptions of the remaining Hispanic architectural heritage of San Antonio.

18. Rena Maverick Green, ed., *Samuel Maverick, Texan: 1803–1870* (San Antonio, 1952), 85.

19. Duval, *Early Times in Texas*, II, 64; J. W. Benedict, "Diary of a Campaign Against the Comanches," *Southwestern Historical Quarterly* 32 (April 1929), 304–305.

20. Edward Stiff, *The Texan Emigrant: Being a Narration of the Adventures of the Author in Texas . . .* (1840; rep., Waco, 1968), 29; Hollon and Butler, eds., *William Bollaert's Texas*, 219.

21. John Holmes Jenkins III, *Recollections of Early Texas: The Memoirs of John Holland Jenkins* (1958; rep. Austin, 1987), 95–96.

22. Hogan, *The Texas Republic*, 260; Jordan, trans. and ed., "Steinert's View of Texas," 62. Various aspects of violence directed at, or occasioned by, Tejanos are treated in Gerald E. Poyo, ed.,

Tejano Journey, 1770–1850 (Austin, 1996). The best of the recent studies on the Texas War of Independence, both of which give considerable attention to Tejano participation, are Stephen L. Hardin, *Texian Iliad: A Military History of the Texas Revolution* (Austin, 1994), and Paul D. Lack, *The Texas Revolutionary Experience: A Political and Social History, 1835–1836* (College Station, 1992).

23. Breeden, ed., *A Long Ride in Texas*, 55; John A. King to William A. Bell, Feb. 10, 1843, quoted in Friend, ed., "Thomas W. Bell Letters," 592.

24. Green, ed., *Samuel Maverick*, 87; Benedict, *Diary of a Campaign*, 305.

25. Carl, Prince of Solms-Braunfels, *Texas, 1844–1845* (Houston, 1936), 57.

26. Muir, ed., *Texas in 1837*, 105.

27. Hogan, *The Texas Republic*, 112, 128, 131. There are no published studies of colonial and Mexican-Texan folklore. A study of the customs and social practices of Mexican Americans in general is John O. West, comp. and ed., *Mexican-American Folklore: Legends, Songs, Festivals, Proverbs, Crafts, Tales of Saints, of Revolutionaries, and More* (Little Rock, 1988). The educational environment in Spanish and Mexican Texas is treated in Max Berger, "Education in Texas During the Spanish and Mexican Periods," *Southwestern Historical Quarterly* 51 (July 1947), 41–53.

28. Muir, ed., *Texas in 1837*, 105; Hollon and Butler, eds., *William Bollaert's Texas*, 218; Benedict, "Diary of a Campaign," 305.

29. Jordan, ed., "Steinert's View of Texas," 192; Green, ed., *Samuel Maverick*, 142; Hollon and Butler, eds., *William Bollaert's Texas*, 217.

30. Muir, ed., *Texas in 1837*, 104.

31. Frétellière, "Adventures of a Castrovillian," 93.

32. William Kennedy, *Texas: The Rise, Progress, and Prospects of the Republic of Texas*, (1925; rep., Clifton, NJ, 1974), 767; McClintock, "Journal of a Trip," 144; Muir, ed., *Texas in 1837*, 106.

33. Hollon and Butler, eds., *William Bollaert's Texas*, 230, 228.

34. Olmstead, *A Journey Through Texas*, 159.

35. Duval, *Early Times in Texas*, II, 70–71.

36. Hogan, *The Texas Republic*, 114–15. A recent study on the role of religion in Tejano efforts to preserve community in antebellum San Antonio is Timothy M. Matovina, *Tejano Religion and Ethnicity: San Antonio, 1821–1860* (Austin, 1995).

37. De la Teja and Wheat, "Bexar," 22; T. C. Allan, "Reminiscences of Mrs. Teal," *By the Way* (July 1897), 5.

38. Green, ed., *Samuel Maverick*, 136; Hollon and Butler, eds., *William Bollaert's Texas*, 224; McClintock, "Journal of a Trip," 147.

39. Duval, *Early Times in Texas*, 53; Muir, ed., *Texas in 1837*, 103.

40. Jordan, "Steinert's View of Texas," 401.

41. Jno. Duff Brown, "Reminiscences of Jno. Duff Brown," *Southwestern Historical Quarterly* 12 (Apr. 1900), 300; Archie P. McDonald, ed., *Hurrah for Texas: The Diary of Adolphus Sterne, 1838–1851* (Waco, 1969), 75; Allan, "Reminiscences of Mrs. Teal," 5. If Hogan is correct on this issue, even the habitual and public form of religion practiced by Tejanos made them more spiritual than the majority of Anglo Texans. According to him, "by the end of 1845 not more than one-eighth of the white population were either active or nominal members of Texas churches." Hogan, *The Republic of Texas*, 194.

42. "Reminiscences of Mrs. Teal," 4; Frétellière, "Adventures of a Castrovillian," 92.

Theodore Gentilz, *La Purísima Concepción de Acuña*. The area around San Antonio saw devastating military actions beginning in the spring of 1813. By the time of the Texas Revolution, the missions had become ruins that visitors to the area often commented resembled ancient European castles. Following the battle of Rosillo on March 29, 1813, the Republican Army of the North took up headquarters at Mission Concepción, much of the compound of which was already in ruins. Courtesy of Daughters of the Republic of Texas Library, San Antonio, Texas.

9

Rebellion on the Frontier*

In January, 1811, at the height of Mexico's insurrection against Spanish colonial rule, a retired military officer from Nuevo Santander living in San Antonio organized the overthrow of provincial authorities. The insurrection quickly removed the governor and other Spanish officials in the province. Dissension and unclear goals among rebel leaders, however, resulted in a counterrevolt in early March. Eighteen months later, between August 1812, and April 1813, the province succumbed again, this time to an invading force of Mexican rebels and Anglo-American filibusters. A royal army, more successful in controlling Texas than the earlier rebels had been, defeated the insurrectionists that summer in a pitched battle.

These events were significant politically and economically, yet the reasons why Béxar residents (Bexareños) teetered between loyalty and disloyalty remain unclear. Some historians have suggested that Tejanos opposed Spanish authority because they believed in the Enlightenment ideals of the day, especially as represented by the United States. Others have viewed rebelliousness in Texas as a result of Spain's inability to promote growth in the province.[1] Recent research on the Mexican independence movement suggests that such explanations are too limited and that clues to Béxar's role should be sought in the complex political, economic, and socioeconomic realities affecting the province as a result of changing circumstances at the beginning of the nineteenth century.[2]

FROM AUTONOMY TO A CROSSROADS PROVINCE

Early nineteenth-century San Antonio de Béxar was a quite different place from what it had been throughout the eighteenth century. From its founding as a military buffer in 1718 to Louisiana's retrocession to France in 1800, Béxar had developed according to the vagaries of Spanish impe-

---

*First published in *Tejano Journey, 1770–1850*, edited by Gerald E. Poyo (Austin: University of Texas Press, 1996).

rial policy. At San Antonio, military settlers mixed with a small group of Canary Island immigrants to produce a population that by the end of the century had clearly established a regional identity.³ As residents of the only chartered civilian settlement in Texas, and enjoying numerical predominance over La Bahía and Nacogdoches, Bexareños came to see their community as representing Texas itself.

Béxar's eighteenth-century economy was simple and limited. Local agriculture was sufficient to provide subsistence to the population and meet the demands of Béxar's and nearby La Bahía's (Goliad's) garrisons. Livestock, mostly wild cattle in the late 1700s and equine stock after the turn of the century, provided the only real, if limited, export earnings. San Antonio's most important economic institution was the presidio, which provided a market for local produce and services and was the settlement's largest employer. All Bexareños were poor by the standards of outsiders looking in, and by their own standards even the wealthiest were men of very limited means.⁴

Béxar was secure, if not entirely content, in its relative poverty and isolation. At least three native sons had successfully studied for the priesthood; another had attained the rank of presidial commander at Agua Verde, Coahuila; one other was a successful lawyer practicing before the Audiencia of Guadalajara. Most Bexareños of some means had small business dealings with neighboring provinces, and there were particularly close ties with the presidial settlement of Rio Grande as well as with Monclova and Saltillo. Some citizens made regular trips to Saltillo to attend the annual autumnal fair, where they sold or traded their cattle and a few other items in return for goods from the interior; others conducted commerce—illegally—with Louisiana. An occasional business trip to Mexico City and a steady stream of litigation over any number of issues were the most notable linkages to Central New Spain.⁵

The nineteenth century opened on an ominous note with Spain's transfer of Louisiana back to France followed by Napoleon's sale of the immense and vaguely defined region to the United States. Spanish concerns over American encroachments into New Spain, exemplified by Philip Nolan's mustanging expeditions, now turned into fear of an American invasion.⁶ What had been the undefended border between two Spanish provinces began to produce refugees who claimed a desire to remain subjects of his Catholic Majesty. As a result, royal policymakers ordered hundreds of troops—from fewer than 200 presidial troops in 1801 to a high of 1,368 in mid-1806—into Texas to protect what was now New Spain's border with the land-hungry United States.⁷

The largest long-term military reinforcement took place at Béxar, where the presence of such a large body of soldiers and their dependents not only swelled the town's population but strained its productive capacity. The troops stationed at San Antonio were for the most part outsiders brought to Texas after 1805 in response to US occupation of Louisiana. In addition to the garrison company of 104, composed chiefly of Bexareños, there were the 69 men of the Parras Company, who had been transferred to San Antonio permanently in 1803—a total of 173 troops who may be considered locals. There were, moreover, 50 soldiers from the Punta de Lampazos garrison, 254 militiamen from Nuevo Leon, and an equal number from Nuevo Santander, for a total of 558 temporarily stationed troops.[8]

THE MEXICAN WAR OF INDEPENDENCE

As if the border difficulties were not trouble enough, Texas was also affected by the increasing political turmoil in both Spain and New Spain.[9] Having participated in the French revolutionary and Napoleonic wars, as both an enemy and an ally of France, Spain faced a deepening economic crisis, which its rulers attempted to remedy by increasing colonial revenues. In 1804, a royal decree confiscated the assets of church charitable funds and placed them at the disposal of the Crown. The action, coming on top of the economic downturn caused by disruptions in overseas trade and bad harvests, created a financial crisis as the church was forced to call in mortgages and loans. As disaffection grew, royal authority suffered its most severe blow when, in 1808, Napoleon invaded Spain, forced Carlos IV to abdicate, and arrested the heir, Fernando. He placed his own brother, Joseph, on the Spanish throne.

Unwilling to accept a French-imposed king, the colonials also could not decide on a clear course of action. Majority sentiment among the *criollo* (white Spanish American) elites seems to have favored some sort of provisional government acting in the name of the legitimate king, Fernando VII. Not only peninsular Spaniards but most white elites in the Americas feared the consequences of involving the Indian and mixed-blood masses, which made up over 80 percent of the population, in any struggle for power. The peninsulars favored rule by the viceroy and Audiencia, the traditional royal authorities, while Mexico City's *criollo* leadership advocated a provisional council, or junta, to manage affairs until Fernando's restoration. When Viceroy José de Iturrigaray sided with the American elites, a force of peninsulars packed him off to Spain, arrested a number of local leaders, and named an aged Spanish field marshal, Pedro Garibay, viceroy.

While Mexico City entered into a period of uneasy calm in 1809, other parts of the viceroyalty became increasingly agitated. Continued disruptions in trade and poor crops in that year led to an economic slowdown and famine in 1810, particularly in the Bajío, the viceroyalty's leading mining center. It was in the area of Guanajuato, capital of the region, that a number of disgruntled *criollos*, hoping to wrest power from the peninsulars, determined to employ the Indian and mixed-blood peasantry in the effort. Among the conspirators was the parish priest of Dolores, a small agricultural town east of Guanajuato. Father Miguel Hidalgo y Costilla formally began the rebellion against "bad government" and Spaniards on the morning of September 16, 1810, from the steps of the parish church, after receiving news that the conspiracy had been exposed.

The early progress of the revolt, particularly the looting of Guanajuato, which was accompanied by the killing of large numbers of peninsulars and *criollos*, led these groups to close ranks behind the viceregal government. The able leadership of Viceroy Francisco Javier Venegas and Gen. Félix María Calleja (who succeeded Venegas as viceroy) soon had Hidalgo's Indian army on the run. In January 1811, Calleja defeated Hidalgo outside Guadalajara, forcing the rebel leadership to flee northward, where they were eventually captured in March. Leadership of the rebellion devolved on José María Morelos, a mestizo priest whose organizational and political skills far surpassed Hidalgo's. Still, Morelos was unable to convince *criollos* to support the insurrection, which now became a mestizo movement for independence. By November 1815, Morelos, too, had been captured, leaving only a handful of ill-equipped and undermanned guerrilla groups in the field.

THE TEXAS INSURRECTIONS, 1811–1813

From 1811 to 1813, the tensions and conflicts associated with the United States' westward movement and the Mexican War of Independence met in Texas and erupted in warfare. Aside from Anglo-American expansionist threats, foreign intrigue was in the air. As Spain succumbed to Napoleonic France, Spanish colonial officials were severely tested in trying to hold the empire together. French agents working to destabilize the colonies were soon joined by disgruntled colonials who began to conspire against Spain. Despite or because of its remote location, Texas did have something to offer the agents of change, a channel through which propaganda, money, arms, and, eventually, men could be introduced into New Spain from the United States. Correspondence between Cmdt. Gen. Nemecio Salcedo and the governors of Texas during this time shows mutual concern over the problem.[10]

As New Spain destabilized following Father Hidalgo's declaration of war on "bad government," Crown officials in the northern provinces prepared for the rebel onslaught. At the end of 1810, the royalist forces rebelled against the governor of Nuevo Santander after orders arrived that they were to be sent to San Luis Potosi to fight the insurgents. In early January 1811, as Governor Antonio Cordero of Coahuila arranged his seven hundred troops to meet an insurgent force of between seven thousand and eight thousand, his entire command mutinied and went over to the rebels. As insurgent forces were sent to Nuevo Leon, local officials there declared for Hidalgo.[11]

The news arriving in Béxar from the surrounding provinces in mid-January indicated the complete overthrow of royalist rule in the region. Governor Manuel Salcedo, who had previously received instructions to prepare a force to march against insurgents in the interior, called for calm and loyalty even as he ordered his troops to prepare for an expedition. Salcedo went so far as to call a meeting of Béxar's ecclesiastical, military, and civilian officials on January 18, 1811, to discuss the situation. The meeting did little to settle the situation, however, for on January 22, Juan Bautista de las Casas, a retired officer living in San Antonio, led a bloodless coup in which royalist officials were removed and all Spaniards arrested.[12] Rebel fortunes collapsed about as quickly as they emerged, however.

Dissatisfaction with Casas as governor combined with the continued loyalist leanings of many among Béxar's elite to produce a counterrevolutionary movement in February. The conspirators were led by Juan Manuel Zambrano, an ordained priest and native of Béxar whose family was among the wealthiest of the town. Working first among the most prominent citizens and then among disaffected military officers, he represented his movement to revolutionary leaders who had arrived in Béxar as wishing only the replacement of the incompetent Casas. Having gained the support of the troops, the counterrevolutionaries took an oath of loyalty to Ferdinand VII and appointed a governing junta of twelve in the early morning hours of March 2, 1811.[13]

The restoration in Texas succeeded because the insurgency was coming apart in the interior as well. Gen. Joaquín Arredondo successfully invaded Nuevo Santander and began its restoration. At Saltillo, Ignacio Allende removed Father Hidalgo from the rebellion's leadership and made plans for a retreat through Texas to the United States. Farther north, Governor Manuel Salcedo was liberated by a counterrevolutionary junta, which also convinced a retired lieutenant colonel and hacienda owner, Ignacio Elizondo, to lead loyalist forces. Taking control of Monclova, Elizondo learned of Allende's plans for the retreat to the United States and, on March 21, 1811, captured Allende, Hidalgo, and their insurgent chiefs. With the exception of pockets of resistance in Nuevo Santander, the northeastern provinces again came under the commandant general's orders.[14]

Not all insurrectionaries were disposed of, although Hidalgo, Allende, Casas, and numerous others lost their heads. One who managed to escape was Bernardo Gutiérrez de Lara. A native of Revilla, Nuevo Santander, who had early adopted Hidalgo's cause, he held a commission as revolutionary ambassador to the United States, where he met with Secretary of State James Monroe and President James Madison as well as French agents and other Spanish-American revolutionaries in late 1811 and early 1812. With limited support from the US government, Gutiérrez de Lara made his way back to the Texas border by way of New Orleans and Natchitoches, where he met Anglo Americans desirous of assisting Mexico in its struggle for liberty and others whose eyes may have looked no farther than liberating Texas for the United States. He had determined to recruit an army capable of taking Texas and revitalizing the rebellion.[15]

It was at Natchitoches, Louisiana, that Gutiérrez de Lara met Augustus Magee, a lieutenant in the US army who had acquired an interest in Mexican affairs. In June 1812, Magee resigned his army commission and went to work for Gutiérrez de Lara as recruiter for the Republican Army of the North. Samuel Davenport, erstwhile Indian agent of the Spanish Crown in Nacogdoches, became quartermaster. Preparations continued through the early summer and, in August 1812, Magee ordered the advance. One of the first victims of the invading force was Manuel Zambrano, who lost a shipment of wool he was taking to Louisiana. Confusion, rumors of an irrepressible force, and Davenport's assurances of good treatment resulted in the flight of those royalist troops who chose to remain loyal and the quick submission of Nacogdoches to the Republican Army of the North.

Magee and Gutiérrez reinforced their troops and sent propaganda to the other Texas settlements before taking their next step. At first they planned to head straight for Béxar, but reports of Salcedo's continued control of the town and the presence of only a small garrison at La Bahía led the Republican Army to redirect itself to the old presidio, which it occupied on November 7, 1812. When Salcedo and his military commander, Simón Herrera, marched their forces to La Bahía, the republicans found themselves under siege. When the governor refused to accept the invaders' requested terms for surrender—safety and pardons for all Texans who had embraced the republican cause and the withdrawal of the Republican Army from the province—the siege continued.

In spite of the early despair of the republicans, it was the royalists who were sapped of strength during the siege. After the pessimistic Magee died in early February, his place was taken by Samuel Kemper, who may have had a more optimistic outlook.[16] Skirmishes between the two forces routinely favored the invaders, whose equipment and munitions were in superior shape and of better quality than that of the royalists. Disheartened, suffering increasing desertions, and unable to prevent resupply of the presidio, Governor Salcedo lifted the siege in mid-February and retired with what remained of his army to Béxar. There, about thirteen miles southeast of Béxar, he dug in at Salado Creek to await the republican advance, which came on March 29, 1813. The Battle of Salado left a hundred royalists dead, their baggage and cannon captured, and the road to Béxar open. On April 2, 1813, the royalist government of Texas surrendered unconditionally to the Republican Army of the North.

Success proved illusory for the republicans as they fell out among themselves. They were also dissatisfied with the form of government established in a constitution written by Gutiérrez de Lara and Tejanos without input from the Anglo Americans. Furloughs granted to Kemper and other officers led to deteriorating morale and discipline, as did the arrival of new recruits whose loyalty was questionable. By the beginning of August, Tejanos and Anglo Americans had determined that the blame for the new republic's ills lay with Gutiérrez de Lara, who was forced to resign and leave Texas. His place was taken by José Alvarez de Toledo, a native of Cuba who had met Gutiérrez de Lara in the United States and shared an interest in liberating Mexico from Spain.

Toledo had little time to regroup. General Arredondo, who had successfully campaigned against insurgents in Nuevo Santander, mustered an army on the Rio Grande and marched on Béxar in early August. Toledo decided to meet the royalist army outside the town and marched his two divisions, one composed of Anglo Americans and the other of Mexicans and Indians, on the road to Laredo. On August 18, 1813, the two armies met southwest of the Medina River, and Arredondo, having outflanked Toledo, led the royalists to a decisive victory. The rout was such that Colonel Elizondo chased the remnants of the Republican Army beyond the Sabine, killed numerous rebels, and captured hundreds of men, women, and children.[16]

The royalist victory in Texas was complete. Despite the almost complete ruin of the province—Nacogdoches was virtually abandoned; Béxar and La Bahía were subject to constant Indian depredations; ranches were deserted and herds either destroyed or taken to safety in the interior—the royalist governors managed to retain control of the province and repulse or dissipate incursions by filibusters, revolutionaries, and French exiles. Independence came to Texas when it arrived for the rest of Mexico, with Iturbide's triumph under the Plan of Iguala in 1821.[17]

SOURCES OF DISAFFECTION

Events in Texas from 1811 through 1813 clearly indicate that disaffection with Spanish rule had existed in Texas at the time of Hidalgo's revolt in 1810. Crown authority, which had begun to increase some thirty years earlier, often conflicted with local interests and irritated some elements in Béxar. A few years prior to the Casas revolt, Governors Antonio Cordero and Manuel Salcedo had introduced local measures to regulate town life and reduce contraband.[18] While the governors attempted to keep Tejanos from trading illegally with Louisiana, however, Spanish officers remained deeply involved in contraband. In 1808, an anonymous informant told the viceroy that Commandant Herrera was involved in a profitable trade of Texas horses and mules for finished goods. The strength of Herrera's ties with the French were such, according to the informant, "that anyone wishing portraits of Napoleon and his field marshals should visit Herrera's own quarters where an assortment would be found."[19] Such contradictory behavior could not but have helped create resentment toward provincial officials.

Another and perhaps more irritating measure to the town's elite was Cordero's *ayuntamiento* (town council) reform. The six governors who held office between 1772 and 1808 all viewed the council as a strong-willed, uncooperative group of ill-qualified yokels. Needless to say, more than one governor called for the council's abolition or its reduction to manageable size from the six *regidores*, two *alcaldes*, and a *procurador* it had had since its founding. It was not until Cordero's administration, however, that a legal opinion was obtained allowing the governor to modify the council as he saw fit, and Cordero lost no time in reducing membership to two *alcaldes*, two *regidores*, and a *procurador*. Disturbed by the abridgment of local prerogatives, a group of town leaders sent a secret complaint against the action to the Audiencia.[20]

Some in Béxar resented the governor's increasing authority. While there is no evidence that Béxar was divided into distinct political factions, some members of the community's oldest elite families were perhaps the most hostile. Some Canary Islander descendants, particularly from the Travieso and Arocha families, who had traditionally exerted undue influence in local affairs, resented the governors and their activities. But it is also true that they were rebuffed by members of their own families who had established cordial relations with the governors. Another prominent family, the Menchacas, also included controversial members who played roles on both sides of the two uprisings that affected the town. The Zambranos also had their share of troublesome family members, particularly Manuel, who had been banished from the province after complaints by the citizenry. Nevertheless, he later served as a counterrevolutionary leader.[21] In general, the close-knit and isolated nature of Béxar society meant that most families were related and that rivalries often took place among kinfolk, albeit sometimes distant ones.

So while it is difficult to identify the branches of the specific families who were unhappy with Spanish rule, it seems they did exist, both at the political and the personal levels. Governor Salcedo, for example, found it necessary to warn the townspeople not to pay attention to the anti-Spanish rhetoric being spread by some.[22] And it is clear that at least some of those who acted against Spanish rule did so with great personal bitterness and a desire for vengeance. Indeed, one of the most cold-blooded acts of the period was the murder of Governor Salcedo, auxiliary-troop commander Simon Herrera, and a dozen other Spaniards taken prisoner in Béxar. According to Father Feliciano Francisco Vela and Guadalupe Caso, who escaped to the royalists with news:

> On the fourth of this month, Governor Manuel de Salcedo, Captain Arrambide, and all the other leaders and officers . . . were executed. They had their throats cut, their anguished requests for spiritual comfort denied. And, in order to perform this sacrifice, they were all stripped and Mr. Salcedo had his tongue taken out. They were all scalped and not permitted burial. That they might not be interred, Indians were left to guard that unfortunate place.[23]

According to one version, Salcedo and Herrera were condemned to death for having participated in Hidalgo's capture and for luring a local rebel, Capt. José Menchaca, to his death, but as the above account suggests, the execution was unduly violent. Another account argues that the Spaniards were executed by Béxar militia commander Antonio Delgado in revenge for the murders of his father and brother.[24] While the specific motivations cannot be confirmed, it is probable that the killings resulted from the combination of a private act of revenge and a general antagonism toward Spanish rule among a small group.

THE CAUTIOUS MAJORITY

It seems that considerable friction existed in Béxar between Spanish officials and local residents, but evidence does not support the idea that the town was a seething revolutionary center waiting to rise against Spain's rule. The thoughts and actions of the local population were cautious, complex, and aimed at preserving their interests.

While many actions of the governor and his officials had no doubt irritated and offended the residents of Béxar, most probably would not have sanctioned the actions against Salcedo and his officials. The reduction of the *cabildo's* size, for example, was unprecedented and outraged many, but by itself it probably did not foster revolutionary and separatist feelings.[25] Indeed, the citizens of Béxar had a long history of opposition to governors' actions and they usually sought relief by appealing to the courts. In most cases, they sought compromises that preserved local prerogatives.[26]

The contraband and corruption issues were also long-standing in the province. Tejanos had traded illegally with Louisiana since early in the eighteenth century, and Crown officials paid only lip service to fighting contraband. Some governors battled more efficiently than did others, and those who acted effectively usually alienated the local population; but most Bexareños found ways to sidestep Spanish officials.

A significant group in Béxar was unhappy with Spanish rule, but most Tejanos remained cautious and seemed reluctant to unconditionally throw in their lot with ill-defined revolutionary movements led by outsiders like Casas, Gutiérrez, and Toledo. These leaders, being unfamiliar to the local population, failed to inspire confidence in the residents and many, perhaps most, Bexareños watched developments closely and changed sides whenever necessary to protect themselves and their community.

The Casas revolt is illustrative. When Casas seconded Hidalgo's revolutionary call in Béxar, he rallied a small group of sympathizers, but they turned against him and deposed him when events suggested that the revolution was not likely to triumph.[27] Casas was not from Béxar, nor was he a long-standing (or influential) member of Béxar's social elite; thus, some may have suspected his interest in the matter. Indeed, the junta that removed Casas took great pains to regain favor with the Spanish authorities. In a communication dated April 28, 1811, the junta expressed its concern that the official government report on the capture of Hidalgo and the crushing of the revolt in Coahuila had not acknowledged the five hundred troops sent by Béxar in support of that goal. The same soldiers who had initially supported Casas willingly collaborated in putting down the Hidalgo revolt. The junta explained its about-face by saying that the military uprising had resulted from the hysteria occasioned by the continual arrival of distressing news from other provinces. Bexareños did not want to support lost causes but, rather, hoped to preserve and protect the town's interests.[28]

Even Gavino Delgado and Francisco Travieso, Casas's two primary civilian supporters named in testimony concerning the insurrection in Béxar, switched sides when the counterrevolt came along. Delgado not only became a member of the junta that deposed Casas, but also was praised for playing an important role in removing the rebel leader. Although Travieso remained under suspicion and was removed from the province after Governor Salcedo's return, he had been selected by the junta as senior alcalde immediately after Casas's overthrow.[29] Both men supported the insurrection when it seemed that victory against the Spanish might be possible, but quickly backed away when success seemed doubtful.

Events at La Bahía substantiate the view that Tejanos acted primarily to protect local interests in these increasingly difficult times. Lt. Luciano García remained loyal to the Crown and was forced to flee when Casas's emissaries arrived to take over the town. José Agabo de Ayala, who replaced García, cooperated with the insurgents but could not muster support from the settlement's prominent citizens. Father Miguel Martínez, presidial chaplain, Postmaster Bernardo Amado, and Manuel de la Concha, royal monopoly administrator, led a resistance against Casas that was coming to a head when the counterrevolt in San Antonio restored loyalists to power.[30]

Similar strategic considerations also influenced the actions of those who supported the Gutiérrez de Lara-led invasion of Texas in 1812–13. Two Bexareños caught bringing seditious material into San Antonio in the fall of 1812, for example, believed they were saving the town from destruction by preparing the citizenry for the filibusters' arrival.[31] An Anglo-American traveler at the time found "everything in confusion, every person alarmed for the security of his person and property. Officers spoke publicly against the Captain General [Don Nemecio]. The Indians had at that time killed fifty-four persons, had stolen 5,000 sheep and 10,000 head of horses and mules."[32] Such conditions created considerable fear that the Spanish forces in Béxar could not hope to protect the citizenry. Bexareños perhaps accepted the invaders out of fear rather than sympathy for their cause.

Military participation during the Gutiérrez-Magee episode rested on equally pragmatic grounds. At first, Governor Salcedo managed to maintain the loyalty of the local population. While there were numerous individual desertions, Salcedo's forces did not go over to the rebels en masse. In fact, Salcedo marched his army to La Bahía, where the Gutiérrez-Magee forces were encamped, and lay siege to the town for four months. The governor eventually retreated to Béxar and surrendered to the filibusters after the battle at Salado Creek.

The soldiery, with families to maintain, was confronted with the choice of becoming prisoners of war or joining the ranks of the Republican Army of the North.[33] It is not surprising, then, that the Republican Army found a contradictory ambiance upon entering San Antonio in April 1813. Though local citizens accepted their presence and often cooperated with them, they did not seem enthusiastic or particularly anxious to embrace the republicans.[34] It is quite possible that residents of Béxar saw the large presence of Anglo Americans as an indication of imminent US occupation, as had happened in Louisiana, and that preservation of property depended on cooperation with the new regime.

Similar attitudes played a role in the acceptance of the filibusters at Nacogdoches and La Bahía. When Capt. Bernardino Montero and Juan Manuel Zambrano attempted to retreat from Nacogdoches with the local militia, they were challenged by a militia captain who declared that they would not abandon their homes and families in the face of an invading force whose intentions were not known. At La Bahía the presidial company and citizenry spent the day before the Republican Army's arrival in chapel, hoping for some miracle. When the filibusters continued their approach, the soldiery abandoned the fort while the residents looked on.[35] Magee did not mince words after taking La Bahía: "we are differently received in this country to what we expected and the treachery of the people is beyond belief."[36]

Testimony from individuals escaping Béxar in the days following the surrender to the American force suggests that many, perhaps most, people acted to preserve themselves rather than to support one cause or the other. Guillermo Saldaña, a servant in the employ of one of the Spanish officers taken prisoner, declared that, while the royal troops from outside the province had been disarmed, the local military units remained under arms. "The day before their entry into Béxar, said troops and militiamen ... and many women went to Mission Concepcion to incorporate themselves to the said Americans."[37] A priest and two civilians who escaped soon thereafter reported on the lukewarm nature of the military companies' support for the invaders. In particular, an expeditionary force of five hundred that

Rebellion on the Frontier

had intended to march south on Presidio del Rio Grande had been reduced to three hundred men, half of them Anglo Americans, because of the neutrality of the Texas companies.[38]

Ignacio Elizondo, who led the vanguard of the royalist army that reconquered Béxar, reported that more than three hundred soldiers, residents, women, and children had escaped to his camp shortly after his arrival. Elizondo continued, describing a phenomenon similar to that exhibited by the population earlier in favor of the filibusters: "the rest of the citizenry has not come out because of the guards maintained by the rebels. Yet, in spite of the guards, I believe that the whole town will leave today, for now they are all disabused and have recognized their error."[39]

AFTERMATH: PARDONS AND RECONCILIATION

With the defeat of the insurgent forces, the authorities set about reestablishing local confidence in Spanish rule. They treated unrepentant insurgents harshly, but left the door open to those who wanted to make peace with Spanish authority. Elizondo, for example, reported sparing the lives of more than one hundred men, including soldiers and civilians, and an equal number of women. Arredondo, however, executed hundreds of men in the aftermath of the battle and chased many into Louisiana. He then turned his attention to restoring confidence in the government and containing only clearly dangerous individuals. A general pardon excepted only four local men—Francisco Arocha, Francisco Ruiz, Juan Veramendi, and Vicente Travieso. The pardon, a tool widely used in other parts of New Spain to pacify rebels, proved effective in quieting the province. Bexareños also moved to lessen tensions by requesting that families and individuals still considered dangerous or suspicious be removed from Texas.[40]

The authorities recognized and distinguished between those who accepted Spanish rule and those who remained firmly rebellious. In the fall of 1813 one individual asked that property confiscated from his father, who had joined the insurgents, be given to him, since he had joined the royalist army and had seen action in Texas twice. The petition was granted. Fernando Veramendi, the town council's choice for teacher in a new primary school, not only had collaborated with the insurgents but had acted as a member of the insurgent junta. Arrested for having provided letters of recommendation for the insurgent José Alvarez de Toledo, Erasmo Seguín refused to accept a pardon, claiming he had provided the letters under duress and wished to be exonerated. The authorities found him to be honest and released him on his own recognizance. Ultimately cleared of all charges, Seguín retook his place as one of Béxar's most prominent citizens.[41] He later represented Texas at the Mexican Constitutional Congress in 1823–24 and remained postmaster and quartermaster until 1835.

Bexareños quickly regained a measure of control over their affairs, most important, in the institution that represented local prerogatives, the ayuntamiento. In December 1813, the appointed *alcaldes* and *procurador* elected their successors, and the following year a council of four *regidores* ruled in Béxar. The council itself selected commissioners for the town's four wards. In the restored elections, old patterns reemerged, with governors having to reject some elected officials on the grounds that they were often out of town on business or were illiterate, among other reasons.[42] Perhaps the most important indicator of returning stability was the governor's declaration in September 1815 that "the ayuntamiento, as is my understanding from what my predecessor told me and the acceptance of various of its actions by the Commandant General, should be considered a legal body entitled to all rights and privileges."[43]

Other local initiatives show that the community reasserted itself beginning in the mid-1810s. During 1815, the town council once again organized the town's official religious feasts, celebrated since the mid-eighteenth century.[44] On February 1, 1816, the municipal council addressed a grievance to the interim governor, Mariano Varela, concerning the townspeople's provisioning of meat and firewood to the troops without payment. The corporation pleaded that Indian hostilities and scarcity of livestock made life impossible for many and that the government therefore should assume the burden of supplying the garrison. A year and a half later the council protested charges made against their honor and their loyalty to the government of Spain.[45] "Since 1813," the council declared, "the only people inhabiting this province were those who, after undergoing a strict examination, were shown to be free from the ugly crime of revolution, together with some former insurgents who had been forgiven because they had not done much damage."[46]

In spite of desperate and almost chaotic conditions in Texas, and Béxar in particular, the province remained squarely in royalist hands. On numerous occasions, troops had to be sent to the abandoned eastern part of the province and to the coast, where filibusters and French exiles were attempting to establish themselves. Troops also had to be sent out frequently in pursuit of Indians who committed depredations at both Béxar and La Bahía. Surprisingly, especially in light of the fact that the troops' pay remained in arrears throughout the entire period and that they received almost no supplies, they executed their orders with remarkable efficiency.

In 1817, near La Bahía, Governor Antonio Martínez defeated a band of filibusters under Henry Perry, a participant in the Gutiérrez-Magee Expedition and, in 1819, he sent a force of 550 men under Colonel Ignacio Pérez to drive James Long's men out of Nacogdoches.[47]

When independence came to Texas in the summer of 1821, it arrived clothed in reserve and respectability. Béxar supported it only after news arrived in San Antonio of Commandant General Arredondo's acceptance of the Plan of Iguala at Monterrey on June 3, 1821. In mid-July the royalist governor, Antonio Martínez, led the military and civilian establishment in the oath to the new Mexican nation with all the decorum and ceremony that might have attended the celebration of a victory by the king's arms.[48]

CONCLUSION

The events of 1811–13 reveal that Tejanos faced a dilemma that would remain a central theme over the next forty years. On the one hand, they had to contend with the turbulence associated with anti-government sentiment in New Spain; on the other, they had to weigh that dissatisfaction with the potential problems connected to the United States' westward movement toward their land. During the years in question, Spanish troops and Anglo-American filibusters occupied Texas. Both posed a threat to local interests and freedom of action, and Tejanos dealt with these difficult times in highly pragmatic and self-interested ways. Though Tejanos certainly had views about whether Mexico should be independent of Spain, and those views naturally varied, their actions in relation to such discussions reflected local imperatives. The same can be said of their reactions to the filibuster invasion. Most residents of Béxar probably had legitimate complaints about Spanish rule, but that certainly did not translate into support for a US takeover of the region. Throughout 1811–13, long-standing loyalties, fears, and grave uncertainties created caution and an interest in self-preservation as guiding principles for many. Buffeted by forces largely outside their control, Bexareños learned to place a priority on their local needs. Not surprisingly, they later became strong supporters of Mexican federalism until their loyalties were once again tested by the Anglo American-led rebellion against Mexican sovereignty in Texas.

NOTES

1. For the more recent writings reflecting these various historical interpretations see David M. Vigness, *The Revolutionary Decades: The Saga of Texas, 1810–1836* (Austin: Steck-Vaughn,

1965); T. R. Fehrenbach, *Lone Star: A History of Texas and the Texans* (New York: Macmillan, 1968). For a general discussion of Anglo-American historians' influence on colonial Texas history writing see Gerald E. Poyo and Gilberto Hinojosa, "Spanish Texas and Borderlands Historiography in Transition: The Implications for United States History," *Journal of American History* 75, 2 (Sept. 1988): 393–416.

2. Timothy E. Anna, *The Fall of the Royal Government in Mexico City* (Lincoln: University of Nebraska Press, 1978); D. A. Brading, *Haciendas and Ranchos in the Mexican Bajío: León, 1680–1860* (Cambridge: Cambridge University Press, 1978); Brian R. Hamnett, *Roots of Insurgency: Mexican Regions, 1750–1824* (Cambridge: Cambridge University Press, 1986); Doris Ladd, *The Mexican Nobility at Independence* (Austin: University of Texas Press, 1976); John Tutino, *From Insurrection to Revolution in Mexico: Social Bases of Agrarian Violence, 1750–1940* (Princeton: Princeton University Press, 1988); Luis Villoro, *El proceso ideológico de la revolución de independencia* (Mexico: Universidad Autónoma Nacional de México, 1983). The best effort among Texas historians to analyze events within the context of local social and economic circumstances is Jack Jackson, *Los Mesteños: Spanish Ranching in Texas, 1721–1821* (College Station: Texas A&M University Press, 1986), 525–35.

3. This and the following paragraphs dealing with the historical background are drawn from the author's "Land and Society in 18th Century San Antonio: A Community on New Spain's Northern Frontier" (Ph.D. diss., University of Texas at Austin, 1988).

4. Nettie Lee Benson, "Texas Failure to Send a Deputy to the Spanish Cortes, 1810–1812," *Southwestern Historical Quarterly* 64, 1 (July 1960): 31–32.

5. Ibid., 23–24; Proceedings concerning the election of a deputy to the Cortes, June 27, 1810, Béxar Archives, The University of Texas Archives, Austin (hereafter cited as BA).

6. The most complete account of Nolan's activities on the Louisiana-Texas frontier is Maurine T. Wilson and Jack Jackson, *Philip Nolan and Texas: Expeditions to the Unknown Land, 1791–1801* (Waco: Texian Press, 1987).

7. Odie B. Faulk, *The Last Years of Spanish Texas, 1778–1821* (The Hague: Mouton, 1964), 124; Mattie Austin Hatcher, *The Opening of Texas to Foreign Settlement, 1801–1821* (reprint, Philadelphia: Porcupine Press, 1976), 61–62, 70–71.

8. Estado que manifiesta la fuerza efectiva de las tropas, May 23, 1810, in May 24, 1810, BA.

9. Aside from the works cited above in note two, an excellent brief account of the Mexican War of Independence is Timothy Anna, "The Independence of Mexico and Central America," in *The Independence of Latin America*, Leslie Bethell, ed. (Cambridge: Cambridge University Press, 1987).

10. For a general survey of Spanish policy toward Texas during this time see Hatcher, *The Opening of Texas to Foreign Settlement*, chapters 1–5. French intrigues and the role of Texas as an avenue to the interior is treated in Julia Kathryn Garrett, *Green Flag Over Texas: A Story of the Last Years of Spain in Texas* (New York: The Cordova Press, 1939), 14–19, 25–26.

11. Alessio Robles, *Coahuila y Texas*, 629–35; Garrett, *Green Flag Over Texas*, 33–35. Garrett writes that Cordero had two thousand troops under his command while Alessio Robles has the figure at seven hundred.

12. Fieles habitantes de la provincia de Texas, Jan. 6, 1811, BA; Salcedo to Sebastián Rodríguez, Jan. 16, 1811, ibid.; Junta convocada por el señor gobernador de la provincia de Texas . . . , Jan. 18, 1811, ibid. The details of the Casas revolt have been well told in a number of works, and documents regarding the coup were published in Frederick C. Chabot, ed., *Texas in 1811: The Las Casas and Sambrano Revolutions* (San Antonio: Yanaguana Society, 1941).

13. The standard narrative of the counterrevolt is J. Villasana Haggard, "The Counter-Revolution of Bexar, 1811," *Southwestern Historical Quarterly* 43, 2 (Oct. 1943): 222–35.

14. Alessio Robles, *Coahuila y Texas*, 639–49. Garrett, in *Green Flag Over Texas* (pp. 61–62), and following earlier historians, maintains that Elizondo was an insurgent convinced by Governor Salcedo to return to the loyalist fold. Alessio Robles maintains, however, that he evidence overwhelmingly points to Elizondo having been a royalist all along.

15. Alessio Robles, *Coahuila y Texas*, 653–54; Garrett, *Green Flag Over Texas*, 83–112. The Gutiérrez-Magee Expedition is one of the most widely written episodes of early Texas history. Among the best narratives are Félix D. Almaráz Jr., *Tragic Cavalier: Governor Manuel Salcedo of Texas, 1808–1813* (Austin: University of Texas Press, 1971), chap. 6; Castañeda, *Our Catholic Heritage in Texas* 6: chaps. 4 and 5; Garrett, *Green Flag Over Texas*, chaps. 25–39.

16. Harry McCorry Henderson, "The Magee-Gutiérrez Expedition," *The Southwestern Historical Quarterly* 55 (July 1951): 49–51.

17. A very readable, yet detailed, survey of the period between the Battle of Medina and Mexican independence is Castañeda, *Our Catholic Heritage*, 6: chaps. 6 and 7.

18. A narrative of Governor Salcedo's administration is Almaráz, *Tragic Cavalier*; for Governor Cordero, see Fabius Dunn, "The Administration of Don Antonio Cordero, Governor of Texas, 1805–1808" (Ph.D. diss., The University of Texas at Austin, 1962). See also, Elizabeth May Morey, "Attitude of the Citizens of San Fernando Toward Independence Movements in New Spain, 1811–1813" (M.A. thesis, The University of Texas at Austin, 1930).

19. Alessio Robles, *Coahuila y Texas*, 622. Author's translation.

20. Jesús F. de la Teja, "Indians, Soldiers, and Canary Islanders: The Making of a Texas Frontier Community," *Locus* 3, 1 (Fall 1990): 94; Morey, "Attitude of the Citizens," 38–39.

21. Muñoz to viceroy, Jan. 7, 1792, Nacogdoches Archives Transcripts, University of Texas Archives, Austin; Case against Tomás Alvarez Travieso, July 12, 1805, BA; Case against Francisco Travieso, Nov. 23, 1810, BA; Vicente Travieso vs. Francisco Travieso, May 23, 1810, BA; Case against José Félix Menchaca, et al., Jan. 27, 1808, BA; Case against Juan Manuel Zambrano, Oct. 27, 1802, BA; Junta to commandant general, June 19, 1811, in copy of same date, BA.

22. Following earlier writers who misrepresented anti-Spaniard sentiments in the population, and by attaching to Béxar's disturbances the same character as the insurrectionary movement in central areas of the empire, recent writers have also concluded that European and class hatreds were rampant in San Antonio. Compare, for instance, Morey, "Attitude of the Citizens," 46, and David J. Weber, *The Mexican Frontier, 1826–1846: The American Southwest Under Mexico* (Albuquerque: University of New Mexico, Press, 1982), 9.

23. [Copy of testimony taken from Br. don Feliciano Franco Vela, Dn. Guadalupe Caso, and D. Antonio Fuentes], April 15, 1813. AGM, vol. 422, p. 309.

24. Warren, *The Sword Was Their Passport*, 50; Garrett, *Green Flag Over Texas*, 180–81.

25. Morey, "Attitude of the Citizens," 53.

26. De la Teja, "Indians, Soldiers, and Canary Islanders," 94.

27. The nature and workings of this group seems to fit Hamnett's description of the "local dissident groups" through which Hidalgo extended his insurrection (pp. 125–26).

28. Decree of the Junta, March 3, 1811, BA; ibid., March 24, 1811, ibid.; Junta to Manuel Salcedo, April 18, 1811, ibid.; Decree of the Junta, April 21, 1811, ibid.

29. Chabot, ed., *Texas in 1811*, 54–55, 58–62, 111; Contra Dn. Francisco Travieso por falta de respeto e inobediente, November 23, 1810, BA; Decree of the Governing Junta, March 3, 1811, ibid.; Junta to Nemecio Salcedo, June 19, 1811, ibid.; Antonio Cordero to Manuel Salcedo, July 4, 1812, ibid.

30. Kathryn Stoner O'Connor, *The Presidio del Espiritu Santo de Zuniga, 1721–1846* (2nd ed., Victoria: Armstrong Printers, 1984), 85.

31. Morey, "Attitude of the Citizens," 100.

32. Garrett, *Green Flag Over Texas*, 176.

33. Alessio Robles, *Coahuila y Texas*, 656–657; [Copy of testimony of Soldier Guillermo Nabarro, of the Lampazos Company, taken at Laredo on April 8, 1813], The University of Texas at Austin, Barker Texas History Center, Archivo General de Mexico, Historia: Operaciones de Guerra, Arredondo (transcripts, hereafter cited as AGM), vol. 422, p. 242.

34. Morey, "Attitude of the Citizens," 106.

35. Garrett, *Green Flag Over Texas*, 151, 167–58.

36. Garrett, *Green Flag Over Texas*, 170.

37. [Copy of testimony taken of Guillermo Saldaña], April 6, 1813, AGM, vol. 422, p. 247.

38. [Copy of testimony taken from Br. don Feliciano Franco Vela, Dn. Guadalupe Caso, and D. Antonio Fuentes], April 15, 1813. AGM, vol. 422, p. 309.

39. Ignacio Elizondo to Arredondo, June 18, 1813, AGM vol. 423, p. 80.

40. Morey, "Attitude of the Citizens," 113–14, 119, 121–22; Hatcher, *Opening of Texas*, 235–38; Elizondo to Arredondo, Sept. 2, 1813, and Sept. 12, 1813, AGM vol. 423, pp. 215, 218; Joaquín de Arredondo to Cristóbal Domínguez, October 10, 1813, BA; Ygnacio Pérez to Benito Armiñán, March 17, 1814, ibid.; Lista de los Presos prosesados por Ynsurgentes y se han puesto en Libertad de orn. del Sor. Governador y Coronl. del Regimiento de estremadura D. Benito de Armiñán, July 4, 1814, ibid.; Noticia de los Ynsurgentes Yndultados, y de las familias que pueden ser sospechosas, y perjudican la quietud y pública tranquilidad de esta Provincia, August 8, 1814, ibid.; [Governor] to Antonio Cordero, January 2, 1815, ibid.

41. Petition of José Felíx Menchaca, September 22, 1813, BA; [Commandant General] to governor of Texas, November 2, 1814, ibid.; Proceso de José Erasmo Seguín, 1813–19, Saltillo, Coahuila, Archivo de la Secretaría de Gobierno, photostatic copy in Saltillo Archives, University of Texas at Austin, Barker Texas History Center.

In inventories of property confiscated from Spaniards during the Gutiérrez-Magee occupation, Fernando Veramendi appears as president, treasurer, or both; e.g.: Ymbentario de los enseres qe. se imbentariaron por el Presidente y Tesorero Dn. Ferndo. Beramendi en la Casa del Sor. Dn. Simón de Herrera, April 17, 1813, ibid. Yet, just over a year later, in an unsigned document, Fernando Veramendi is listed as the town's choice for school teacher, there not being a more qualified individual, see [May 31, 1814], ibid.

42. Election report, December 28, 1813, BA; ibid., December 28, 1814, ibid.; Benito Armiñán to council, December 28, 1814, ibid.; council to Armiñán, January 5, 1815, ibid.; election report, December 21, 1815, ibid.; ibid., December 21, 1816, ibid.; new election, December 23, 1816, ibid.; Ygnacio Pérez to council, December 22, 1816, ibid.; election report, December 23, 1816, ibid.

43. Governor to José Dario Sambrano, September 21, 1815, BA.

44. Minutes of the council, January 25, 1815, and October 5, 1815, BA.

45. Town council to Interim Governor Mariano Varela, February 1, 1816, BA.

46. Morey, "Attitude of the Citizens," 122.

47. Chipman, *Spanish Texas* 238–41; Castañeda, *Our Catholic Heritage in Texas* 6:126–69.

48. For a discussion of the coming of independence to San Antonio, see Félix D. Almaráz Jr., *Governor Antonio Martínez and Mexican Independence in Texas: An Orderly Transition* (reprint, Béxar County Historical Commission, 1979).

Theodore Gentilz, *Stick Stock*. San Antonio's elite generally welcomed and supported Anglo-American settlers, whose interests in Texas as farm country made land the province's most valuable resource. Combining Anglo-American surveying techniques with Spanish-Mexican measures and concepts of land use, Texas developed a unique surveying system during the fifteen years of Mexican government. Land hunger and land speculation brought Tejanos and Texians together and contributed some of the principal factors of the Revolution. Courtesy of Mr. Larry Sheerin, San Antonio, Texas.

10

The Colonization and Independence of Texas: A Tejano Perspective*

The traditional historiography of Texas' Mexican period (1821–35) and the Texas War of Independence (1835–36) often has neglected the Tejanos (Texans of Mexican heritage). When they do appear in the record it is to validate the acts of the ascendant Texians (Anglo-American Texas residents) or to demonstrate the untrustworthy nature of Mexicans. One needs only to read editorials, letters to editors, and journals of the period to see that Texian patriotism was couched in the language of the American Revolution and the virtues of the Great Republic, not in a Mexican context. Texians, in fact, were fighting to recreate the United States on virgin soil, whereas Tejanos were struggling, as were their Mexican countrymen from other regions, to consolidate their position in the new Mexican nation.

Relegated by the Texians to the status of foreigners in the aftermath of Texas' War of Independence from Mexico, most Tejanos, whether fourth-generation natives or recent immigrants, found only a marginal place in the new order. Tejanos inherited the negative stereotypes that were ascribed to the Spanish process of colonization. Recently, this sentiment has been eloquently expressed by T. R. Fehrenbach in his popular history of the state of Texas: "Rigid adherence to outmoded ideas—always the mark of a society in decline—certainly played a major role in Spanish failure. In Texas, Spain met new and different conditions, and the Spanish secular and ecclesiastical mind was never able to adjust. . . . Only an expanding, pragmatic, decentralized, adaptable culture could have penetrated the region and put down roots in the face of the Apache-Comanche threat. And this was precisely what Spain lacked. Spain failed to put people in Texas."[1]

In such an environment, Tejanos were representatives of the defeated

---

*First published in Jaime E. Rodríguez O. and Kathryn Vincent, eds., *Myths, Misdeeds, and Misunderstandings: The Roots of Conflict in U.S.-Mexico Relations* (Wilmington, DE: Scholarly Resources, 1997).

Spanish-Mexican culture; they were guilty by association of obstructing the "rise, progress, and prospects of the republic of Texas," to borrow from William Kennedy's title for his 1841 book on the subject. Kennedy's chapter on Spanish settlement is a model of Black Legend writing, and he sums it up thus: "A population, consisting chiefly of expatriated friars, vagabond soldiers, enthralled and savage Indians, with the motley offspring of Mexican licentiousness, was eminently adapted for retaining Texas, consistently with the policy of Spain, in the condition of an unimproved and unexplored wilderness."[2]

The possibility that Tejanos may have had an agenda separate from, though compatible with, the recently arrived Anglo Americans has been ignored or dismissed. The historiography of the victorious Texians and their descendants could not acknowledge Tejanos as important actors because it would expose their ill behavior toward Mexican Texans from 1835 onward. It is not surprising that books about this period of Texas history continue to appear without the slightest mention of Tejanos or with the mere token presence of those few who achieved political prominence.[3] Nevertheless, Tejano society was complex and led by an elite that represented the region in Spain's legislature, the Cortes, and in Mexico's congress. Their story is important to a better understanding of how Texas fell under Anglo-American control and to a more sympathetic perception of all parties concerned.

TEXAS IN INDEPENDENT MEXICO

Tejano attitudes during the Mexican period were forged in the experience of the Mexican War of Independence. During the decade-long struggle, Texas suffered not only from internal rebellion but also from filibustering expeditions and Indian depredations. As a result, Texas entered the independence era drained of human resources and in economic ruins. Conditions were so bad that in 1819 Governor Antonio Martínez, after pointing out that barely two thousand residents remained in the province, proposed the settlement in Texas of Tlaxcaltecan Indians from Saltillo.[4]

Tejanos were not timid in presenting their own case, however. When the Spanish Constitution of 1812 was restored in New Spain in 1820, Tejanos followed a constant policy of seeking national government assistance to strengthen the province. The recently established Ayuntamiento of La Bahía (Goliad) in November 1820 decried the deplorable conditions the settlement had endured over the previous eight years: incessant Indian hostilities; nonpayment of the garrison; and the high turnaround in commanders, sixteen since 1813. "And although this place should be wealthy because of its good lands and plentiful water, barely enough corn can be raised for the inhabitants." The council's request was simple: an increase in population and a remedy to the ills plaguing the presidio (garrison).[5] The Ayuntamiento of San Antonio de Béxar had much the same to say about that place. Since 1813 the twin blows of Indian depredations and a destitute and desperate military had advanced the province, "at an amazing rate, towards ruin and destruction."[6] The third Texas settlement, Nacogdoches, had been so thoroughly decimated by the vicissitudes of the 1810s that it had fewer than one hundred residents in early 1821 and was the prime example of the need for government attention to the province.[7]

Consequently, one theme that appeared repeatedly in the Tejanos' dialogue with Mexico City, even after the beginning of Anglo-American colonization, was the establishment of a string of additional presidios on the western frontier. These garrisons not only would protect the settled areas from Comanche attacks but also would provide a market for local produce. Another often-repeated proposal was to open one or more ports on the Gulf of Mexico. Since the eighteenth century, Tejanos had argued that opening the coast to commerce would be a boon, not only to Texas but to neighboring provinces, including New Mexico. In presenting these various proposals, Tejanos assumed that they would be acting in concert with the citizens of three neighboring provinces, Tamaulipas, Nuevo León, and Coahuila, who had interests in many of the same matters and whose provinces during the late-colonial period had formed part of the administrative unit called the Provincias Internas (Interior Provinces).[8] Tejano complaints regarding a port were finally satisfied with the establishment of a customs house at La Bahía for authorized landings in San Bernardo Bay. Garrisons began to arrive in 1830, not for Indian defense or to promote economic development, but to stem the tides of contraband trade and illegal immigration from the United States.[9]

Tejanos also were capable and more than willing to take charge of their own affairs. Ayuntamientos often challenged the authority of the governor, who by late 1820 was called *jefe político* (political chief). After independence, Tejanos continued their efforts to be heard in the new imperial government of Mexico. They quickly filled the vacuum of political authority when Emperor Agustín de Iturbide abdicated in March 1823. The following month, the citizens of San Antonio de Béxar, known as Bexareños, led the way in establishing a *junta gubernativa* (governing committee) for the province, made up of seven representatives from Béxar and one from each of the other two settlements. The junta gave way in July to Luciano Garcia, appointed *jefe político* by the national provisional government.

The governing body was restored in the fall when the national government authorized the establishment of provincial deputations in all the northern provinces. (The provincial deputation was created by the Spanish Constitution of 1812 in an effort to provide more local representation to the provinces of Spain and America. It consisted of locally elected deputies and a governor, the *jefe político*, appointed by the national government. After independence, Mexico retained the laws and institutions of Spain while it drafted its own constitution.) Although Texas' representatives to the Constituent Congress would have liked to establish their own state, they realized that the province lacked sufficient population to become a separate political entity. They therefore agreed to become part of a larger state, Coahuila y Tejas, with its capital in Saltillo. Because the provincial deputations transformed themselves into state legislatures, the new state of Coahuila y Tejas disbanded its two provincial deputations and created a state legislature in Saltillo.[10] But having acquired a taste for self-rule, Tejanos were reluctant to give up the provincial deputation to a legislature in far-off Saltillo.

Support for Texas was sought in Mexico City through the deputies elected to represent the province at national congresses. San Antonio's parish priest, Refugio de la Garza, represented Texas at the First Constituent Congress, in 1822–23. While in Mexico City, De la Garza worked from instructions that ran along the lines of pre-independence memorials and declarations: organization of a campaign against hostile Indians, establishment of a string of presidios to protect from both Plains Indians and undesirable Anglo Americans, support for immigration to Texas from the interior of Mexico, and final secularization of the missions and distribution of their agricultural lands to Tejanos. De la Garza was soon frustrated in most of his efforts, reporting in July that even as he knew and had protested the misery in which Texas troops found themselves, he too was out of funds with which to maintain himself.[11] Optimism still reigned in May 1823, however, when De la Garza wrote to the ayuntamiento regarding the establishment of a federal order:

> Mexico today happily enjoys the most inalienable rights and the utmost liberty, which the first Mexican congress victoriously restored to it after a year of sorrowful war against despotism.
>
> To repeat what I have written in my previous letters: Arbitrariness is ended, as are oppression, despotism, and tyranny. Today [Texas] enjoys unlimited freedom, without obstacles or hindrances. [Texas] may dispose

of everything which prodigal nature has bestowed upon it, land and sea, without regard to any laws other than those which the province may itself liberally impose.[12]

Matters soon took a turn toward the sober reality of an isolated and underpopulated province faced with external forces beyond even the national government's means to manage. By the time he arrived in Mexico City in late 1823, Erasmo Seguín, Texas' deputy to the Second Constituent Congress (which drafted the federal Constitution of 1824), was aware that the Tejano assumptions about local autonomy and joint action with the other northeastern provinces were no longer valid. Furthermore, he was confused by the news that San Antonio de Béxar's municipal government recommended union with Coahuila as the proper course. Independently assessing the political situation in terms of financial resources, Seguín reasoned that territorial status under the national government was preferable to association with Coahuila. As a territory, Texas would be provided by the national government with the necessary resources for development. Union with Coahuila, however, would be detrimental, he wrote, as "the inhabitants of Coahuila will not help us with money to get us out of the difficulties in which we find ourselves, nor to preserve our lives and vital interests."[13]

The Texas provincial deputation shared Seguín's letter with the Ayuntamiento of Béxar, which convened a town meeting on February 15, 1824. The citizenry discussed the province's status, and the resulting resolutions were not unpredictable. They proposed that Texas should join with the three other northeastern provinces to form a single state, although each province was to retain its distinct provincial character and government; that Texas would not be required to make any contribution to such a state until it had the means to do so; that some provision should be made for allowing each province, on attaining the necessary requirements, to form a separate state; and that if the other provinces refused to participate, Texas was to form a state on its own, relying on the national government to supply the necessary resources to maintain it.[14]

By the time the city's wishes reached Seguín he had experienced a change of heart in the matter. The successful efforts of Nuevo León to form a separate state, the feeling among the other potential partners that Texas could be only a burden, and the political instability of the emerging national government all led the Texas representative "to go about begging for refuge, and as the Saltilleros [the representatives from Saltillo] are the most determined, they are predisposed to protect and help us, up to a point.

This is a solution which appears to me we should adopt (although it brings us little advantage, for they can give us nothing) rather than be given the status of territory."[15] Statehood with Coahuila would be more beneficial to Texas, however, than remaining a separate territory because the new Mexican colonization law granted control of public lands to the states whereas the federal government administered public lands in the territories. Seguín proposed to include a measure that guaranteed Texas separate statehood once it had the necessary resources.[16] Indeed, the congressional decree of May 7, 1824, which created the poorest state in the Mexican federation, Coahuila y Tejas, contained a clause granting Texans the right to inform the national government when they felt capable of sustaining a separate state government.

Seguín also felt responsible for representing the interests of the newly arrived Anglo-American colonists, who now represented the province's best chance for quick economic development. Stephen F. Austin, the *empresario* (contractor) in charge of the first colonization effort, had made a number of guarantees to potential settlers regarding their civil and economic rights. His father, Moses Austin, had originally received permission to settle from the Spanish government before the Cortes passed the 1821 colonization law that prohibited the importation of slaves into Spanish territories and freed those brought there. Austin, nevertheless, had enticed a number of slaveholders to bring cotton culture to Texas. Naturally, therefore, Austin and his group were concerned about the status of the institution of slavery in the new Mexican congress, and Seguín seemed agreeable to taking up their cause. Even so, as a group Tejanos had no clear position on slavery; they saw it as less important than the political status question, which had a direct relationship to the availability of aid for Texas. Although a few Tejanos owned slaves at the time, these were domestic servants. Only a handful of Tejanos had firsthand knowledge of field slavery from business trips to Louisiana. Having been named to the Mexican congress's Colonization Commission (organized to develop rules for colonization of Mexico's less-populated territories), Seguín was well placed to intercede on behalf of the colonists, to whom he promised: "As to the slaves, I will say everything that occurs to me in favor of that colony when this matter is discussed—be it in regard to those slaves the colonists may bring, or be it in regard to those born in our territories—taking very careful consideration of the observations you have made to me on this issue, in view of the benefit that may result to those settlers, in whom I am so interested."[17]

Seguín argued in Congress that preservation of slavery was the means to assuring the immigration of wealthy men who could do much to further regional development. Without slavery only poor farmers would come, adding little to the Texas economy. His congressional colleagues did not agree, however. Seguín later explained to Austin: "But my friend, in this congress no one wanted to hear such arguments. To the contrary, the whole congress was electrified when the subject of slavery was spoken of and in consideration of the miserable state of that portion of humanity."[18]

By late March 1824, the Texas delegate believed the battle had been lost, but he tried to make the best of the situation. He wrote to Baron de Bastrop, the state commissioner of colonization, "A law has just passed for the general abolition of slavery, but to remedy this problem, which may have great consequences for the colony because of the shortage of labor, I have already spoken to the government and we agree it will send 800 or 1,000 vagrants to the colony." He knew these people were not the best settlers possible, but he believed that those who established themselves permanently could only help the province.[19] Enough questions remained, however, that the congress apparently reconsidered abolition and rescinded its actions. Subsequently, the matter of slavery was left out of both the new national colonization law and the federal constitution. In the end, the congress abolished only the slave trade, leaving unclear whether the prohibition extended to owners bringing slaves for their own use.[20]

That Seguín was not alone in favor of a continuation of slavery is clear from the actions of San Antonio de Bexar's city council in 1826, at the same time that the Coahuila y Tejas state legislature was debating a constitution. In August James E. B. Austin reported from San Antonio to his brother Stephen that the ayuntamiento, deliberating on the matter, had reached a decision favorable to the colonists. "Since . . . they have given it the attention it merited—and by the last mail *have sent* up a *representation couched* in the strongest language they could express in *favor* of the *admission* in the New *Colonies*—they *declare* it to be *indispensable* to the prosperity of this Department; in fact they have said all they can say."[21] These were the same arguments that San Antonio's city council later would make in their 1832 memorial to the state legislature in protesting the restrictive Law of April 6, 1830.

Another potential impediment to Anglo-American settlement also loomed for Stephen Austin in the deliberations of the Constituent Congress about the religious requirement for colonists. Seguín assured the *empresario* that only non-Catholic public worship was not permitted. "As to the requirement that all who immigrate precisely be Catholic, I do not find a reason that will convince me, as even under the old government religious toleration was permitted, and I believe this cannot be prevented. What I cannot argue for is that public worship be permitted, for according to the constitutional act that governs the matter, there shall be no other cult than the Christian Catholic."[22]

Seguín's opinion appears to have been correct in light of the Mexican congress's earlier response to efforts by one delegate to make Catholicism an issue. In August 1824, Seguín notified Austin that "a proposal has been made in Congress by one of the deputies to require the colonists who are admitted into our territories to be Roman Apostolic Catholics, and it was rejected by a unanimity of votes, as only the deputy who made the proposal voted for it."[23] The Constituent Congress understood the difference between the terms *Christian* and *Roman Catholic* and, as in the case of the slavery issue, chose to employ ambiguous language that permitted maximum flexibility in the admission of new colonists.

EFFORTS TO CONTROL IMMIGRATION IN TEXAS

Tejanos did not act blindly, carelessly, or recklessly in supporting Anglo-American immigration. On a number of occasions during the early 1820s, when settlers began to come across the border on rumors of free land, Texas authorities made attempts to control the flow. In the January 1822 instructions for the Texas deputy to the Constituent Congress of the Mexican Empire, Tejanos took a very cautious approach to immigration from the United States. They justified a call for the fortification of the recently resettled town of Nacogdoches by citing the need to prevent Anglo Americans from trading with Texas Indians and from illegally settling in the province. Anglo Americans should not be allowed to settle without government permission and only "under the specific condition that they be Catholics, have property, a craft or useful profession, and that if after five years of residency they should not wish to remain in the country but return to their own, they may take only the capital or property that they introduced."[24] Laws requiring that immigrants report to the nearest authority were, however, flagrantly violated. The warnings that the national government should pay serious attention to the squatter problem went unheeded. Attempts to have the national government assume responsibility for removing undesirables and making worthy squatters comply with regulations proved unavailing.[25]

Settlement by honest, industrious, and substantial farmers was another matter altogether. If Stephen F. Austin opened the door to colonization from the United States, it was a door that San Antonio's elite Tejanos helped open. As Austin labored to expand the scope of his operations, he received the assistance of José Antonio Saucedo, the political chief, and Gaspar Flores and Miguel Arciniega, who served as commissioners for two of his contracts, as well as from Erasmo Seguín. In return, he asked for and received a contract in 1827 to settle one hundred families along the Old San Antonio Road to Nacogdoches at the crossing of the Colorado River, near the present community of Bastrop. This he did to satisfy local wishes that some of the colonists be settled closer to San Antonio in an area where they could help defend against Comanche raids.

Other *empresarios* were soon at work in Texas, and those who occupied areas near San Antonio made sure to enlist the support of the local elite. Not surprisingly, law and order increased with distance from the US border and in the direction of San Antonio. South of the Austin colony, Martín de León, who was the only Mexican *empresario* to fulfill the terms of his contract, obtained permission for a settlement before the national colonization law of 1824 was promulgated from the provincial deputation sitting in San Antonio. The colony came to include more than one hundred fifty families, most from the Mexican interior, some from San Antonio and Goliad, and others from the United States. Green DeWitt, who had been with Austin and other would-be *empresarios* in Mexico City seeking contracts from Emperor Agustin in 1822–23, finally obtained one for four hundred families from the state government of Coahuila y Tejas in 1825. For commissioner he chose José Antonio Navarro, a prominent San Antonio merchant, who would later be one of only two Tejano signers of the Texas Declaration of Independence. The partnership of John McMullen and James McGloin, which established a small Irish colony on the Nueces River, appointed first José Antonio Saucedo and then José María Balmaceda as commissioners.

Cooperative efforts between the Tejano elite and non-Mexican *empresarios* were not devoid of friction. Conflicting land grant boundaries and disagreements over interpretation of contraband laws and livestock ownership soon created among the Tejanos an undercurrent of suspicion of Anglo-American intentions. One recent historian of the period has discovered in Rafael Antonio Manchola a prime example of Tejano ambivalence toward the new colonists. Presidial commander of La Bahía from 1828 to 1830 and alcalde (magistrate) of Goliad in 1831, Manchola also was son-in-law to the only resident Tejano *empresario*, Martín de León. As early as 1826, Manchola warned the military commander for Texas of the Anglo colonists' lack of respect for Mexican law:

> No faith can be placed in the Anglo-American colonists because they are continually demonstrating that they absolutely refuse to be subordinate, unless they find it convenient to what they want anyway, all of which I believe will be very detrimental to us for them to be our neighbors if we do not in time, clip the wings of their audacity by stationing a strong detachment in each new settlement which will enforce the laws and jurisdiction of a Mexican magistrate which should be placed in each of them, since under their own colonists as judges, they do nothing more than practice their own laws which they have practiced since they were born, forgetting the ones they have sworn to obey, these being the laws of our Supreme Government.[26]

Manchola's voice proved to be in the minority, however. Despite continued problems in getting the Anglo settlers to accept their new nationality, Tejanos found no other alternatives for developing the vast stretches of fertile land on which the province's economic prosperity would rest.

Land became what Texas was all about. For almost three centuries Texas land had held little value. Although the fertility of its soil had been noted by early explorers, it took the threat of foreign penetration of northern New Spain to compel Spanish authorities to settle the region. During the eighteenth century, when presidios and missions shared the province with only two sizeable civilian settlements, San Antonio (established in 1718) and Nacogdoches (1779), hostile Indians and remoteness kept settlement to a minimum. But with the arrival of the Anglo-American settlers in the early 1820s, Texas land began to assume an economic potential that quickly led to speculation. Settlement meant increasing land values and expanded markets for Tejano merchants and producers. Additionally, because various colonization laws made Anglo-American ownership of more than one *sitio* (4,428 acres) of land difficult, Anglo-American speculators commonly employed Mexican fronts to gain control of tens of thousands of acres. A Mexican national, usually a well-connected Coahuilense or Tejano, would petition the governor for a grant of up to eleven *sitios*, the maximum amount allowed; once the grant was received, he would sell the land to the speculator through a power of attorney.[27] In these ways Bexareños, who as children knew firsthand the dangers of an unpacified countryside, now had the opportunity to turn a profit on that very land. Francisco Ruiz made clear the underlying concern of the Tejano leadership: "I cannot help seeing advantages which, to my way of thinking would result if we admitted honest, hard-working people, regardless of what country they came from . . . even hell itself."[28]

Tejanos therefore reacted forcefully when threatened by a cessation of immigration from the United States. Although enacted by opposing political groups in Mexico City, two pieces of legislation drew immediate protests, not only from the Anglo-American settlements, but from the Tejanos of San Antonio as well: President Vicente Guerrero's emancipation decree of September 1829 and, after he was overthrown, the conservative Colonization Law of April 6, 1830, which both prohibited the introduction of slaves and barred the entry of foreign settlers to "those states and territories bordering on their nations of origin," a clear exclusion of Anglo Americans. Ramón Múzquiz protested as shortsighted the emancipation of Texas slaves when the region was only then beginning to rise to its potential. Both Tejano representatives to the Coahuila y Tejas legislature, Rafael Antonio Manchola and José María Balmaceda, after protesting the conservative legislation and making their liberal leanings known, soon found themselves under attack. By the fall of 1830, Balmaceda had been expelled from the legislature and Manchola censured, to the protests of the San Antonio, Goliad, and San Felipe ayuntamientos. The political situation in Texas became increasingly complicated as the issues of slavery and immigration became intertwined with the national debate over the need to strengthen the country's government—federalism versus centralism. Because conservative centralists favored stricter control over both immigration and public lands, Texans—Tejanos as well as Texians—found liberal federalism more compatible with their interests. When the next state legislature convened, the Texas representatives, Stephen F. Austin and Manuel Músquiz, like Manchola and Balmaceda before them, were squarely and openly in the federalist camp.[29] In December 1832, San Antonio's city council backed the Texian protests of the Law of April 6, 1830, and acts of the state legislature inspired by the centralists. In a memorial to the state legislature the council complained that immigration from the United States was being stopped when nothing was being done to foster Mexican migration to Texas, "which, without a doubt, would be the most convenient for Texas."[30] The Ayuntamientos of Goliad and Nacogdoches also expressed displeasure with Coahuila's domination of Texas, although in more general terms. Supporting Béxar's memorial, they complained of rule by far-off officials ignorant of local conditions and, therefore, susceptible to the fraudulent designs of disreputable *empresarios* and speculators.[31] All the Texas memorials contained the threat of seeking separation from Coahuila if reforms did not materialize. Austin commented at the time, "They [the Tejano elite] are as anxious for separation [from Coahuila] as we are, but wish to show to the world that they are right and stand on just ground in case force must ultimately be resorted to."[32]

The roughest description of the Texas economy in the period just before the war of independence provides some idea of the problems faced by Tejanos. During his 1834 inspection tour on behalf of the national government, Juan N. Almonte found vast differences between the commercial activities of the predominantly Tejano and the overwhelmingly Texian areas. Referring to the former, he stated: "At the moment the products of this department [Bexar] being so few, none of them are exported; and it so happens that at present the only export commerce is reduced to 8 to 10 thousand skins of all kinds and the importation of some goods from New Orleans, which are expended in Béxar in exchange for skins."[33] In contrast, Almonte described commercial activity in the department of the Brazos, that is, the Austin and DeWitt colonies, as amounting to six hundred thousand pesos. For 1834 the expectation was that five thousand bales of cotton and fifty thousand pelts would be exported.[34] The story was much the same for the department of Texas, which had just been formed and included the eastern settlements. Export estimates for 1834 included two thousand bales of cotton, ninety thousand pelts, and five thousand head of cattle.[35] With the exception of Nacogdoches, which had been all but abandoned during the 1810s, the population, settlement, and productivity of the Brazos and Texas departments had risen only since 1821, the beginning of Anglo-American immigration. Meanwhile, San Antonio and Goliad, the oldest settlements in Texas, were economically backward and demographically dwarfed. The Anglo Americans brought development, which many Tejanos hoped would sooner or later rebound to their benefit, but the newcomers were also dangerous because of their strength.

THE WAR FOR TEXAS

Amid the crisis over immigration and slavery, the state government became hostage to the passions of competing political forces. In March 1833 federalist deputies managed to remove the state capital from Saltillo (a centralist stronghold) to Monclova, which had the support of other areas of Coahuila y Tejas that resented Saltillo's power. Yet the treasury was empty, and the temptations offered by speculators lobbying for more access to Texas land proved overwhelming. Shady transactions by individuals had already made settlers suspicious of the government in Coahuila; then in March and April 1834 the legislature in Monclova decided to sell Texas land to raise revenue. The sales led Texians to perceive the state government as corrupt and insensitive to their needs despite the significant reforms it passed during this period: new municipalities were chartered in

Anglo-American parts of Texas. Texas was subdivided into three districts, thus expanding its legislative representation from two to three. The use of English was legalized for all public acts except communications with the legislature and state executives. Freedom of conscience was legislated, and the state's legal system was overhauled to provide an Anglo-American style court system in Texas.[36]

Caught between the rising enmity between federalists and centralists in Coahuila and the mounting discontent in the Anglo-American colonies, Bexareños attempted to find a middle ground. When Stephen F. Austin passed through San Antonio on his way to Mexico City bearing the demands of Texians who met at San Felipe in April 1833 for separate statehood and resumption of legal immigration from the United States, he found the San Antonians unwilling to go along with the project, despite their feelings of having been neglected by the state government. José María Balmaceda, the former Texas delegate to the state legislature who also had served the McMullen-McGloin colony as commissioner, raised the issue of the Anglo Americans going directly to the federal government with their complaints with José Francisco Madero, former land commissioner and a deputy of the state legislature: "The political situation of the Mexican part of Texas is very difficult and compromised at present, and we all wonder very much that the state's authorities have not dictated some measures to preserve even the appearance of the laws and respect for the authorities entrusted with enforcing them."[37]

If Tejanos were cautious, they were not passive. Clashes between militia units loyal to the rival state governments in Saltillo and Monclova, as well as the arrival of the federal army general Martín Perfecto Cos in Monclova to take control of matters in Coahuila, suggested to Béxar's interim *jefe político*, Juan Nepomuceno Seguín, that an effective state government had ceased to exist. At a meeting held in early October 1834, Bexareños decided to call a new convention in which Texans could decide on a course of action. Seguín made the appropriate announcements on October 13 and 14 to the ayuntamientos in his jurisdiction and sent word to the *jefes* of the Nacogdoches and Brazos departments, from whom the response was less than enthusiastic. Henry Rueg of Nacogdoches failed to take any action. Henry Smith, *jefe político* of the Brazos department and long an advocate of Texas independence, saw an opportunity for launching a separatist movement, but a majority of residents in the district refused to participate in the meeting. For San Antonio federalists, the lack of support proved an embarrassment. Compounding their chagrin was President Santa Anna's acceptance of the Monclova regime as the legitimate government of Coahuila y Tejas until new elections were held in the state, and General Cos's chastisement of Seguín for having taken matters into his own hands.[38]

Throughout the spring of 1835, only Bexareños showed an interest in supporting the state government at Monclova. The merchants José María Balmaceda and the brothers José Antonio and Eugenio Navarro offered to lend the one thousand pesos that the governor, Agustín Viesca, had requested from the department, and Juan Seguín raised a company of militia to assist the governor in evacuating Coahuila's federalist government to Texas. For Bexareños the issue throughout this period remained the preservation of federalist rule. The struggle for control of Texas, for radically different reasons by Texians and Tejanos in eastern and western Texas, had begun.

Whereas the first shots of the Texas "revolution" were fired by Anglo Americans outside the town of Gonzales on October 2, 1835, it was the Tejanos who suffered the first consequences. Late in the month, General Cos, who had just occupied the city of San Antonio, removed Erasmo Seguín from his postmaster's position, humiliating him and other prominent townspeople with threats of forcing them "to sweep the streets."[39] Although most Tejanos opted to remain on the sidelines, and some remained loyal to the Mexico City government throughout the war, many chose to join the ranks of rebellion.[40] Juan Seguín and two Flores brothers raised companies from San Antonio and the neighboring ranches. In the Victoria area, Plácido Benavides, a son-in-law of Martín de León, also raised a company. Although little research has been done on their motives, their numbers and their actions provide some indication of their intentions. By the end of 1835 more than one hundred Tejanos had enlisted in the Federal Army of Texas, ostensibly organized to defend the Constitution of 1824 against growing centralist arbitrariness.

It is evident, however, that many Tejanos did not fully agree with the secessionist tendencies of the Texians. Most Tejanos' loyalties lay with the federalists, and they seem to have been unprepared to accept the change in goal from separate statehood under the Constitution of 1824 to complete independence, the opinion prevalent among Texians by early 1836. Tejanos probably also were alienated by the growing anti-Mexican tenor of Anglo-American rhetoric. Consequently, following the Texas Declaration of Independence, many Tejanos appear to have bowed out of the fight and headed home, among them Benavides. By the battle of San Jacinto on April 21, 1836, only Seguín's company remained in the service, and more than half of it was attending to escort and scouting duties. Only nineteen Tejanos, led by Seguín, fought on the secessionist side with the Anglo Americans that day.[41]

The war's aftermath brought forth praise from Texian military commanders for those Tejanos who had remained under arms for the republic, but increased hostility from an Anglo-American population that equated Mexicans and Tejanos strictly on the basis of appearance, language, and religion. In June 1836, Gen. Thomas J. Rusk, headquartered at Victoria, ordered the arrest and exile of all Mexicans suspected of collaborating or sympathizing with Mexico. Among those affected by the turn of events were members of the Martín de León clan, founders of Victoria, supporters of the Texas cause, and prominent members of the Victoria community. Benavides, who had raised a cavalry company at the beginning of hostilities, was compelled to move to Louisiana, where he died the following year.[42]

Forced from their homes in Nacogdoches and the Goliad-Victoria area and threatened in the vicinity of San Antonio, Tejanos began to disappear from the record. By and large, they were no longer policymakers, judges, and military men—makers of society. In the land records they became the sellers, not the buyers; in court records they were more often the defendants, not the plaintiffs; in the military records they appeared as the pursued, not as the pursuers. At best, they were tolerated as leaders only within their own isolated communities. In the newly independent Texas, Tejanos became outsiders in the land of their birth.

NOTES

1. T. R. Fehrenbach, *Lone Star: A History of Texas and the Texans* (New York: Collier Books, 1980), 73.

2. William Kennedy, *Texas: The Rise, Progress and Prospects of the Republic of Texas* (1841; reprint, Clifton, NJ: Augustus M. Kelley Publishers, 1974), 226.

3. Most writers not only ignore Tejanos but fail to distinguish between politically prominent Tejanos and the well-known Mexican politician and *empresario*, Lorenzo de Zavala, who had only tangential impact in Texas. In *Rise of the Lone Star: The Making of Texas* (College Station: Texas A&M University Press, 1989), Andreas V. Reichstein mentions Martín de León, Erasmo Seguín, José Antonio Navarro, Francisco Ruiz, and Juan Martín Veramendi very briefly and Juan Seguín not at all. The only Tejano mentioned in Sam Haynes's *Soldiers of Misfortune: The Somervell and Mier Expeditions* (Austin: University of Texas Press, 1990) is José Antonio Navarro. Robin W. Doughty, in his *Wildlife and Man in Texas: Environmental Change and Conservation* (Austin: University of Texas Press, 1983), dismisses the writings of Tejanos and Hispanic travelers to Texas, going straight to Anglo-American views of the region. Even the most widely used college-level Texas history reader, *The Texas Heritage*, 2nd ed., ed. Ben Procter and Archie P. McDonald (Arlington Heights, Illinois: Harlan Davidson, 1992), almost completely ignores the Tejanos in the three essays dealing with the Anglo colonization, independence, and republic of Texas. Instead of forming an integral part of these dramas, Tejanos are relegated to a separate essay toward the back of the book.

4. Carlos E. Castañeda, *Our Catholic Heritage in Texas*, 7 vols. (1936–58; reprint, New York: Arno, 1976), 6:183.

5. Commandant General to governor of Texas, March 29, 1821, Nacogdoches Archives, transcripts, Barker Texas History Center, University of Texas at Austin (hereafter cited as NAT).

6. Report of the Ayuntamiento of San Fernando de Béxar in compliance with the provisions of the Royal Decree of July 11, 1820, NAT.

7. James M. McReynolds, "Family Life in a Borderlands Community: Nacogdoches, Texas, 1779–1861" (PhD diss., Texas Tech University, 1978), 23–25.

8. Instructions for the Texas deputy to the provincial deputation, November 15, 1820, Béxar Archives, Barker Texas History Center, University of Texas at Austin (hereafter cited as BA); City Council minutes of June 10, 1822, in Ayuntamiento Minute Book (1821–25), January 17, 1821, ibid.; Instructions for the deputy from Texas to the Constituent Congress of the Mexican Empire, January 30, 1822, NAT; Instructions to the commissioners of the junta who are to represent Texas at the provincial deputation in Monterrey, in copy book of documents certifying the amounts of money in Bank of Texas currency held by individuals making demands on the Junta Gubernativa, May 2, 1823, BA.

9. Jesús F. de la Teja and John Wheat, "Béxar: Profile of a Tejano Community, 1820–1832," *Southwestern Historical Quarterly* 89, no. 1 (July 1985): 30–31; Vito Alessio Robles, *Coahuila y Texas desde la consumación de la independencia hasta el tratado de paz de Guadalupe Hidalgo*, 2 vols. (1945–46; reprint, Mexico: Editorial Porrúa, 1979), 1:373.

10. José Félix Trespalacios to ayuntamiento and commander at la Bahía, April 17, 1823, BA; Trespalacios to junta gubernativa, April 24, 1823, ibid.; Juan Martín Veramendi to Luciano García, July 8, 1823, ibid.; Luciano García to ayuntamiento, Sept. 25, 1823, ibid.; Deputation to ayuntamiento, September 30, 1824, ibid.; Deputation to *jefe político*, October 1, 1824, ibid. See also Nettie Lee Benson, *The Provincial Deputation in Mexico: Harbinger of Provincial Autonomy, Independence, and Federalism* (Austin: University of Texas Press, 1992), 51–60.

11. Instructions for the deputy from Texas to the Constituent Congress of the Mexican Empire, January 30, 1822, NAT; De la Garza to ayuntamiento, July 17, 1822, BA.

12. De la Garza to ayuntamiento, May 28, 1823, BA.

13. Seguín to provincial deputation of Texas, December 23, 1823, in deputation to ayuntamiento, February 12, 1824, Eugene C. Barker, ed., *Austin Papers*, 3 vols. (vols. 1 and 2, Washington, DC: American Historical Association, 1924, 1928; vol. 3, Austin: University of Texas, 1927), 1:741.

14. Ayuntamiento Minute Book I, for February 15, 1824, BA.

15. Seguín to Bastrop, April 21, 1824, *Austin Papers*, 1:775.

16. Jesús F. de la Teja, ed., *A Revolution Remembered: The Memoirs and Selected Correspondence of Juan N. Seguín* (Austin: State House Press, 1991), 9.

17. Erasmo Seguin to Austin and Bastrop, January 14, 1824, *Austin Papers*, 1:723.

18. Seguín to Austin, July 24, 1825, *Austin Papers*, 1:1157.

19. Seguin to Bastrop, March 24, 1824, *Austin Papers*, 1:758.

20. Eugene C. Barker, *The Life of Stephen F. Austin, Founder of Texas, 1793–1836* (1925; reprint, Austin: University of Texas Press, 1969), 355.

21. James E. B. Austin to Stephen F. Austin, August 22, 1826, *Austin Papers*, 1:1430–31.

22. Seguín to Bastrop, March 24, 1824, Barker, *Austin Papers*, 1:758.

23. Seguín to Austin, August 11, 1824, *Austin Papers*, 1:874–75.

24. Instructions from the Ayuntamiento of Béxar for the deputy from Texas to the Constituent Congress of the Mexican Empire, January 20, 1822, NAT.

25. Juan A. Seguín to governor, August 15, 1821, BA; Santiago Dill to governor, October 22, 1821, ibid.; Refugio de la Garza to Ayuntamiento of Béxar, March 27, 1822, ibid.; Ayuntamiento to governor, March 28, 1822, ibid.

26. Manchola to Mateo Ahumada, Oct. 29, 1826, BA, cited in Andrés Tijerina, "Tejano Identity under the Mexican Flag," (manuscript in possession of author), 43–44.

27. De la Teja, *A Revolution Remembered*, 17.

28. David J. Weber, *The Mexican Frontier, 1821–1846: The American Southwest Under Mexico*

(Albuquerque: University of New Mexico Press, 1982), 176.

29. Weber, *The Mexican Frontier*, 176; Vito Alessio Robles, *Coahuila y Texas*, 1:383–86; Tijerina, "Tejano Identity," 33–34.

30. Memorial, ayuntamiento to state congress, December 19, 1832, NAT.

31. Alessio Robles, *Coahuila y Texas*, 1:429–37.

32. Eugene C. Barker, *Life of Stephen F. Austin*, 355.

33. Celia Gutiérrez Ibarra, ed., *Cómo México perdió Texas: Análisis y transcripción del informe secreto (1834) de Juan Nepomuceno Almonte* (Mexico: Instituto Nacional de Antropología e Historia, 1987), Apéndice, 23.

34. Ibid., 30.

35. Ibid., 34–35.

36. Alessio Robles, *Coahuila y Texas*, 1:490–97; Barker, *Life of Stephen F. Austin*, 393, 403–405; Paul Lack, *The Texas Revolutionary Experience: A Political and Social History, 1835–1836* (College Station: Texas A&M University Press, 1992), 7–8.

37. Balmaceda to Madero, April 6, 1833, published in the *Gaceta del gobierno del estado de Coahuila y Tejas*, May 27, 1833, reproduced in Ibarra, *Cómo México perdió Texas*, Apéndice, 5.

38. De la Teja, *A Revolution Remembered*, 21–22.

39. James Bowie and William Fannin to Stephen F. Austin, October 22, 1835, in John J. Jenkins, ed., *The Papers of the Texas Revolution*, 10 vols. (Austin: Presidial Press, 1973), 2:191.

40. Paul Lack, *The Texas Revolutionary Experience*, 183–207.

41. Lack, *The Texas Revolutionary Experience*, 55–57, 78–81; see also chap. 10, "Los Tejanos."

42. Kathryn Stoner O'Connor, *Presidio La Bahia del Espiritu Santo de Zuniga, 1721–1846* (1966; reprint, Victoria, Texas: private printing, 1984), 253.

Bibliographic Essay

Early Texas and San Antonio cannot and should not be understood strictly from an American history perspective. Texas was part of an indigenous world upon which Europe intruded in the sixteenth century, and so the region enters Western history as part of the modern age of Spanish imperialism. Spaniards' quest for riches, adventure, and souls eventually brought them to what later came to be known as Texas, where they interacted with a wide variety of cultures; soon began demographic, economic, and cultural processes still at work in the Lone Star State today. In other words, Texas history is not at all parochial; it is a rich mixture of world and local events. And so, to properly understand the story of Texas, we need to understand indigenous stories, European stories, Mexican stories, as well as American stories.

This essay focuses on those works more accessible to a general audience focusing on Spanish, Mexican, and Republic Texas and therefore is subject to some limitations. There is a rich Spanish-language historiography of the colonial and nineteenth-century Hispanic world, some of which is cited in individual chapters of this book, but discussion of which lies beyond the scope of this essay. Moreover, I make no claims to being comprehensive in coverage, chronologically, geographically, or thematically. I mention some of those recent works I have found useful in the course of my studies, investigations, and classroom experiences. I make no effort to systematically cite items to be found in the notes to the individual essays, instead focusing on studies that supplement or expand upon my writings. A more complete survey of the literature produced in the last quarter-century can be found in F. Todd Smith's essay "Spanish, Mexican, and Republican Texas to 1845" in *Discovering Texas History*, edited by Bruce A. Glasrud, Light Townsend Cummins, and Gary D. Wintz (2014).[1]

World histories rarely make room for early Texas, so it is difficult to get that level of perspective from any single source. However, books dealing with Spanish history, even when they do not cover Texas directly, still provide the necessary context to understand Texas. A good place to start is

William D. Phillips Jr. and Carla Rahn Phillips, *A Concise History of Spain* (2010) and J. H. Elliott, *Imperial Spain, 1469–1716* (2nd ed., 2002). The former provides a grounding in Spanish history from prehistoric times to recent events and the latter focuses on Spain in the age when it struggled to form a modern nation state at the same time that it established the first worldwide empire. Elliott's more recent *Empires of the Atlantic World: Britain and Spain in America 1492–1830* (2006) provides a comprehensive overview of the two empires most engaged in transforming the Americas into extensions of the Western world. In *American Colonies*, Alan Taylor attempts to bring a multicultural perspective to the history of North America. Although not as generous with coverage of Texas as might be hoped, the book provides a good corrective to the mid-Atlantic seaboard chauvinism of most American history. My own brief overview of imperial rivalries in the context of Texas can be found in chapter 1, "European Competition for the New World," of La Belle: *The Ship that Changed History*, edited by James E. Bruseth (2014).

From an imperial perspective, Texas was part of what before 1821 was known as the Viceroyalty of New Spain. There are numerous good histories of Mexico from which to choose, any one of which can provide the necessary background to understanding the story of Texas. For decades *The Course of Mexican History* (9th ed., 2010), by Michael C. Meyer, William L. Sherman, and Susan M. Deeds, has been the most popular textbook treatment, and the most recent editions have tried to incorporate some earlier history of Texas and the borderlands before it gets to the events surrounding Mexico's loss of Texas and the war with the United States. A denser, more analytical approach is taken by Oxford historian Alan Knight in his three-volume history of Mexico, the first two volumes of which, *Mexico: From the Beginning to the Conquest* (2002) and *Mexico: The Colonial Era* (2002) are particularly noteworthy. For those willing to delve even deeper, the impressive cast of contributors to *The Oxford History of Mexico* (2010), edited by William Beezley and Michael Meyer, cover a broad range of topics in very sophisticated ways. Still useful for gaining a good foundation in Mexican colonial history and society, many elements of which played a vital role in Texas, is *The Forging of the Cosmic Race: A Reinterpretation of Colonial Mexico* by Colin M. MacLachlan and Jaime E. Rodríguez O. (1980).

We are very fortunate to have a handful of works that provide a solid foundation for understanding early Texas in its borderlands context. Two surveys from very different perspectives combine to tell the full story of Spain north of the Rio Grande. David J. Weber's *The Spanish Frontier in*

North America (1992) is a comprehensive survey of what is now the southern half of the United States from the early sixteenth century to Mexican independence. John L. Kessell's more geographically limited *Spain in the Southwest: A Narrative History of Colonial New Mexico, Arizona, Texas, and California* (2002) nevertheless offers a colorful account of the western part of Spanish North America. Oakah L. Jones Jr. synthesized the available secondary literature to tell the story of Hispanic settlement on Mexico's colonial frontier in *Los Paisanos: Spanish Settlers on the Northern Frontier of New Spain* (1979, 1996). This is a very different book from Weber's and Kessell's in its emphasis on demographic and social processes that brought Spanish colonial civilization to what is now the US side of the border from neighboring Mexican provinces. Although now somewhat dated, it remains a sound introduction to the region and Texas' place in it.

There is another side to the story, however, one that centers on the indigenous experience. Charles C. Mann's *1491: New Revelations of the Americas before Columbus* (2005) tells a hemispheric story of what Europeans found when they encountered the original Americans, emphasizing the development of Indian societies over time in relation to New World environments. Brian M. Fagan's *The Great Journey: The Peopling of Ancient America* (2004) is a well-illustrated and clearly written introduction to North American prehistory that begins with the theories regarding the Old World origins of the American Indian populations. A highly entertaining—and informative—alternative is *The Eternal Frontier: An Ecological History of North America and Its Peoples* by Tim Flannery (2001), which does not even get around to introducing human beings until halfway through the book. Flannery does take the story into the twentieth century, however, so he treats Indians, Europeans, and others as just waves of migrations with distinct ecological effects on North America. William C. Foster's *Climate and Culture Change in North America AD 900–1600* (2012) is another ambitious work, arguing for the movement and transformation of groups across the continent in response to environmental conditions. For Texas proper, Timothy K. Perttula's edited volume, *The Prehistory of Texas* (reprint, 2013), is a comprehensive volume that makes sense of the latest findings about the cultural landscape of the region from earliest times to the eve of European intrusion.

General histories of Texas during the three centuries of a Spanish presence are available from very different perspectives. Carlos E. Castañeda's monumental seven-volume *Our Catholic Heritage in Texas, 1519–1936* (1936–58) remains important for serious scholars, but at six volumes covering the story up to 1836 and its rather dated sensibilities, it is not suitable for the contemporary general audience. The best one-volume effort is Donald E. Chipman, *Spanish Texas, 1519–1821* (rev. ed., 2010), which offers a solid narrative employing more recent research findings to tell the story from the Spanish perspective. In part 1 of *Texas: Crossroads of North America* by Jesús F. de la Teja, Ron Tyler, and Nancy Beck Young (2016), I tell the story of the region as an integral part of the Mexican frontier, stressing how colonial Mexican social, economic, and political developments created the world that Anglo Americans would quickly come to dominate following Mexican independence.

The general trend in American historiography over the past thirty years or so to more systematically include the indigenous side of the story has resulted in a number of recent works that tell the story of Texas from very different viewpoints. Although the first three quarters of the twentieth century produced numerous studies telling stories of Spanish-Indian interactions, Elizabeth A. H. John's *Storms Brewed in Other Men's Worlds: The Confrontation of Indians, Spanish, and French in the Southwest, 1540–1795* (reprint, 1996) was one of the first major efforts to give native peoples "agency." The Texas portions of the book are indispensable for gaining an appreciation of just how complex the story of European-Indian relations actually was. F. Todd Smith's *From Dominance to Disappearance: The Indians of Texas and the Near Southwest, 1786–1859* (2005), explicitly built on *Storms Brewed in Other Men's Worlds*, is a thoughtful survey of the decline of Indian fortunes, particular those of the Caddos, at the turn of the nineteenth century. Gary Clayton Anderson uses the social science concept of ethnic re-creation, ethnogenesis, to tell the indigenous side of the story of the greater Texas region in *The Indian Southwest, 1580–1830: Ethnogenesis and Reinvention* (1999). More restricted in chronological scope, but more expansive in bringing issues of gender and native sovereignty to the story of Indian-European interactions, is *Peace Came in the Form of a Woman: Indians and Spaniards in the Texas Borderlands* by Juliana Barr (2007). She summarized her major argument that Indians were actually the ones who controlled Texas in "Beyond Their Control: Spaniards in Native Texas," in *Choice, Persuasion, and Coercion: Social Control on Spain's North American Frontiers*, edited by Jesús F. de la Teja and Ross Frank (2005). For a very readable general survey of the Texas Indian story, there is David La Vere's *The Texas Indians* (2004), which, like Barr's work, emphasizes inter-Indian dynamics independent of Euroamericans. Finally, William C. Foster helps clarify some of the confusion over the region's indigenous cultural landscape in *Historic Native Peoples of Texas* (2008).

The broader interest in indigenous Texas and the Southwest has produced considerable new work on specific groups. Among these, none has received more attention than the Comanches, who from the time they entered Texas history in the mid-eighteenth century until their final defeat in the 1870s were at the center of regional events. In *The Comanche Empire* (2008), Pekka Hämäläinen makes the argument that although not an "empire" in the European sense, the Comanches' expansionist economic domination of the southern Plains qualifies them as an imperialist power. Thomas A. Britten's *The Lipan Apaches: People of Wind and Lightning* (2009) is the story of the Comanches' chief rivals east of New Mexico, who although progressively pushed south of the San Antonio area by their more powerful Indian rivals still managed to remain autonomous until the mid-nineteenth century. In *The Wichita Indians: Traders of Texas and the Southern Plains, 1540–1845* (2000), F. Todd Smith tells the story of yet another migrant native group that by the mid-eighteenth century had crossed the Red River and established control over a large portion of North-Central Texas as far south as the Brazos River.

It was not just Plains Indians whose activities challenged Spanish efforts in Texas; so too did the peoples of the eastern parts of the state. Archeologist Robert A. Ricklis has brought together the most important findings on one of the most misunderstood groups in *The Karankawa Indians of Texas: An Ecological Study of Cultural Tradition and Change* (1996), while Kelly F. Himmel takes the story forward to its tragic end in *The Conquest of the Karankawas and the Tonkawas, 1821–1859* (1999). Although it followed a different trajectory, the story of the Caddo Indians of the Texas-Louisiana-Arkansas-Oklahoma border region is no less tragic. The title of F. Todd Smith's study, *The Caddo Indians: Tribes at the Convergence of Empires, 1542–1854* (2000), highlights the "in-between" existence of a people that tried to preserve their autonomy in the face of Spanish and French interests. David La Vere takes an even longer view of the Caddos in *The Caddo Chiefdoms: Caddo Economics and Politics, 700–1835* (1998), which stresses the sophistication of the westernmost of the North American woodlands people.

European exploration of North America generally is beyond the scope of this essay, but Robert S. Weddle's three-volume study of the exploration and settlement of the Gulf of Mexico is worthy of attention. In *Spanish Sea: The Gulf of Mexico in North American History, 1500–1685* (1985), Weddle lays to rest some long held misconceptions about Spanish activity in the Gulf. In *The French Thorn: Rival Explorers in the Spanish Sea, 1682–1762* (1991), he analyzes how the fears of Frenchmen and Englishmen prodded Spain to pay attention to the neglected upper-Gulf Coast region. Finally,

Weddle tells the story of Spain's struggles in the face of English and Anglo-American challenges in *Changing Tides: Twilight and Dawn in the Spanish Sea, 1763–1803* (1995).

The exploration of what we now know as Texas by Europeans began on an inauspicious note, the shipwrecked conquistador Álvar Núñez Cabeza de Vaca and his three fellow survivors of the Pánfilo de Narváez expedition to conquer Florida. A veritable cottage industry has grown up around the man who introduced what became Texas to the Western world and who remains the earliest ethnographic source on the region. Cabeza de Vaca recounted his travels through what are today Texas, Coahuila, Chihuahua, New Mexico, Sonora, and Sinaloa in a work titled *Relación*. It has been translated numerous times, including the very readable and well-illustrated *Castaways: The Narrative of Alvar Núñez Cabeza de Vaca*, edited by Enrique Pupo-Walker, translated by Frances M. López-Morillas (1993). Cabeza de Vaca's writings have been analyzed from anthropological, ethnohistorical, historical, and literary criticism perspectives, and Andrés Reséndez's *A Land So Strange: The Epic Journey of Cabeza de Vaca* (2007) is the best at making sense of the tale.

Cebeza de Vaca was followed by the Coronado and De Soto-Moscoso expeditions. Perhaps because De Soto died on the banks of the Mississippi River before his expedition traveled through eastern Texas, relatively little has been written about the Texas portion of that story. Luis de Moscoso, De Soto's second in command, brought the still formidable force of Spaniards into Texas in an attempt to reach Spanish territory overland. The best analysis of the available evidence in the effort to learn their route is James E. Bruseth and Nancy A. Kenmotsu, "From Naguatex to the River Daycao: The Route of the Hernando De Soto Expedition Through Texas," *North American Archaeologist* (1993). Analysis of the De Soto campaign from a variety of disciplinary perspectives is found in Patricia Kay Galloway's edited volume *The Hernando de Soto Expedition: History, Historiography, and "Discovery" in the Southeast* (2006). Although Francisco Vázquez de Coronado's expedition never entered the territory of Spanish Texas, Richard Flint's *No Settlement, No Conquest: A History of the Coronado Entrada* (2008) is worth mentioning for its effort to explain the thinking behind Spanish exploratory activity in the sixteenth century.

The occupation of Spanish Texas and development of communities and institutions has not received nearly enough attention, but there are some basic works of note. In *Spanish Expeditions into Texas, 1689–1768* (1995), William C. Foster attempts to untangle the often confusing information regarding the routes of travel of the Spanish *entradas* and reconnaissance expeditions into Texas. Juan Bautista Chapa's *Texas and Northeastern Mexico, 1630–1690* (1997), edited and annotated by Foster, provides considerable insight into the nature of Mexico's northeastern frontier on the eve of the occupation of Texas. Still unsurpassed for telling the story of Spain's efforts to locate La Salle, and therefore of Spain's initial interactions with Texas, is Robert S. Weddle's *Wilderness Manhunt: The Spanish Search for La Salle* (1973), which is counterbalanced by his more recent look at the French expedition in *The Wreck of the Belle, the Ruin of La Salle* (2001). William C. Foster has made readily available the best source on the French side of the La Salle fiasco in a new translation of La Salle's secretary's diary: *The La Salle Expedition to Texas: The Journal of Henri Joutel, 1684–1687* (1998). Biographical sketches of the men involved in these early activities as well as other Spaniards important to understanding Spanish Texas can be found in Donald E. Chipman and Harriett Denise Joseph's *Notable Men and Women of Spanish Texas* (1999).

It is impossible to appreciate the Spanish Texas story without a working knowledge of the institutions on which Spain built its frontier provinces. As I argue in some of the chapters in this book, Texas was first and foremost a military province. The institutional dimension of the military system at work in Spanish Texas is the subject of Max L. Moorhead's *The Presidio: Bastion of the Spanish Borderlands* (1975). A good update to Moorhead's work is V. A. Vincent, "The Frontier Soldier: Life in the Provincias Internas and the Royal Regulations of 1772, 1766–1787," *Military History of the Southwest* (1992). However, the operation of the far-flung frontier defensive system proved an ultimately insurmountable problem for Spanish policymakers, as Elizabeth A. H. John's edited volume *Views from the Apache Frontier: Report on the Northern Provinces of New Spain by José Cortés, Lieutenant in the Royal Corps of Engineers, 1799* (1989) makes clear. Another example of the effort to define the problem and propose solutions is "Ramón de Murillo's Plan for the Reform of New Spain's Frontier Defenses," edited and annotated by Jesús F. de la Teja, *Southwestern Historical Quarterly* (2004).

Unfortunately, there is as yet no stand-alone synthesis of the presidio system in operation, but a handful of works provide a good foundation for understanding it. Of the various studies that discuss the military inspections of Pedro de Rivera and the Marqués de Rubí, the latter of which produced critical changes in the operation of Texas government, the best for a basic understanding of what happened is *Imaginary Kingdom: Texas as Seen by the Rivera and Rubí Military Expeditions, 1727 and 1767*, edited by Jack Jackson and annotated by William C. Foster (1995). Donald C. Cutter's *The Defenses of Northern New Spain: Hugo O'Conor's Report to Teodoro de Croix, July 22, 1777* (1994) makes clear the frustrations of dealing with a frontier that Spain held largely in name only. Historical archeologist James E. Ivey covers the evolution of Béxar's garrison in "The Presidio of San Antonio de Béxar: Historical and Archaeological Research," *Southwestern Historical Quarterly* (2004).

Like the presidio, the mission was critical to Spain's efforts to incorporate Texas into the imperial fold. From the appearance of Herbert E. Bolton's critical essay "The Mission as a Frontier Institution," *American Historical Review* (1917), the story of the Spanish colonial missions has been viewed from the perspective of the goals and efforts of missionaries and Spanish policymakers. A newer generation of scholars has come to focus on the negative effects of the missionary project on the target populations, however. See, for example, David Sweet, "The Ibero-American Frontier Mission in Native American History," in Erick Langer and Robert H. Jackson, editors, *The New Latin American Mission History* (1995). Jackson's survey *From Savages to Subjects: Missions in the History of the American Southwest* (2000) serves as a useful general survey of missionary enterprise on the northern frontier.

As in the case of the presidio, however, a general synthesis of Franciscan efforts in Texas is lacking, but the introductory chapter in Marion A. Habig, *The Alamo Chain of Missions: A History of San Antonio's Five Old Missions* (1968), remains a very useful survey of the institution from the Spanish viewpoint. Two essays by Gilberto M. Hinojosa provide a more contemporary perspective on Spanish-Indian interactions in the San Antonio area. In "Friars and Indians: Towards a Perspective of Cultural Interaction in the San Antonio Mission" (1990), Hinojosa attempts to break away from the older approach that treated the neophytes as little more than objects, while in "Religious-Indian Communities: The Goals of the Friars," in *Tejano Origins in Eighteenth-Century San Antonio*, edited by Gerald E. Poyo and Gilberto M. Hinojosa (1991), he provides a concise and objective overview of the missionary enterprise in general. Another useful essay in appreciating some of the causes of the decline in the mission system is Félix D. Almaráz Jr., "San Antonio's Old Franciscan Missions: Material Decline and Secular Avarice in the Transition from Hispanic to Mexican Control," *Americas* (1987). Almaráz followed up with *The San Antonio Missions and Their System of Land Tenure* (1989), which examines the process of land acquisition and loss from their founding through final breakup in the mid-nineteenth century.

Spaniards did not rely solely on soldiers and friars to carry on the work of developing the frontier; civilian settlers were always a critical component. Gilbert R. Cruz surveys the founding of settlements on the frontier in *Let There Be Towns: Spanish Municipal Origins in the American Southwest, 1610–1810* (reprint, 1996). Although uncritically accepting of Spanish settlement activities and overemphasizing the democratic character of the cabildo system, Cruz does provide a good grounding in Spanish colonial civil government institutions. In the case of Texas, the story of La Bahía has yet to receive comprehensive scholarly treatment, but Craig H. Roell provides a good introduction in *Remember Goliad! A History of La Bahía* (1994). Also lacking a comprehensive survey is the often neglected East Texas Tejano community, which is the subject of Francis Xavier Galán, "Presidio Los Adaes: Worship, Kinship, and Commerce with French Natchitoches on the Spanish-Franco-Caddo Borderlands, 1721–1773," *Louisiana History* (2008), and Patrick J. Walsh, "Living on the Edge of the Neutral Zone: Varieties of Identity in Nacogdoches, Texas 1773–1810," *East Texas Historical Journal* (1999). For the part of South Texas that was colonial Nuevo Santander, Omar S. Valerio-Jiménez's *River of Hope: Forging Identity and Nation in the Rio Grande Borderlands* (2013) tells the story of the region's development from a socio-economic perspective.

The best-developed civilian settlement was San Antonio, the province's largest and most diverse community. Aside from my book, *San Antonio de Béxar: A Community on New Spain's Northern Frontier* (1995), different aspects of the city's early story are told in the various essays in Poyo and Hinojosa's *Tejano Origins in Eighteenth-Century San Antonio*. In a follow-up volume edited by Poyo, *Tejano Journey, 1770–1850* (1996), his essay "Community and Autonomy" discusses Tejanos' development of a strong sense of independence through an examination of the conflicts between governors and townspeople. The critically important issue of water in the town's early development is the subject of I. Wayne Cox, *The Spanish Acequias of San Antonio* (2005) and Charles R. Porter Jr., *Spanish Water, Anglo Water: Early Development in San Antonio* (2009), both of which take their subject from colonial times into the twentieth century. Aside from his examination of the presidio, James E. Ivey is the author of an article exploring aspects of San Antonio's physical development, "A Reconsideration of the Survey of the Villa de San Fernando de Béxar in 1731," *Southwestern Historical Quarterly* (2008). No Spanish colonial town could exist without a proper church, construction of which was not an exclusively religious exercise, as Adán Benavides explains in "Sacred Space, Profane Reality: The Politics of Building a Church in Eighteenth-Century Texas," *Southwestern Historical Quarterly* (2003).

One other institution of northern Mexican frontier life that deserves attention is ranching. Livestock, both horse culture and cattle raising, is an integral part of the region's Hispanic identity, and Spanish-Mexican practices are often credited for serving as the foundations of American (and Texan) cowboy culture. Cultural geographer Terry G. Jordan attempted a comprehensive survey of livestock culture in *North American Cattle-Ranching Frontiers: Origins, Diffusion, and Differentiation* (1993), which was a follow-up to the somewhat controversial *Trails to Texas: Southern Roots of Western Cattle Ranching* (1981). Partly as a response to that work, which seemed to downplay the Mexican roots of ranching, Jack Jackson produced a comprehensive narrative history of ranching in *Los Mesteños: Spanish Ranching in Texas, 1721–1821* (1986). The difficulties of creating a safe environment for cattle operations in Spanish Texas is one of the principal subjects of *El Fuerte del Cíbolo: Sentinel of the Béxar-La Bahía Ranches* by Robert H. Thonhoff (1992). The development of ranching below the Nueces River is well told by Armando Alonzo in *Tejano Legacy: Rancheros and Settlers in South Texas, 1734–1900* (1998). And, the relationship of land, water, and the law is the subject of Jesús F. de la Teja's "'Only Fit for Raising Stock': Spanish and Mexican Land and Water Rights in the Tamaulipan Cession," in *Fluid Arguments: Five Centuries of Western Water Conflict*, edited by Char Miller (2001).

Of course, society is made up of more than economic, political, and religious institutions; it is people and their culture. Women's history has come in for more attention in the past twenty years, and a good place to begin is *Las Tejanas: 300 Years of History* by Teresa Palomo Acosta and Ruthe Winegarten (2003), and "Colonial Women," in *Notable Men and Women of Spanish Texas* (1999). Amy M. Porter explores Spanish frontier women's lives, including at San Antonio, in *Their Lives, Their Wills: Women in the Borderlands, 1750–1846* (2014). Much has been made of the differences in the legal status of women between the Hispanic and English worlds and how that applied to Texas. That is the subject of *Hers, His, and Theirs: Community Property Law in Spain and Early Texas* by Jean A. Stuntz (2005) and of *Homesteads Ungovernable: Families, Sex, Race, and the Law in Frontier Texas, 1823–1860* by Mark M. Carroll, which picks up the story in the Mexican era. Among the variety of collections focusing on women, Mary L. Scheer's *Women and the Texas Revolution* (2011) includes essays dealing with native and Hispanic women that remind us that within a generally marginalized group there are subgroups even more isolated from the main currents of historical memory.

What is needed is more spade work in the bountiful primary sources to uncover new and different stories. Studies of families and individual women remain too few, but there are some prominent examples. Patricia De León, matriarch of the De León clan after her husband's passing, is a central subject of *De León: A Tejano Family History* (2003) by Ana Carolina Castillo Crimm. Nora Ríos McMillan narrates the story of one of the best-documented women of late colonial and Mexican Texas in "A Woman of Worth: Ana María del Carmen Calvillo," in *Tejano Epic*, edited by Arnoldo De León (2005).

The political organization and jurisdictional history of the Spanish borderlands is a complicated topic, much of which is of limited interest to the general audience. However, for those interested in understanding the demographics, political and ecclesiastical jurisdictions, and relationships between Texas, its neighboring provinces, and the viceroyalty as a whole, Peter Gerhard's *The North Frontier of New Spain* (2nd ed., 1993) is indispensable. Among the most complex jurisdictional issues in Texas history was the claim that the Thomas Jefferson administration made to the territory north and east of the Rio Grande following the Louisiana Purchase. That story is brought up to date, although from a decidedly American perspective, by J. C. A. Stagg in *Borderlines in Borderlands: James Madison and the Spanish-American Frontier, 1776–1821* (2009). Spain's fears about the loss of Texas to the United States is treated in Maurine T. Wilson and Jack Jackson's *Philip Nolan and Texas: Expeditions to the Unknown Land, 1791–1801* (1987) and *Jefferson and Southwestern Exploration: The Freeman and Custis Accounts of the Red River Expedition of 1806* by Dan L. Flores (1984).

A decade after the Louisiana Purchase put a new rival on Spain's Texas doorstep, the crisis deepened with the outbreak of Mexico's War of Independence. A good survey of the decade-long conflict is Timothy J. Henderson, *The Mexican Wars of Independence* (2009). For anyone wishing to delve deeply into the processes of the Mexican independence movement, Eric Van Young's prodigious study, *The Other Rebellion: Popular Violence, Ideology, and the Mexican Struggle for Independence, 1810–1821* (2002) is an examination of the thinking of over one thousand rebels from trial records. For the northeastern frontier, including Texas, *A World Not to Come: A History of Latino Writing and Print Culture*, by Raúl Coronado (2013), is an intellectual history that focuses much of its attention on José Bernardo Gutiérrez de Lara, the Hidalgo supporter who was never caught, led an invasion of Texas, and went on to become an important early national political leader in his home state of Tamaulipas.

A number of more specialized studies add to or provide different perspectives on events. The bloodiest and largest battle ever fought on Texas soil is the subject of Ted Schwarz, *Forgotten Battlefield of the First Texas Revolution: The Battle of Medina, August 18, 1813*, edited and annotated by Robert H. Thonhoff (1985). In the 1850s, José Antonio Navarro published personal reminiscences of events from his participation in the war as a teenager: *Defending Mexican Valor in Texas: José Antonio Navarro's Historical Writings, 1853–1857*, edited by David R. McDonald and Timothy M. Matovina (1995). Ed Bradley's "Fighting for Texas: Filibuster James Long, the Adams-Onís Treaty, and the Monroe Administration," *Southwestern Historical Quarterly* (1999), brings the international conflict to the local level. In "Take Pity on Our Glory: Men of Champ d'Asile," *Southwestern Historical Quarterly* (1984), Kent Gardien updates the story of the French Napoleonic exiles who briefly sought to establish a new homeland at the upper reaches of Galveston Bay.

Just as he later did for the Spanish colonial period, David J. Weber produced a masterful survey of borderlands history from 1821 to 1848 in *The Mexican Frontier, 1821–1846: The American Southwest Under Mexico* (1982). The work remains the starting point for considering Texas' place in the clash of nations that ultimately produced today's American Southwest. A more focused examination of the transformations in local Mexican frontier societies occasioned by the turmoil of the decades of Mexican independence is found in Andrés Reséndez's thoughtful *Changing National Identities at the Frontier: Texas and New Mexico, 1800–1850* (2004).

However, as in the case of the Spanish era, a good grounding in the history of Mexico's first decades as an independent nation is useful to understanding the dynamics of the Texas case. Two very different works offer in-depth coverage: Timothy E. Anna's *Forging Mexico, 1821–1835* (1998) and Stanley C. Green's *The Mexican Republic: The First Decade, 1823–1832* (1987). In addition, it is helpful to understand the leading figure of the time, Antonio López de Santa Anna, who first came to Texas as a junior officer in 1813 during the royalist campaign to regain control of the province, later bore personal responsibility for losing Texas at the battle of San Jacinto, and ultimately contributed to Mexico's loss of the territory that today comprises California, Nevada, Arizona, New Mexico, Colorado, and Utah. The best of these biographies is Will Fowler's *Santa Anna of Mexico* (2007).

Underpopulated and underdeveloped, Texas could not hope to join the other states of the Mexican union as a full partner. The result was a forced union with neighboring Coahuila, a coupling the consequences of which have not been fully appreciated by American historians. Among the handful of scholars who have paid attention to the issue, Nettie Lee Benson offers a sound overview of the politics in "Texas as Viewed from Mexico, 1821–1834," *Southwestern Historical Quarterly* (1987). Still the best brief explanation of the process that brought about the State of Coahuila y Texas is Charles A. Bacarisse's "The Union of Coahuila and Texas," *Southwestern Historical Quarterly* (1958). Andrés Tijerina's *Tejanos and Texas under the Mexican Flag, 1821–1836* (1994) argues that Mexican Texans had well-established and effective institutions when the Anglo Americans arrived, an argument furthered in the essays on eleven Tejano leaders in Jesús F. de la Teja, editor, *Tejano Leadership in Mexican and Revolutionary Texas* (2010).

The considerable historiography on Anglo-American settlement, the Texas Revolution, and the Republic would take this essay far afield from the story of Hispanic Texas, so I will focus on only those studies that offer considerable departures from the traditional historiography and emphasize Tejano themes. First is Gregg Cantrell's *Stephen F. Austin: Empresario of Texas* (1999), which supersedes Eugene C. Barker's classic biography and provides a more balanced account of the empresario's role in the transformation of Texas into an extension of American southern society by taking greater consideration of Mexican and Tejano figures in the story. Next is Gary Clayton Anderson's *The Conquest of Texas: Ethnic Cleansing in the Promised Land, 1820–1875* (2005), which, as its title makes clear, takes a radically different view of the warfare between westward moving Anglo Americans and the native and Hispanic peoples of the region. A more focused study of the process of Indian removal in Texas is found in Kelly F. Himmel's *The Conquest of the Karankawas and the Tonkawas, 1821–1859* (1999).

Béxar during the Mexican period underwent a political devolution, first in losing its status as a provincial capital, when Saltillo became the seat of government for Coahuila y Texas, and later when it lost territory as department capital with the creation first of the Department of the Brazos and later a third department centered at Nacogdoches. Nevertheless, San Antonio remained the largest urban center and the gateway to the Mexican interior. An overview of San Antonio during the Mexican era is presented in Jesús F. de la Teja and John Wheat, "Béxar: Profile of a Tejano Community," in *Tejano Origins in Eighteenth-Century San Antonia*, edited by Gerald E. Poyo and Gilberto M. Hinojosa (1985). Raúl A. Ramos's *Beyond the Alamo: Forging Mexican Ethnicity in San Antonio, 1821–1861* (2008) is an important attempt to understand the stresses Tejano society underwent in the 1820s and 1830s, while Timothy M. Matovina's *Tejano Religion and Ethnicity, San Antonio, 1821–1860* (1995) explores the increasing tensions that the monolithically Catholic community in 1821 faced in the decades following Texas independence.

As the entrepôt between Texas and the rest of Mexico, San Antonio was battered by warfare from the early 1810s through the early 1840s. No period was more destructive, however, than the six months from October 1835 to March 1836, when it was at the heart of the struggle for Texas independence. Stephen L. Hardin's *Texian Iliad: A Military History of the Texas Revolution* (1994) is the most balanced general history of the war available, providing good coverage of the fights in and around Béxar and taking particular notice of the Tejano role in the warfare. One other important work on the revolution that takes into account Tejano aspects of the story is Paul D. Lack, *The Texas Revolutionary Experience: A Political and Social History, 1835–1836* (1992).

Tejano perspectives on the war, although largely marginalized in the traditional historiography until recently, are readily available. Timothy M. Matovina's *The Alamo Remembered: Tejano Accounts and Perspectives* (1995) brings together and analyzes the stories of the women and children who survived the siege and battle of the Alamo. The most prominent Tejano military figure in the war of independence, Juan N. Seguín, had command of the city following the retreat of the Mexican Army. Jesús F. de la Teja fills in the details and provides a good annotation of Seguín's recollections in *A Revolution Remembered: The Memoirs and Selected Correspondence of Juan N. Seguín* (reprint, 2002). Events in and around San Antonio from the Mexican War of Independence to the Mexican War form the major portion of José Antonio Menchaca's reminiscences, which have been edited and introduced by Timothy Matovina and Jesús F. de la Teja in *Recollections of a Tejano Life: Antonio Menchaca in Texas History* (2013). And, in David McDonald's *José Antonio Navarro: In Search of the American Dream in Nineteenth-Century Texas* (2010), San Antonio's most distinguished Tejano leader for a good portion of the nineteenth century has finally received the thorough biographical treatment he deserved.

Finally, there is the question of visualizing early San Antonio, a particularly intractable problem. For a long time historians relied on the few maps that had been found in the archives of Mexico and Spain, or old photographs, lithographs, and paintings from a later time, and in some cases on original artwork, especially in recent decades that of the renowned José Cisneros of El Paso. Important in understanding the Franciscan project in San Antonio and a helpful way of understanding the remaining cultural landscape of early San Antonio is Jacinto Quirarte's *The Art and Architecture of the Texas Missions* (2002). Since the 1970s, however, the works of

Theodore Gentilz, a Paris-born artist and surveyor contracted by Henri Castro to work in his Texas colony, have become the "go-to" images to depict Hispanic Texas society. I have relied on his empathetic vision of Tejano San Antonio on many occasions, including the illustration of this volume. His life and art are the focus of Dorothy Steinbomer Kendall and Carmen Perry, *Gentilz, Artist of the Old Southwest* (1974). Finally, the recently reissued *History and Legends of the Alamo and Other Missions in and Around San Antonio* by Adina de Zavala and edited by Richard Flores (1996) reminds us that the legacy of Hispanic Texas reaches well beyond the bricks and stones of missions, houses, and forts.

NOTES

1. The essay originally appeared as "Texas through 1845: A Survey of the Historical Literature of Recent Decades," *Southwestern Historical Quarterly* 113, no. 3 (January 2010): 310–41.

Index

acequias (irrigation ditches), 25, 42, 59, 121. *See also* irrigation
Adaes. *See* Los Adaes
Adaesaños, 100, 101–2
agriculture: corn, 25, 43, 140–42; fertility of soil, 37–38; Spanish era profiles, 40–43, 162; Spanish technology, 141. *See also* farming; ranching
aguardiente (brandy), 131
Aguayo, Marqués de San Miguel de (and expedition), 18, 20, 28, 36, 56, 69–70
Aguilar, José Marcos, 95, 107–8
Akokisa Indians, 22
Alabama-Coushatta Indians, 13
Alamo. *See* Valero (Alamo)
Alarcón, Martín de (and expedition), 18, 19, 54, 56, 57, 70
albures (card game), 130
alcabalas (excise tax), 88
alcaldes (magistrates), 61, 132*n* 20, 168, 174. *See also ayuntamiento* (town council)
alcohol, 27, 131–32
Alessio Robles, Vito, 80, 84
Allende, Ignacio, 165–66
Almazán, Fernando Pérez de. *See* Pérez de Almazán, Fernando
Almazán, Juan Antonio de. *See* Pérez de Almazán, Juan Antonio
Almonte, Juan N., 192
Angelina River, 21
Anglo American, definition, 48*n* 1
Anglo bias in literature, 2–3, 139–40, 181–82
Anglo immigration, 30, 31, 186–92
Apache Indians: attacks by, 15, 58, 68–70, 72, 147; early settlement profiles, 12, 13; missions for, 16, 22, 68–69; peace ceremony with, 72

Arocha family, 109, 169, 173
Arredondo, Joaquín, 8, 165, 167, 173, 175
artisans, 24–25, 27, 28, 59, 76, 156*n* 4. *See also* market economy of early settlements
At Home in Texas (Doughty), 35
Austin, James E. B., 187
Austin, Moses, 30, 186
Austin, Stephen F., 186, 187–89, 191, 193
Ayala, José Agabo de, 171
ayuntamiento (town council), 168, 174. *See also alcaldes* (magistrates); *regidores* (aldermen)

Bahía. *See* La Bahía (Goliad)
Balmaceda, José María, 189, 191, 193, 194
Barker, Eugene C., 8
Barrio, Pedro del, 128
Battle of Medina, 8, 167
Battle of Salado Creek, 167, 172
Battle of San Jacinto, 194
Bell, Thomas W., 141, 143
Benavides, Plácido, 194, 195
Benedict. J. W., 146, 148, 149
Bergamo, Ilarione da, 125
Berlandier, Jean Louis, 144
Béxar (settlement). *See* San Antonio de Béxar
Bexareños, definition, 43, 119
Bidai Indians, 13
birds, native, 37, 38, 41
bison, 38–39, 43, 46
Black Legend writing, 182
blankets, Mexican, 145
bolas (game), 123–24
Bollaert, William, 142, 144–45, 147, 149, 150, 151, 153
Brahan, Robert, 144
Braudel, Fernand, 80–81

Brazos River, 22, 192, 193
Bucareli (settlement), 13, 21, 22
buffalo, American. *See* bison
bullfighting, 83, 84, 123, 133

caballada (horse herd), 67
Caballero de Croix. *See* Croix, Teodoro de (and inspection tour)
Cabello, Domingo, 18, 45, 67–68, 75, 95, 104, 106, 124, 129
Cabeza de Vaca, Álvar Núñez, 11
Caddo peoples, 11–12, 13, 15, 16, 140
calidad (race), 99, 109
Calleja, Félix María, 164
Camberos, José María, 94, 95, 104
Camino Real, 21, 85, 89
Canary Islanders: Béxar settlement profile, 18, 20, 25, 53, 71; disputes with other settlers, 60–61; lack of suitability as settlers, 61–62; racial identity and social status, 23–24, 85
Capistrano, 1, 20, 71
card games, 130–31
Casas, Juan Bautista de las, 165, 170–71
Castañeda, Carlos, 54
Castañeda, Felix, 98, 99–100
castas (Spanish-Indian-African), 99
caste system. *See* racial hierarchy
Catholicism, 8, 153–54, 187–88. *See also* religion
cattle, 26, 44–46, 86, 121, 143
celebrations, 81, 83–84, 123, 124, 132–33, 152–54
centralism *vs.* federalism, 175, 191–94
Central Texas settlements, 15–16, 21, 22, 41. *See also* San Antonio River Valley
Cherokee Indians, 12–13
Chihuahua fairs, 82–83
children's games, 123–24
chinguirito (rum), 27
Christian, William, 81
Chuchumbé (song), 125–26
cíbolo (bison), 38
Cíbolo post, 67–68, 74, 75
citizen militias, 23, 72, 75, 79, 172, 194

Clemente Arocha, José, 109, 111
climate, 37–38, 40, 45, 48, 144, 150. *See also* drought
clothing and fashion, 139, 142, 144–45, 152
Coahuila province, 19, 53, 55
Coahuila y Tejas, 184, 192–94
Coahuila y Texas en la epoca colonial (Alessio Robles), 80
Coahuiltecan Indians, 11, 16, 96–97
coastal development proposals, 183
coastal missions, 16–17, 20–21
coastal plains, 38, 40
cockfighting, 128, 129–30
colonization efforts, 186–87, 189–90. *See also* recruitment efforts for settlers
colonization laws, 186, 188, 190, 191
Colorado River, 22, 36
color quebrado (broken color, mixed bloods), 99
comales (griddles), 144
Comal River, 36
Comanche Indians, 12, 13, 73–74, 147–48
Comandancia General de las Provincias Internas, 75
commerce. *See* market economy of early settlements
communication/isolation issues. *See* isolation issues
Concepción, 20, 71, 183
contraband trade, 26, 143, 168, 170, 183
Cordero, Antonio, 22, 165, 168
corn, 25, 43, 140–42
Coronado, Francisco Vásquez de, 11, 12
Cortés, Hernan, 83
Cos, Martín Perfecto de, 193, 194
Coushatta Indians, 13
Cow People (Jumanos). *See* Jumano Indians
credit and trade, 79, 87, 88, 89
Creek (Seminole) Indians, 12–13
criollos (white Spanish Americans), 163–64
Croix, Teodoro de (and inspection tour), 14, 44–45, 101–2
cultural entertainment, 122, 151–52

cultural identity. *See* Spanish racial/cultural identity
Cutter, Charles, 7

dancing, 125–27, 131–32, 149, 150–51, 152–53
De la Garza, Refugio, 184–85
De la Mata, José Francisco, 108, 124
De la Peña, Juan Antonio. *See* Peña, Juan Antonio de la
De la Santa, José, 93, 106–7
De la Santa, Juan José, 107, 132
Delaware Indians, 12–13
De León, Alonso, 39, 54
De León, Arnoldo, 5, 140
De León, Martín, 189–90, 194, 195
Delgado, Gavino, 171
De los Santos, Francisco, 98
De los Santos, Luisa, 97
De Soto-Moscoso expedition, 11, 12
DeWitt, Green (colony), 189, 192
disease, 13–14, 15–16
Dolores, Mariano Francisco de los, 44, 68–69
domestic activities, 141–42, 144, 149, 150
don/doña honorific, 24, 102–3
Doughty, Robin, 35
drought, 42–43, 45, 48
Duval, J. C., 142, 146, 152, 153
dwellings/structures, 40, 46–47, 59–60, 122, 145–47

Early Texas period, 139–55
East Texas settlements, 13, 15, 20, 21, 71, 84–85. *See also individual settlements*
economic profiles: credit and trade, 79, 87, 88, 89; Mexican Texas, 182–83, 192; Spanish colonial period, 18, 24–28, 55, 76, 162. *See also* Saltillo Fair; trade
education, 107–8, 122, 124
Elguézabal, Juan Bautista, 46
Elizondo, Ignacio, 166, 167, 173
empresarios (colonization contractors), 186, 189–90
entertainments. *See* recreation

entrepreneurship, 6, 85, 89–90. *See also* artisans; trade
epidemics, 13–14, 15–16
Escandón, José de, 20, 23
Espada, 20, 25, 71
Espinosa, Isidro, 36, 39, 40, 41, 70
Espíritu Santo de Zúñiga, 16, 20
European goods, desire for, 14–15, 27, 82
exclusionist policies, 191
expansionist proposals, Mexican Texas, 183

fairs, 80–83. *See also* Saltillo Fair
Fandango (Gentilz painting), 124, 127
fandangos, 125–27, 131–32, 150–51
farming, 25, 41–43, 59
fauna, native, 37, 38, 39–40, 41, 43–44, 46, 47
Federal Army of Texas, 194
federalism *vs.* centralism, 175, 191–94
Fehrenbach, T. R., 181
Fernández de Santa Ana, Benito, 69
firearms (and Indians), 12, 26–27
fish, native, 38, 41
Five Civilized Tribes, 12–13
floods, 21, 48
flora, native, 36–37, 39–40, 41, 46, 47
Flores de Abrego, Nicolás, 58, 73
food and cooking, 141–42, 144, 150
Franciscans. *See* missions, overviews
Franquis de Lugo, Carlos Benites, 130
French invasion and fear of, 22, 54, 56, 69, 84–85, 120
Frétellière, Auguste, 127, 143, 150, 154
Fuentes, Pedro, 29, 93–94, 104–5, 129

Galveston Bay settlements, 22
Gálvez, Bernardo de, 18, 26
gambling, 123, 128–31, 149, 150–51
games. *See* recreation
Games, Ana María de la Trinidad, 93–96, 98–99, 100, 102, 103, 106–7, 111
Games, Felipa, 94, 95, 104
Games, Ildefonso, 103
Games, José Mariano, 102–3

Games, María Trinidad. *See* Games, Ana María de la Trinidad
Games brothers. *See* Sales Games, Francisco; Sales Games, José Miguel
García, Luciano, 171, 183–84
García Larios, Francisco, 132
Garibay, Pedro, 163
gendered social structure, 94, 96, 108
Gentilz, Theodore, 124, 127
geoecology of Spanish Texas, 36–43, 46–48, 70
Goliad. *See* La Bahía (Goliad)
Goliad, Texas, 16, 20
González, Rafael, 129
Governor's Palace, 73
Guadalupe River, 22
Guanajuato, Mexico, 164
Guerrero, Coahuila, Mexico, 120. *See also* San Juan Bautista del Río Grande
Guerrero, Vicente, 191
Gutiérrez de Lara, Bernardo, 8, 166, 167, 171
Gutiérrez-Magee expedition, 29, 166–67, 171–72, 175

Hasinai Indians, 70, 71, 84
Hernández, Carlos, 100–101
Hernández, Pedro, 100–101
Herrera, Simón, 166, 168, 169
Hidalgo y Costilla, Miguel, 164, 165–66, 169, 170–71
hidalguía (nobility), 108
Hinojosa, Gilberto, 5
Hinojosa, Urbano, 93–97, 104, 105, 106, 111
Hispanic, definition, 48n 2
History of Texas (Morfi), 14, 15
Hogan, William Ranson, 139–40, 141, 144, 146, 147, 148, 149
holiday festivities, 123, 132, 152–53
horsemanship contests, 123, 124–25, 149, 152
horses: and bison withdrawal, 46, 48; Indian attacks, 58, 69–70, 148; presidio herds, 67–68, 69; Spanish introduction of, 12, 15; trade in, 26, 27, 143; wild herds, 43–44
horticulture, 42
huertas (vegetable gardens), 59
Hurley, Alfred, 5

illiteracy, 106. *See also* education
Indian attacks, overviews, 25–26, 44, 69–70, 72, 147–48
Indian removal programs/policies, 12–13
Indians in Texas, early settlement profile, 11–18. *See also individual tribes*
insect pests, 37, 42
intermarriage, 18, 19, 24, 57–58. *See also Chapter 6*
irrigation, 24, 25, 40, 42, 70. *See also acequias* (irrigation ditches)
Isleños. *See* Canary Islanders
isolation issues, 19, 24–26, 48, 56, 57–60, 112, 162, 169
Itturigaray, José de, 163
Iturbide, Agustín de, 168, 183

jacales (thatch-roof hut), 59, 145–46
Jackson, Robert H., 3–4
jefe político (political chief), 183
Jenkins, John Holland, 147
Jones, Okah, 4, 55
jornalero (farmhand), 29, 99
Jumano Indians, 12, 13, 140
junta gubernativa (governing committee), 183
justicia mayor (chief magistrate), 60

Karankawa Indians, 11, 16–17, 21
Kemper, Samuel, 167
Kennedy, William, 151, 182
Kikapoo Indians, 13
King, John A., 148

La Bahía (Goliad), 16, 20, 21, 121, 166–67, 171, 182–83
labrador (farmer), 29
land ownership, 24, 28, 60–61
land speculation, 190–91, 193

language issues, 14, 193
Laredo, Texas, 22–23
limpieza de sangre (purity of blood), 108–9
Lipan Apache Indians. *See* Apache Indians
livestock. *See* cattle; horses; ranching profiles
lobo (Indian-African), 99
Long, James, 175
López, Alberto, 61, 126, 131
López, José Francisco, 43
Los Adaes, 21, 22, 37, 74, 101, 120, 121
Los Paisanos (Jones), 4
Louisiana: French period, 22, 54, 56, 69, 84–85, 120; US period, 19–20, 21, 22, 76, 162

Madero, José Francisco, 193
Madison, James, 166
Magee, Augustus, 166–67
maiz (corn), 140–42
malilla (card game), 130
Manchola, Rafael Antonio, 189–90, 191
marginalization of Tejanos, 8, 148–49, 155, 181–82, 194–95
market economy of early settlements, 18, 24–28, 55, 76, 162. *See also* artisans; trade
marriage age, 93, 98
Martínez, Antonio, 27–28, 30, 175, 182
Martínez Pacheco, Rafael, 42–43, 45, 79, 88, 101
Martos, y Navarrete, Angel de, 98
Matagorda Bay, 16, 20
Maverick, Mary, 146, 148, 150, 152, 153
McClintock, William, 144, 145, 151, 153
McMullen-McGloin colony, 189, 193
Meléndez Valdez, Francisco, 87
Menchaca, José, 169
Menchaca, Luis Antonio, 73, 86
Menchaca, Mariano, 87, 89
mercantile economy. *See* market economy of early settlements
mesteña (livestock tax), 88
mestizos, definition, 99
metate and *mano* (grinding device), 141

Mexican Texas period, 182–88
Mexican War of Independence: Béxar's position on rebellion, 168–70, 175; impact of, 20, 21, 22, 27, 29, 76, 182; New Spain rebellion, 163–64; Spain, instability of, 162–63; Spanish authority, reestablishment of, 173–75; Texas, insurrection in, 164–68
Mier y Terán, Manuel de, 144
military presence: citizen militias, 23, 72, 75, 79, 172, 194; importance of, 5, 24–25, 53, 58–59, 67–76, 121, 162–63. *See also* presidios
militias, citizen. *See* citizen militias
Miranda y Flores, Bernardo de, 28
miscegenation, 19, 23. *See also* intermarriage
missions, overviews: and decline of Indian populations, 13–14; description of, 122; Indian experience with, overview, 14–17, 68–69; and ranching disputes, 26; secularization of, 17–18, 106. *See also individual missions*
Monclova, Mexico, 166, 192–93
Monroe, James, 166
monte (card game), 130
Montero, Bernardino, 172
Moorhead, Max, 82
morality issues, 125–26, 128, 129, 131–32
Morelos, José María, 164
Morfi, (Fray) Juan Augstín, 14, 15, 39, 41, 44
Moscoso, Luis de, 11, 12
mosquitos, 37
moss, Spanish, 40
mulata (Spanish-African), 99
mulattoes, definition, 99
mules, trade in, 26, 143
Muñoz, Manuel, 29, 45, 67, 101, 131–32
Múzquiz, Ramón, 191

Nacogdoches, Texas: abandonment of, 21, 27; early settlements, 19, 21; geoecological profile, 37; insurgency in, 167, 175; Mexican period, 183; Seguíns in, 29; and separatist movement, 193

Napoleon's invasion of Spain, 163
Narváez, Pánfilo de, 11
Natchitoches, Louisiana, 13, 26, 166
Nations of the North (Norteños). See Norteño Indian tribes
Navarrete, Angel Martos y, 68, 73
Navarro, Ángel, 106–7
Navarro, Eugenio, 194
Navarro, José Antonio, 189, 194
New Braunfels area, 36–37
New Mexico, 5, 83
New Orleans, Louisiana, 26, 143, 192
New Views of Borderlands History (Jackson), 3–4
Norteño Indian tribes, 68, 72, 73, 75
Nueces River, 13, 16, 22, 189
Nuestra Señora del Guadalupe de los Nacogdoches, 21
Nuestra Señora del la Concepción, 20. *See also* Concepción
Nuestra Señora de los Dolores de los Ais, 21, 23
Nuestra Señora del Pilar de los Adaes, 21. *See also* Los Adaes
Nuestra Señora del Refugio, 17. *See also* Refugio
Nuestra Señora del Rosario, 20. *See also* Rosario
Nuevo León province, 185; settlers from, 19, 53
Nuevo Santander province, 19, 22, 23, 165

Oconor, Hugo, 105
Olivares, Antonio de San Buenaventura, 54
Olmstead, Frederick Law, 142, 151–52
Oñate, Juan de, 83
Orcoquisac (mission/presidio), 22, 37, 74
Osage Indians, 12

Palafox (settlement), 22
pares y nones (parlor game), 130
"passing," 23, 58, 110. *See also* Spanish racial/cultural identity
Payaya Indians, 96–97
pecans, 47, 86, 121

Pedernales River, 68–69
pelota (sport), 122–23
Peña, Juan Antonio de la, 36–37, 38
peninsular Spaniards, 163–64
Pérez, Gertrudis, 93, 95, 103, 111–12
Pérez, Ignacio, 175
Pérez de Almazán, Fernando, 56, 57, 60
Pérez de Almazán, Juan Antonio, 69, 71, 73
Perry, Henry, 175
piloncillo (brown sugar cones), 27
Plains Indians, 16
Plan of Iguala, 175, 183
plants, native. *See* flora, native
pobladores (settlers), 57
population data, 12–14, 18–20, 30, 56–57, 103, 120
Poyo, Jerry, 5, 8
Pragmática Sanción, 93, 94, 95
presidios: economic profile, 24–25, 55; jurisdictional structure, 73–75, 79; settlement profile, 53–62, 71–72, 120–21
primeros pobladores, 24
procuradors, 168, 174
prostitution, 128
Pueblo Indians, 13

Querecho Indians, 12

racial hierarchy, 19, 23–25, 57–58, 85, 98–102, 108–11. *See also* Chapter 6; Spanish racial/cultural identity
rainfall. *See* drought
Ramón, Domingo (and expedition), 18, 21, 37, 38–39
Ramos Arizpe, Miguel, 47–48
ranching profiles, 25–26, 28, 29, 43–46, 142–43. *See also* cattle; horses
Reconquista, 83
recreation: bowling, 124; bullfighting, 83, 84, 123, 133; card games, 130–31; celebrations, 81, 83–84, 123, 124, 132–33, 152–54; children's games, 123–24; cockfighting, 128, 129–30; dancing, 125–27; gambling, 123, 128–31, 149, 150–51;

INDEX

horsemanship contests, 123, 124–25, 149, 152; overviews, 119, 149; prostitution, 128; sports, 122–25; theater/plays, 151–52. *See also* fairs
recruitment efforts for settlers, 54, 56, 62, 71. *See also* colonization efforts
Refugio, 17, 21
regidores (aldermen), 61, 135n 28, 168, 174. *See also ayuntamiento* (town council)
Reglamento of 1772, 74–75
religion: Catholicism, 8, 153–54, 187–88; celebrations, 81, 83–84, 123, 124, 132–33, 152–54; and commerce, 80–82
Republican Army of the North, 166–67, 172
Republic of Texas. *See* Texas, Republic of
Revilla (settlement), 23
A Revolution Remembered (De la Teja), 8
Riddell, John Leonard, 145–46, 148
Rio Grande River, 22–23, 54. *See also* San Juan Bautista del Río Grande
Ripperdá, Juan María, Barón de, 45, 68, 74, 105, 128–29, 131
Rivera, Pedro de, 37, 58, 59, 70–71
Robeline, Louisiana, 120. *See also* Los Adaes
Rodríguez, Francisco Javier, 87
Rodríguez Mederos, Antonio, 128
Ronda, James, 7
Rosario, 16, 17, 20, 30
Rubí, Marqués de, 37, 74–75
Rueg, Henry, 193
Ruiz, Francisco, 173, 190
Rusk, Thomas J., 195

Saint James, feast of, 83–84, 88
Salado Creek, 167, 172
Salas, José María, 93, 94–95, 105–6
Salcedo (settlement), 22
Salcedo, Manuel, 124, 126, 131, 165, 166–67, 168, 169, 172
Salcedo, Nemecio, 164–65
Saldaña, Guillermo, 172
Sales Games, Francisco, 93, 100
Sales Games, José Miguel, 93, 95, 100, 102

Saltillo, Coahuila, Mexico, 19, 165, 185, 192. *See also* Saltillo Fair
Saltillo en la historia y la leyenda (Alessio Robles), 80
Saltillo Fair, 5–6, 26, 79–80, 83–90. *See also* fairs
San Antonio de Béxar: founding of and early profiles, 36, 54, 119, 120–22, 161–62; geoecological profile, 41–43; late colonial profile, 27–28; Mexican period, 183–84, 187, 189–90, 191–92, 193–95; present perspective, 1–2; pro- and anti-Spanish sentiments, 168–70, 168–73; Texas period, 144–47, 148–49, 151–55
San Antonio de Béxar (De la Teja), 1, 4
San Antonio de Valero (Alamo), 20. *See also* Valero (Alamo)
San Antonio River, 25, 41
San Antonio River Valley: geoecological profiles, 41–43, 70; settlements, overviews, 16, 20, 54, 120 (*See also individual missions*)
San Carlos del Alamo de Parras, 121, 163
Sánchez, José María, 144
Sandoval, Manuel de, 61, 86, 97
San Fernando de Béxar (chartered settlement), 20, 53. *See also* San Antonio de Béxar
San Francisco de la Espada, 20
San Gabriel River, 15
San Jacinto, Battle of, 194
San José y San Miguel de Aguayo, 20, 71
San Juan Bautista del Río Grande, 22, 36, 70, 120
San Juan Capistrano, 20, 71
San Marcos de Neve (settlement), 22
San Marcos River, 22
San Pedro Creek, 25
San Saba River/Mission, 16, 19, 22, 72
Santa Anna, Antonio López de, 193–97
Santiago, Feast of, 83–84, 88
Santísima Trinidad de Salcedo (settlement), 22
Santo Cristo de la Capilla, 84

San Xavier (mission/presidio), 19, 22
Saucedo, José Antonio, 189
Schmitz, Joseph, 140
secularization of missions, 17–18, 106
Seguín, Erasmo, 29–30, 173–74, 185–88, 189, 194
Seguín, Esmeregildo, 28–29
Seguín, Juan Nepomuceno, 30, 193–94
Seguín, Santiago (nephew of elder Santiago), 28–29
Seguín family, 28–30. *See also individual family members*
Seminole (Creek) Indians, 12–13
separatist movement, 192–94
settlement patterns, 18–23, 55
Shawnee Indians, 12–13
sheep, 43
silver mines of Los Almagres, 28
sitio (4,428 acres), 190
slaughtering of cattle, 44–45
slavery, 186–87, 191
smallpox, 13, 15–16
Smith, Henry, 193
social structure/status: and Canary Islanders, 60–61; frontier opportunities, 56; Seguín family profile, 28–30; Spanish colonial period, 23–24, 59. *See also* racial hierarchy
soldier-settlers, profile of, 53–62, 121
Solís, José de, 37, 39, 40, 42, 43–44
Solms-Braunfels, Prince Carl of, 148
Spain, Napoleon's invasion of, 163
The Spanish Frontier in North America (Weber), 3–4
Spanish racial/cultural identity: and bullfighting, 123; Canary Islanders, 23–24, 85; caste system, 19, 57–58, 98–102, 108–11; colonialist culture, 181; military code, 19, 109–10; and recreational activities, 133–34; and Saltillo Fair, 88. *See also Chapter 6*
sports, 122–25
squatters, 188
Steinert, W. (German settler), 143, 145, 147, 149–50, 154

stereotyping of Tejanos, 149–50, 181–82
Sterne, Adolphus, 154
Stiff, Edward, 146–47
structures/dwellings. *See* dwellings/structures
sugar/sugarcane, 27, 42

tamales, 141–42
Tamaulipas, 23. *See also* Nuevo Santander province
taxes/fees: dances, 127; fairs and markets, 81, 87–88; feral livestock, 44–45
The Tejano Community 1836–1900 (De Leon), 140
Tejano Epic (De León, Arnoldo), 5
Tejano history, 3
Tejano Leadership in Mexican and Revolutionary Texas (De la Teja), 8
Tejanos: culture and community, 139–55; definitions, 3, 113n 10, 139; marginalization of, 8, 148–49, 155, 181–82, 194–95; stereotyping of, 149–50, 181–82
Terán, General. *See* Mier y Terán, Manuel de
Terán de los Ríos, Domingo (and expedition), 36, 37, 38, 43, 54
terminology: jurisdictional, 77n 10, 134n 12; racial, 3, 48n 1, 91n 27, 98–99, 113n 9–10, 135n 20, 139, 163. *See also individual terms*
territorial *vs.* state status, 185–86
Texas, Republic of, 48n 4, 139–55
Texas in 1837 (Muir, ed.), 142
Texas in 1840 (Lawrence, ed.), 143
The Texas Republic (Hogan), 139–40, 141, 147. *See also* Hogan, William Ranson
Texas War of Independence, 30, 181, 194–95
Texians, 3
Teya Indians, 12
theater/plays, 151–52
Thus They Lived (Schmitz), 140
Tijerina, Andrés, 3
timber resources, 46–47
Tlaxcaltecan Indians, 83, 182
Toledo, José Alvarez de, 167, 173

tortillas, 141

trade: agricultural, 25, 121; cattle and byproducts, 26, 44–46, 86, 121, 143; contraband, 26, 143, 168, 170, 183; and credit, 79, 87, 88, 89; with Indians, 12, 26–27, 47, 82, 86. *See also* market economy of early settlements; Saltillo Fair

Travieso, Francisco, 171171

Travieso, Tomás, 47, 89

Travieso, Vicente Alvarez, 68, 173

treinta y una (card game), 130

Trinity River, 21, 22

Urrutia, José (Joseph) de, 73, 86

Urrutia, Manuel de, 131–32

Urrutia, Toribio de, 61, 72, 73

US War of Independence, 26

Valero (Alamo), 20, 25, 29, 54, 68–69, 70–71

vaqueros (cowboys), 142

Varela, Mariano, 174

Vargas, Rita, 102–3

Vázquez, Josefina Zoraida, 8

vecino, 24

Venegas, Francisco Javier, 164

Veramendi, Fernando, 106–7

Veramendi, Juan, 173

Victoria, Texas, 194, 195

Viesca, Agustín, 194

"Villa de Béxar," 57. *See also* San Antonio de Béxar

Villa de Santiago del Saltillo, 83

Villanueva Saldivar, María, 81

Villaseñor, Santiago, 129

weather. *See* climate

Weber, David J., 3–4

"whiteness," 23. *See also* Anglo bias in literature; Spanish racial/cultural identity

Wichita peoples, 12, 13

wildlife. *See* fauna, native

Wildlife and Man in Texas (Doughty), 35

Winthuisen, Tomás Felipe de, 46–47

women: clothing and fashion, 144; domestic activities, 141–42, 144, 149, 150; and gendered social structure, 94, 96, 108; prostitution, 128; shortage of in early settlements, 19, 70

Ybarbo, Antonio Gil, 100

Zambrano, Juan Manuel, 165, 169, 172

www.ingramcontent.com/pod-product-compliance
Lightning Source LLC
Chambersburg PA
CBHW070134080526
44586CB00015B/1685